Germanic Philology

Perspectives in Linguistics and Literature

Edited by
Tina Boyer
Wake Forest University

Heiko Wiggers
Wake Forest University

Series in Language and Linguistics

Copyright © 2024 by the authors.

All rights reserved. No part of this publication may be reproduced, stored in a retrieval system, or transmitted in any form or by any means, electronic, mechanical, photocopying, recording, or otherwise, without the prior permission of Vernon Art and Science Inc.

www.vernonpress.com

In the Americas:
Vernon Press
1000 N West Street, Suite 1200
Wilmington, Delaware, 19801
United States

In the rest of the world:
Vernon Press
C/ Sancti Espiritu 17,
Malaga, 29006
Spain

Series in Language and Linguistics

Library of Congress Control Number: 2024932848

ISBN: 979-8-8819-0168-4

Also available: 978-1-64889-897-6 [Hardback]; 979-8-8819-0031-1 [PDF, E-Book]

Product and company names mentioned in this work are the trademarks of their respective owners. While every care has been taken in preparing this work, neither the authors nor Vernon Art and Science Inc. may be held responsible for any loss or damage caused or alleged to be caused directly or indirectly by the information contained in it.

Every effort has been made to trace all copyright holders, but if any have been inadvertently overlooked the publisher will be pleased to include any necessary credits in any subsequent reprint or edition.

Cover design by Vernon Press. Cover image by JL G from Pixabay.

For H. – a courageous heart.

Table of Contents

	Acknowledgments	vii
	List of Tables	ix
	List of Figures	xi
	Contributors	xiii
	Abbreviations	xvii
	Introduction Tina Boyer *Wake Forest University*	xix
Chapter 1	**On Language History and Extralinguistic Periodization in Germanic** Adam Oberlin *Princeton*	1
Chapter 2	**Metaphor and Metonymy in Germanic Noun Periphrasis** John Paul Ewing *Indiana University Bloomington*	27
Chapter 3	**Scribal Errors and Peculiarities in the *Hildebrandslied*** Robin Cummins *University of Wisconsin Madison*	55
Chapter 4	***gedencken der pender*: A New Reading of Hugo von Montfort's "min dienst und gruzz me tausent stunt" (no. 6)** Alexander Sager *University of Georgia*	75

| Chapter 5 | **Yiddish, Power, and Compassion: Emotive Language in Wagenseil's Belehrung (1699)** | 91 |

Annegret Oehme
University of Washington

| Chapter 6 | **Gendered Variation in Spoken German: Has Prescriptivism Affected the Vernacular?** | 111 |

James M. Stratton
Pennsylvania State University

| Chapter 7 | **Dialect contact and language death: Morphological leveling in an Indiana German heritage variety** | 137 |

Karen Rösch
Indiana University - Purdue University in Indianapolis

| Chapter 8 | **Nineteenth-Century American Translations of German Philology** | 177 |

Ulrike Wagner
Bard College Berlin

Index 203

Acknowledgments

We feel an overwhelming sense of gratitude towards all those who contributed to bringing this book to life. Writing and editing it was no easy feat. But it was certainly a rewarding journey, and we are deeply thankful for the unwavering support and dedication of everyone who made it possible.

We want to extend our heartfelt appreciation to all the contributors of this book. Your expertise, insights, and passion enriched its content and brought depth to the discussions within its pages. Each one of you played a crucial role in shaping this work, and we are truly grateful for your commitment to excellence.

We also want to express our sincere gratitude to the MLA discussion forum on Germanic Philology for providing the foundation for this project. The group's encouragement and scholarly environment, along with the intellectual stimulation and collaborative spirit within the forum and conference meetings, were instrumental in developing the ideas presented in this book.

We extend our deepest appreciation to all those who provided assistance and support at various stages of this project. To our colleagues, mentors, reviewers, and editors who generously shared their time and expertise, thank you for your invaluable contributions. Your guidance was instrumental in refining the ideas presented in this book.

Writing a book requires both solitude and collaboration, and it demands immense patience and perseverance. To everyone who patiently navigated the challenges, revisions, and iterations, your resilience has been inspiring. We are grateful for the collective dedication and determination that propelled this project forward.

Lastly, we want to express our gratitude to our families and friends for their unwavering support, understanding, and encouragement throughout this endeavor. Your belief in us sustained our motivation and made this journey all the more meaningful.

The completion of this book is a testament to the collaborative efforts and support of a remarkable community. We are humbled and grateful for the opportunity to work with such talented and dedicated individuals. Thank you all for being an integral part of this journey and for contributing to the realization of this endeavor.

List of Tables

Table 6.1:	German Participant Profiles	119
Table 6.2:	Swiss Participant Profiles	119
Table 6.3:	Distribution of Variants for Describing Mixed-Sex Referents (real words)	124
Table 6.4:	Distribution of Variants for Describing Mixed-Sex Referents (pseudowords)	124
Table 6.5:	Logistic Regression of Factors Conditioning Use of Generic Masculine to Describe Mixed-Sex Referents	127
Table 7.1:	Gilbert Translation Task: 'he's putting the chair under the tree'	156
Table 7.2:	Gilbert Translation Task: 'the dog bit that bad man'	156
Table 7.3:	Gilbert Translation Task: 'boil that egg in hot water'	157
Table 7.4:	Gilbert Translation Task: 'he's helping me now'	158
Table 7.5:	Gilbert Translation Task: 'he came with me'	158
Table 7.6:	Gilbert Translation Task: 'give her two pieces'	159
Table 7.7:	Gilbert Translation Task: 'he is already in the room'	160
Table 7.8:	Gilbert Translation Task: 'there is something in your left eye'	161

List of Figures

Figure 2.1:	Subtypes of Metaphor in Germanic Noun Periphrasis	35
Figure 2.2:	Subtypes of Metonymy in Germanic Noun Periphrasis	45
Figure 3.1:	Manuscript Evidence	62
Figure 3.2:	Manuscript Evidence	63
Figure 3.3:	Manuscript Evidence	63
Figure 3.4:	Manuscript Evidence	64
Figure 3.5:	Manuscript Evidence	65
Figure 3.6:	Manuscript Evidence	65
Figure 3.7:	Manuscript Evidence	65
Figure 3.8:	Manuscript Evidence	66
Figure 3.9:	Manuscript Evidence	66
Figure 3.10:	Manuscript Evidence	67
Figure 3.11:	Manuscript Evidence	67
Figure 3.12:	Manuscript Evidence	67
Figure 3.13:	Manuscript Evidence	68
Figure 3.14:	Manuscript Evidence	68
Figure 3.15:	Manuscript Evidence	68
Figure 3.16:	Manuscript Evidence	69
Figure 3.17:	Manuscript Evidence	69
Figure 3.18:	Manuscript Evidence	69
Figure 3.19:	Manuscript Evidence	70
Figure 6.1:	Image R – *Zwei Selfiemacherinnen*	122
Figure 6.2:	Image T – *Ein Dabtänzer*	122
Figure 6.3:	The Use of the Generic Masculine in Apparent Time	126
Figure 7.1:	Dubois County Townships: Location of Jasper and Ferdinand, IN	143
Figure 7.2:	Occurrence of Nominative Forms in SG Accusative and Dative Contexts	147
Figure 7.3:	Jasper Area Participants	150
Figure 7.4:	Ferdinand Area Participants	151
Figure 7.5:	SG Masculine Definite Article Declinations for 'The Man'	153

Contributors

Adam Oberlin is a Senior Lecturer in the Department of German at Princeton University, where he coordinates the intermediate and advanced German language program, directs the summer program in Vienna, and teaches language and history courses. He remains active in the fields of medieval studies and Germanic philology and currently serves as the Vice President of the Society for Medieval Germanic Studies.

John Paul Ewing is a Ph.D. candidate (ABD) in the Germanic Studies Department at Indiana University Bloomington. His research has spanned literary and philological topics in Old Saxon, Old English, Old High German, Old Norse, and Middle High German. He has taught German, Latin, and various literature and humanities courses.

Robin Cummins is a graduate student in German at the University of Wisconsin Madison, studying Germanic philology and medieval paleography, linguistics, and literature. Her research focuses on medieval people's relationship to language and writing. Currently, her work investigates the scribal process in the *Hildebrandslied*.

Annegret Oehme is an Associate Professor in the Department of German Studies at the University of Washington. Her research interests include medieval and early modern German and Yiddish literature and pre-modern cultural transfers within a German-Jewish context. Her publications have appeared in *Arthuriana*, *Ashkenaz*, *Euphorion*, *PaRDeS*, and *Speculum*, among others. Her recent publications include the co-edited volume (together with Caroline Gruenbaum) *Medieval and Early Modern Jewish Romance* (ARC Humanities Press: Yorkshire), the co-edited special issue (together with CJ Jones) of *German Quarterly: Premodern German Studies* (96.2, 2023), and the monograph *The Knight without Boundaries: Yiddish and German Arthurian Wigalois Adaptations* (Leiden: Brill, 2022).

Alexander Sager is an Associate Professor of German at the University of Georgia (Athens). He is the author of *Minne von maeren: On Wolfram's Titurel* (Göttingen 2006) as well as articles and essays on Albrecht's *Jüngerer Titurel*, German courtly love poetry, the *Carmina Burana*, and Old Saxon biblical verse. In one way or another, all his work centers on the interaction between early vernacular literature and Latin learning, and between secular and religious modes of literary and cultural experience.

James Stratton received his Ph.D. in linguistics from Purdue University. He is a Germanic linguist with a specialization in Language Variation and Change, Historical Linguistics, and Corpus Linguistics. His research explores aspects of language variation and change both synchronically and diachronically using a corpus-based variationist (Labovian) framework. He is currently engaged in two long-term research projects. The first investigates intensification in Germanic languages, a project that involves examining the longitudinal variegated nature of intensifying adverbs, their ebb and flow, and their sensitivity to a number of linguistic and social factors. The second attempts to establish a variationist tradition in work on German language variation and change by examining a number of linguistic variables using tried and tested quantitative methods in the field of variationist sociolinguistics. He has published in a number of linguistic journals such as the Language Variation and Change, the Journal of Historical Linguistics, and the Journal of Germanic Linguistics.

Karen Rösch received her doctorate in Germanic Linguistics with specializations in sociolinguistics and pedagogy from the University of Texas at Austin in 2009. She retired in 2019 from Indiana University - Purdue University Indianapolis (IUPUI), where she also served as Director of the IUPUI Max Kade German-American Research and Resource Center. For most of the 40 years of her teaching career in public and private schools and universities, she has taught German language, linguistics, and culture in various countries abroad (Germany, Australia, Japan) and in the U.S. (New York, Ohio, South Carolina, Texas, Vermont), during which she also received an M.A. in Curriculum and Teaching in 2000 from Michigan State University in Valbonne, France. Her publications are based on her fieldwork in Texas and Indiana from recorded interviews with German heritage speakers to document and preserve these varieties for teaching and research. They include a monograph on Texas Alsatian, Language Maintenance and Language Death: The decline of Texas Alsatian (2012, John Benjamins) and several articles and chapters on Texas and Indiana German varieties and culture: "The Texas German Dialect Project," (Boas, Pierce, Rösch (2010) JGL), "The History of Front Rounded Vowels in New Braunfels German," (Pierce, Boas, Rösch (2015), Germanic Heritage Varieties in North America; "Mir reda ka richtiges Dietsch: Self-stigmatization in German-American dialects;" Yearbook of German-American Studies (2017); "Wyneken: Thunder on the Indiana Frontier;" (2018), Lutheran Quarterly, "Dialect Contact in Texas German: Linguistic Variants as Sociolinguistic Markers;" The Polymath Intellectual: A Festschrift in Honor of Prof. Robert D. King (2020); and "Texas Alsatian;" Varieties of German in North America (YGAS Supp. Vol. 6), forthcoming (2023). Prof. Rösch currently enjoys teaching ESL to migrant workers in the Texas Hill Country.

Ulrike Wagner is director of the German Studies Program at Bard College Berlin. She received her Ph.D. in German and Comparative Literature from Columbia University an M.A. in North American Studies and German Literature from the Free University of Berlin. She was a visiting Fulbright scholar in the Department of Comparative Thought and Literature at Johns Hopkins University. At Bard College Berlin, she has developed a variety of courses on European and American Romanticism, Germany's Jewish Enlightenment, the literature and culture of the Weimar period in Berlin, contemporary debates in the German public sphere, and an OSUN network course on Feminism and Community. Her current research interests concern the global history of the humanities and practices of philology; relations between German Romanticism and American Transcendentalism in the context of religious debates, historicism, classicism, and aesthetics; German-Jewish women writers; and feminist theory and practice. She has published, among others, in *Literature and Theology*, the *Hegel Bulletin*, *Herder Jahrbuch/Herde Yearbook*, the *Oxford Handbook* series, and *Amerikastudien/American Studies*. She is currently completing a monograph titled *Transcendental Philology: Emerson, Fuller, Nietzsche, and the Migrations of a Method*

Abbreviations

acc	=	accusative
b.	=	born
con.	=	contraction
dat.	=	dative
def.	=	definite article
dem.	=	demonstrative
Eng	=	English
fem.	=	feminine
Fig.	=	Figure
gen.	=	genitive
IPA	=	International Phonetic Alphabet
J-F	=	Jasper-Ferdinand (German heritage variety)
jf	=	J-F determiner forms described by Freeouf (1990)
LAlem	=	Low Alemannic
masc.	=	masculine
neut.	=	neuter
nom.	=	nominative
NP	=	Noun Phrase
pos.det.	=	possessive determiner
pro.	=	pronoun
red.	=	reduced
SG	=	Standard German
OHG	=	Old High German
MHG	=	Middle High German
OS	=	Old Saxon
OE	=	Old English

Introduction
Germanic philology in the twenty-first century

Tina Boyer
Wake Forest University

Philology in the twenty-first century is a complicated topic. This complication stemmed from the turmoil of the twentieth century. In the context of Germanic languages and their study, the century turned into a political, social, and ideological battleground. As a result, philology faded into the shadows. Some scholars reduced its status to historical linguistics, which was true, and others considered it a waste of time, old-fashioned, and unnecessary. Consequently, since the end of the century was influenced by critical theory, philology was categorized as a branch of linguistics. In contrast, critical theory took over Germanic language studies' social and cultural aspects.

However, what do we mean by philology, specifically Germanic philology, as a concept and field of study? The definitions for philology are endless. Haruko Momma's study provides a philological excurse on philology and philologists.[1] Some essential takeaways are:

> The first one, which is popularly accredited to Roman Jakobson, states that 'philology is the art of reading slowly' (see, for example, Watkins 1990, p. 25, and Ziolkowski 1990b, p. 11, n. 7). This dictum, whose underlying concept may be attributed to Nietzsche, tells us that philology is less concerned with *what* we read than *how* we read (see Pollock 2009, p. 933, n. 11).[2]

Reducing the practice of philology to "how we read" improves all other definitions. The essential task of a researcher is to read and read well. This type of reading constitutes open-mindedness and critical thinking. With these assets, philology focuses on the text and adds specializations as necessary.

---

[1] See Haruko Momma, "Introduction: Where Is Philology?," in *From Philology to English Studies: Language and Culture in the Nineteenth Century* (Cambridge: Cambridge University Press, 2012), 1–27.
[2] Ibid., 26.

Therefore, philology can expand into various approaches and use countless disciplines on how to read a text.³ Momma continues:

> [t]he second definition states that philology is 'what philologists do.' However tautological this definition may sound, it reminds us that studies of language and literature are philological if they are so recognized by those who conduct them, and that students of language and literature *become* philologists when they acknowledge themselves as such.⁴

Essentially, philology is self-determined. Therefore, when researchers read philologically, they are philologists.⁵ The text or medium of knowledge lies at the heart of philology. Without it, there is no research. Consequently, as long as we have language and conveyors of these languages, we can and should read philologically. The challenge, however, rests in Germanic philology's faded and tainted reputation.

One reason for Germanic philology's fading influence in the academy appears in its beginnings. In the German context, for example, philologists of the nineteenth century (Herder, Grimm) anchored their research in the desire to create national unity among the many states of Germany and as an answer to Napoleon's march across Europe. For these philologists, national unity would follow by providing an origin of the language and its people.⁶ Myths, folklore, and other forms of cultural transmission were integral in this work. Germany's unity in the nineteenth century did derive in part from philological research; however, the political and ideological currents, like the belief in Social Darwinism and eugenics, some of the worst examples, mixed with philological research (myths, folklore, language studies, medieval literature) and set the stage for the horrors of the twentieth century. Germanic philology became

---

³ We also want to add that words in and of themselves are worth reading and that language is a text. Chapters six and seven in this volume are language studies, one interested in language change and the other a case study of marginalized languages in the United States.
⁴ Momma, "Introduction: Where Is Philology?," 26.
⁵ Chapter eight discusses how to read philologically.
⁶ While the argument for national identity formation in the nineteenth century is predominant; the early modern period provided a good foundation for the ideologies of the nineteenth century. See: Karl Enenkel and Konrad Ottenheym, "Introduction - The Quest for an Appropriate Past: The Creation of National Identities in Early Modern Literature, Scholarship, Architecture, and Art," in *The Quest for an Appropriate Past in Literature, Art and Architecture* (Leiden: Brill, 2018), 1–11. Also see chapter eight on the prominence of philology in the nineteenth century.

enmeshed with racist and bigoted pseudo-sciences to validate northern Europe's white supremacy. To this day, Germanic philology is a thorny topic.

On the one hand, it is alive in historical linguistics and other linguistic analyses, but on the other hand, the field of influence has diminished not only in publications but in the genuine lack of academic positions at universities. Philology will diminish even more by not providing academic freedom and financial support. Young scholars struggle to find posts to continue their research; older scholars do not receive wider recognition than the very small circle of historical linguists within which they exist. In North America, philology is going extinct.

This collection focuses on the Germanic branch of philology and seeks to continue what was started (with goodwill) in the early modern period and gained significance in the nineteenth century, looking to redeem the loss of reputation and abuse of knowledge. Philology, in this respect, is an umbrella term encompassing different ways to understand the text.[7] It is vital to continue defining the concept of philology because, in the very essence of its being — *philo* and *logia* — it allows many different approaches to understand and love words. There is no reason that philology cannot exist and thrive in the twenty-first century. On the contrary, philology's growth to include the knowledge of the twentieth-century hints at a continued future.

In a way, the chapters in this edition mirror the 'old-fashioned' approaches (rhetorical analyses, paleography, etymology). However, they also show what has been learned in the last century (cognitive and social linguistics, textual interpretation with critical theory, and culture). The goal of this edition is simple. It grew from the Germanic Philology sessions at the Modern Language Association and provides an overview of some of the ongoing philological research. It ensures that Germanic philology (with a healthy dose of criticism of its tainted past) has a future.

Since this book resulted from presentations on Germanic philology at the MLA, regarding this publication, we found that the MLA never initiated a Germanic linguistics project as an edited edition.[8] In fact, in the English-

---

[7] In his essay, Nikolaus Wegmann defines philology by way of Nietzsche: "Nietzsche employs an ambivalent neologism—*vielspältig*, multi-columned—to indicate that philology's traditional heterogeneity comprises things that are not only diverse but ultimately incongruous" ("Philology - An Update," in *The Future of Philology: Proceedings of the 11th Annual Columbia University German Graduate Student Conference*, ed. Hannes Bajohr et al. (Newcastle-upon-Tyne, UK: Cambridge Scholars Publisher, 2014), 28). It seems that incongruity and ambiguity define philology very well.

[8] The MLA has published many editions and anthologies between 2005 and 2020, mainly dedicated to English literature and Critical Theory.

speaking market (specifically North America, Great Britain, and Australia), hardly any edited volumes on Germanic philology have been published in the last fifteen years.[9]

However, several edited volumes have been published in Germany in the previous two decades, with Germanic philology as their topic.[10] On the other hand, many books by individual authors in the Anglophone market discuss general or specific aspects of Germanic philology. Often, these books have as subject the history of a specific Germanic language in its entirety,[11] or they discuss particular elements of a Germanic language.[12] Unfortunately, only a handful of edited volumes were published between 2005 and 2020. These are, however, either dedicated to one topic[13] or so-called Handbooks, i.e., large-scale anthologies about a general topic.[14] The closest publication related to our project is a series of monographs by Routledge called *Routledge Studies in*

---

[9] Although English is a Germanic language, our intention from the beginning was to exclude contributions that dealt with English directly due to the over-emphasis on English-language studies in linguistics (and in many other academic disciplines). We believe it is essential to provide different philological approaches for various Germanic varieties, including English, but not as the primary research target in this volume.

[10] These are so-called *Festschriften* (books that honor respected scholars). They are usually edited volumes and consist of contributions by the scholar's colleagues, students, friends, etc. An example would be Stefan J Schierholz et al., *Die deutsche Sprache in der Gegenwart: Festschrift für Dieter Cherubim zum 60. Geburtstag* (Frankfurt am Main: Peter Lang, 2001).

[11] For example Joseph Salmons, *A History of German: What the Past Reveals about Today's Language* (Oxford: Oxford University Press, 2018); Ruth H. Sanders, *German: Biography of a Language* (New York; Oxford: Oxford University Press, 2012); Neal Karlen, *The Story of Yiddish* (New York: Harper Collins, 2014), http://rbdigital.oneclickdigital.com; Christopher Young and Thomas Gloning, *A History of the German Language through Texts* (London: Routledge, 2004), https://www.worldcat.org/title/history-of-the-german-language-through-texts/oclc/931149543&referer=brief_results.

[12] For example Östen Dahl, *Grammaticalization in the North: Noun Phrase Morphosyntax in Scandinavian Vernaculars*, Studies in Diversity Linguistics 6 (Berlin: Language Science Press, 2015); Anne Breitbarth, *The History of Low German Negation* (Oxford: Oxford University Press, 2014); Christopher D. Sapp, *The Verbal Complex in Subordinate Clauses from Medieval to Modern German*, Linguistik Aktuell 173 (Amsterdam; Philadelphia: John Benjamins Pub. Co., 2011).

[13] Valentine A. Pakis, *Perspectives on the Old Saxon Heliand: Introductory and Critical Essays, with an Edition of the Leipzig Fragment* (West Virginia University Press, 2010).

[14] Michael T. Putnam and B. Richard Page, eds., *The Cambridge Handbook of Germanic Linguistics*, Cambridge Handbooks in Literature and Linguistics (Cambridge and New York: Cambridge University Press, 2020); Claire Louise Bowern and Bethwyn Evans, eds., *The Routledge Handbook of Historical Linguistics*, Routledge Handbooks in Linguistics (London and New York: Routledge, 2019).

Germanic Linguistics.¹⁵ However, it is the nature of monographs that they also only discuss a single topic per volume.¹⁶

Another important aspect of this volume for us as editors is that the authors are in varying stages of their respective careers and bring well-founded, familiar, new, and innovative research topics. The contributing authors consist of American scholars researching and teaching at American universities, German scholars studying and teaching at German universities, and German scholars researching and teaching at American universities. Our book represents the current state of research in Germanic philology on both sides of the Atlantic. This joint transatlantic effort, particularly during the last few years, has been mostly absent and is sorely needed in Germanic philology to advance the discipline with vibrant, new research.

The fields of Germanic and philology carry complex connotations, making it important for contemporary new Germanic philology to remain an inclusive and adaptable category. This adaptability is a reflection of the diverse approaches encompassed by the study of language, culture, and literature. In fact, the historical inclusivity of philology can be traced back to the pioneering work of philosophers like Johann Gottfried Herder, whose ideas on the connections between language, culture, and national identity continue to influence the field to this day.

Although Herder did not delve into the intricate comparative linguistic analysis that future philologists would undertake, his philosophical concepts were foundational in creating a culturally informed approach to studying language. His influence on the relationship between language, culture, and national identity has had a long-lasting impact on the advancement of philology and related fields, a viewpoint that has been widely accepted throughout the twentieth and twenty-first centuries. Herder's cultural theory

---

[15] For more information see https://www.routledge.com/Routledge-Studies-in-Germanic-Linguistics/book-series/SE0257. The Routledge series encompasses sixteen titles and ran from 2011 until 2016, i.e., even the closest publication to our book project was discontinued years ago. The only other outlet for the range and variety of topics on Germanic philology that our book project offers are professional journals: *The Journal of Germanic Linguistics* (University of Cambridge Press) in North America and *Zeitschrift für germanistische Linguistik* (de Gruyter) in Germany. *Amsterdamer Beiträge zur älteren Germanistik* (Brill) is another renowned outlet for articles on historical Germanic linguistics. There are presently, however, no books that would match the format of these journals. Since the market is dominated by "one-topic books," we believe that the variety of topics our book offers will be a welcome and necessary addition to readers interested in Germanic philology.

[16] A monograph from the series for example Volker Gast, *The Grammar of Identity: Intensifiers and Reflexives in Germanic Languages* (London: Routledge, 2015).

was deeply rooted in the concept of cultural particularism and the distinctiveness of each cultural group. He stressed the authenticity of individual cultures, arguing that each group possessed its unique spirit, language, and character.

Even though his ideas were groundbreaking for his time, they also emphasized distinction and separation between cultures. He believed that a people's unique spirit (Volksgeist) is expressed through their language, and each language carries the specific cultural characteristics of its speakers.[17] This idea influenced the development of linguistic and cultural nationalism, suggesting that a people's identity is embedded in their language. The concept of national identity formation via language also had a detrimental effect on the development of philology when combined with politics, religion, and eugenics.[18] In effect, monoculturalism lent itself to destructive cultural and political ideologies in the late nineteenth century that culminated in the mid-twentieth century.

Wolfgang Welsch has introduced the concept of transculturalism to alleviate the problem of cultural separatism. He states, "[..] the description of today's cultures as islands or spheres is factually incorrect and normatively deceptive. Cultures de facto no longer have the insinuated form of homogeneity and separateness. They have instead assumed a new form, which is to be called transcultural in so far as it passes through classical cultural boundaries. Cultural conditions today are largely characterized by mixes and permeations."[19] Contrary to Herder's emphasis on cultural particularism, transculturalism takes a more interconnected and dynamic approach. Herder's view tends to stress the boundaries and purity of individual cultures, where transculturalism recognizes the constant flow and interaction between cultures. It challenges the notion of fixed cultural identities and boundaries, highlighting the blending, borrowing, and hybridization of cultural elements.[20] A modern definition of

---

[17] Wolfgang Welsch, "Transculturality: The Puzzling Form of Cultures Today," in *Spaces of Culture: City, Nation, World*, ed. Mike Featherstone and Scott Lash (London: Sage, 1999), 3.
[18] "Put harshly, it tends – as a consequence of its very conception – to be a sort of cultural racism. The sphere premise and the purity precept not only render impossible a mutual understanding between cultures, but the appeal to cultural identity of this kind finally also threatens to produce separatism and to pave the way for political conflicts and wars." Ibid
[19] Welsch, "Transculturality: The Puzzling Form of Cultures Today," 5.
[20] "Transculturality, according to Welsch, alters the nature of the mode of diversity in the world for diversity in the form of single cultures will increasingly disappear. This means a movement from the perspective that differences are to be conceived in terms of the juxtaposition of delimited cultures, as we find in a mosaic format, to differences seen as the result of transcultural networks which have some things in common while differing in others. Hence the mode of differentiation has become more complex and we have

philology can gain a lot from transculturalism, which emphasizes the interconnectedness of cultures, recognizing that cultural boundaries are not rigid and that cultural exchange and adaptation are inherent aspects of human societies, especially in the context of increased globalization and intercultural interactions.

While Welsch describes modern cultures, Ingrid Kasten has applied the concept to a historical context. In her edited edition, *Transkulturalität und Translation*, the authors approach the topic within a medieval context.[21] Transculturality works very well in a historical and linguistic context. It provides the field of philology an inherently more holistic definition of how the different tools of interpretation (linguistic, literary theory, history, religion, politics) are all a part of a common and interchanging approach to the texts we study.

Since our collection brings together scholars at various stages of their careers, one crucial consideration born out of the MLA discussion forum for Germanic philology was encouraging younger scholars and providing them with a platform to share their research. This edited volume presents a step away from traditional philological work published in article format or one author's monograph study. As editors, we found it vital to give a picture of the current work done in Germanic philology's ever-expanding field. In essence, philology is the bridge between literature, linguistics, and history, and so are the contributions in this volume. The approaches range from rhetorical and speech analysis, grammatical and lexical analysis, and paleography to sociolinguistic case studies.

Chapter Summaries

The volume is ordered chronologically because each chapter presents a different facet of philological inquiry and language, and a chronological order seemed best suited to show the diversity of languages and their change in time. The first chapters deal with Old Saxon, Old English, Old Norse, and Old High

---

overlaps and distinctions at the same time." Mike Featherstone and Scott Lash, "Introduction," in *Spaces of Culture: City, Nation, World* (London: Sage, 1999), 10.

[21] She introduces the contributions arguing that: "Komparatistische und interdisziplinäre Methoden sind daher, wie auch der vorliegende Band zeigt, ein grundlegendes Fundament der germanistischen Mediävistik. Sie überschreiten sowohl fachliche als auch nationale Grenzen. In der Konfrontation mit der Alterität der mittelalterlichen Literatur kann das Fach einen relevanten Beitrag zu den Debatten über die gegenwärtige Kultur Europas und seiner Geschichte entwickeln, indem es zeigt, dass diese Debatten eine lange Geschichte haben und dass es viele verschiedene Möglichkeiten gibt, (europäische) Gemeinschaften zu entwerfen und zu leben." Ingrid Kasten, "Einleitung," in *Transkulturalität Und Translation: Deutsche Literatur Des Mittelalters Im Europäischen Kontext* (Berlin: De Gruyter, 2017), 3–4.

German dialects. The following two chapters look at developments in the Early New High German era, one in comparison to Middle High German and the other at Yiddish texts in a German-speaking environment. The last chapters present case studies in modern German. One focuses on gendered language in different speech communities of Low and High German speakers, and the other focuses on German-language heritage in the United States, the Indiana German Project. We believe this range of languages and dialects shows current Germanic philology's interactive nature.

Periodization has always been one of the foundational issues of philology. In the first chapter, Adam Oberlin outlines and contextualizes these difficulties, calling for a reassessment of the current system; considering this first chapter as a call to action, the book endeavors to provide a wide range of approaches that fall under the umbrella of philology.[22]

Adam Oberlin sets the stage with pertinent questions for periodization ("... to what extent is the traditional tripartite [old, middle, new] division of language history valid? What does it mean for a language to be at a particular stage? Which quanta lend themselves to analysis? What discriminatory means can one apply to chronologies or systems of chronology? Can a language be assigned to a stage asynchronously from generalized, cross-linguistically-defined periods?").[23] He asserts that these issues stem from the lack of including other fields in the historical framework, such as philosophy, literary, and social history. The inclusion of this would help in finding a more cohesive periodization.

His thorough examinations of different schemas build a foundation for this edition. After all, periodization is a philologist's major interest. Pointing to the problems of these schemas, Oberlin shows us the logical and cultural weaknesses of periodization. Historically bounded and sharing a common cultural mindset, the schemas often reflect philologists' concerns within their times. This acknowledgment of social, political, and cultural influences is noteworthy as they explain the ideologies behind language periodization. He looks to "language-external periodization criteria" to provide a deeper understanding outside of strictly linguistic phenomena, for example, literary-historical trends.

Old Saxon, Old Frisian, and Crimean Gothic offer examples for his arguments. He points to the co-existence of "old" and "middle" languages. He states, "As

---

[22] James Turner discusses the beginnings of European philology and examines literary studies, classical studies, archaeology, history, and religious studies in the second part of his book: *Philology: The Forgotten Origins of the Modern Humanities* (Princeton, N.J.: Princeton University Press, 2014), 167–230.

[23] See Chapter 1 for the entire line of questions, pgs. 2-3.

Introduction

with the example of Old Frisian, it is the assumed or demonstrable age of textual content rather than the date of composition or copying that facilitates such common comparison with Old English literary monuments in service to both literary and linguistic arguments."[24] However, he states that the age of the composition of a text and its intertextual companions in other geographical and linguistic areas are now the focus of researchers in North Germanic literature. The antiquity of the language (Old Norse) withstanding, the examination of the literature within its synchronic context provides more profound insight than the search for the source of the text.

He proposes instead that analyses of social history and time could be an alternative way to approach linguistic periodization. These "extralinguistic modes" are beneficial because they provide varied and synchronized patterns on top of added linguistics insights. Following Oberlin's claim, we argue that including extralinguistic factors is crucial for periodization and any approach to an old text where it is applicable. Adding anthropological, archeological, and sociological research to this mix can only enhance our knowledge of ancient texts and languages. The same goes for rhetorical and grammatical approaches that can benefit from a solid placement of the texts or corpora in time and space.

Each following chapter shows different facets of philological diversity. The second chapter analyzes Old English and Old Saxon metaphorical and metonymical constructions in kennings. While a wealth of such kennings is attributed to Old Norse literature, John Paul Ewing demonstrates that these constructions warrant research in skaldic poetry and a sharpened interest in Old English and Old Saxon figurative language. He uses the base word of the construction to discuss the use of metaphor and metonymy and provides a comprehensive table of subcategories that describe the semantic transfer.

Utilizing the existing rhetorical categories, he analyses the "figurative process" in Germanic noun periphrasis. Ewing's premise places him firmly in the ongoing scholarly dialogue. Moreover, while his rhetorical analysis is superb, he is also concerned with clearly understanding metaphorical terminology and subcategorizing them to clarify the current scholarly discussion on the topic. He asserts that clear definitions of each category will help to reconcile the classical rhetorical tradition with modern methods. Furthermore, he looks at how these metaphors structure the text semantically and the "linguistic means of implementation." Finally, he wants to clarify that Old English and Old Saxon periphrasis do not avoid "colorful figurative expressions" as previously assumed and provide a counterpoint to Old Norse kennings.

---

[24] See Chapter 1 pg. 11.

He uses examples from *Beowulf* and the *Hêliand* to show the complexity of metaphorical construction and their differences from skaldic kennings. He finds that in Old English and Old Saxon, there is not as an extreme level of abstraction as in Old Norse. Instead, he observes that "literal-descriptive modalities" are more common.[25] Ewing opens the discussion for further research into the complexity of tropic expression, which has been hitherto not as in-depth in Old English and Old Saxon. Furthermore, there are social and cultural questions. Why are the kennings in these languages and literary works less abstract than in Old Norse? Is it a matter of genre, difference in time, and literary development, or are other factors at play? Ewing presents a precise analysis of metaphorical language that, according to Lakoff and Johnson, is at the heart of communication and understanding culture.[26]

Ewing affirms that his findings and further research into metaphorical structures in nominal periphrasis show the 'potential to clarify various Germanic poetic corpora."[27] It demonstrates patterns of creation of metaphorical devices, common usage, origin, and path of influence. Furthermore, metaphors have the remarkable ability to show insight into the cultural and social environment of a speech community. The analysis promises a better understanding not only of the devices but also of the speakers and writers and the texts themselves.

The third chapter employs paleography to analyze scribal errors within the *Hildebrandslied* manuscript, showing insight into its creation. Robin Cummins states that the text was copied from a different manuscript due to scribal errors. Furthermore, Cummins asserts in the analysis that two scribes were responsible for the text and that it was originally written in Old High German. Finally, Cummins analyzes the manuscript in detail based on Bernard Muir's study of the *Exeter Book*, Timothy Price, and Emma Danielowski's analysis of scribal features.

Chapters two and three present the work of scholars who are at the beginning of their careers. The goal was that their voices would contribute new facets to texts that had been studied for over 200 years. They are now part of a greater dialogue spanning into the distant future, ensuring new perspectives and analyses. The implication is that despite what has already been said about texts and the various methodologies used to analyze them, there is still much to discover. Ewing's rhetorical analysis lays the groundwork for a more in-depth look at metaphors in OHG and OS. Ewing shows that speech analysis is closely

---

[25] See Chapter 2, pg. 52.
[26] Lakoff and Johnson state: "[...] metaphor is pervasive in everyday life, not just in language but in thought and action. Our ordinary conceptual system, in terms of which we both think and act, is fundamentally metaphorical in nature" (*Metaphors We Live By* [Chicago: University Of Chicago Press, 1981], 30.
[27] See Chapter 2, pg. 53.

interlinked with cultural and societal phenomena within each speech community. The analysis also provides the overarching similarities in speech acts between OE, OS, and OHG. The author works with large corpora to find commonalities and differences between language groups, whereas Cummins dives into a detailed analysis of a single text. The results are fruitful, adding to the discussion of how many scribes wrote the *Hildebrandslied*.

The fourth chapter analyzes a late fourteenth-century German canso in the minnesong tradition by the Styrian poet Hugo von Montfort. At the heart of the chapter is a crux concerning the term "pender" (an upper German form of NHG "Bänder," from "Band"), for which a convincing interpretation has been lacking hitherto. Drawing upon early modern historical sources, Alexander Sager proposes a new reading of the word as a term for the relationship between a parent and his/her natural child. This interpretation illuminates the parent-and-child analogy within the poem, employed as a metaphor for the relationship between the courtly lady and the singer. Sager's careful analysis of the social meaning and autobiographical details leads to a new interpretation, giving the reader more profound insight into the poet's life and also showing Montfort's innovative and creative poetic style.

Chapter five represents Early New High German and looks at a seventeenth-century textbook to learn Yiddish and its real purpose. Finally, Annegret Oehme investigates a Christian author, Johann Christoph Wagenseil, and the impact of his *Belehrung* in his effort to Christianize Jewish communities. Oehme points to the one-sided monologue of the *Belehrung* and its missionary objective. She rejects that the text provides an impetus for Christian and Jewish co-existence. Her conclusion points to Wagenseil's goal of Christianizing Jewish people to aid in their full integration into German society through a complete linguistic transformation and the elimination of Yiddish.

She maintains that Wagenseil's call to Christians to learn Yiddish is not to foster a better understanding of different religious communities but to help convert Jewish people with the help of their language. The influence of Wagenseil's work shaped the negative impression of Yiddish, so the language attained a lasting shadow partly because of him and his influence. Oehme's contribution provides insight into the history of Yiddish. The attitude of the Christian German language community shows that the status of Yiddish as a separate language was called into question. Instead, Wagenseil's hostile attitude, shared by the majority of his speech community, reveals how religious intolerance and ideologues can further negatively influence the minority status of a language.

However, the irony of the situation cannot be ignored because *Belehrung* was the "most influential pre-modern Yiddish textbook" in teaching Yiddish.[28]

Both Sager and Oehme provide new readings of texts in different time periods. They offer insight into established scholarship and present their findings, adding to said scholarship but also new ways of thinking. For example, Sager shows the relationship between intimate autobiographical details, the representational nature of courtly poetry, and the poet's social status. Oehme points out a seventeenth-century textbook's polemical and antisemitic language. She maintains that this negative attitude of the Christian author ultimately eradicates Yiddish. The same language he purports to teach in his text.

Leaving Yiddish and Early New High German, we turn to the end of the twentieth century and the beginning of the subsequent language change in speech and text. While some minority varieties of German (such as Amish, Indiana, and Texas German) struggle with their changes and diminishment in an all-English environment (see Chapter 7). Some cultural changes trigger, in this case, German, a language change that has been under discussion since the last century.

The conversation around gender in a social and cultural context (this is not limited to a binary male/female divide but encompasses a fluid non-binary approach to gender) influences not only change in the language but also political change. As fluid as spoken language can be, an essential agreement on terminology and legal use of such terms is critical on the bureaucratic level where language and policy changes meet. In chapter six, James Stratton looks at gendered language in Modern German. In this case study, he analyzes whether prescriptive attempts to make German more gender-inclusive are reflected in everyday spoken German. His research considers language change on a social and cultural level, where gendered language has become an intense discussion regarding equity, legality, and use in public spaces such as schools. Cultural changes are reflected in language change, innovations, and neologisms that seek to provide a solution for more accessible communication.

His variationist sociolinguistic study considers the factors that influence the use of gender-inclusive language in everyday conversation. Observing this change is exciting and warrants more research in the area. First, he examines which variants of gender inclusivity are chosen in two speech communities: Westoverledingen in East Frisa and Basel in Switzerland. Second, he investigates the impact of social and linguistic factors on gender inclusivity. His preliminary conclusions were the preference of the generic masculine over gender-inclusive variants in spoken language. Stratton points to the difference in the

---

[28] See pg. 94.

Introduction   xxxi

written language. He finds that social and linguistic factors restricted gender-inclusive variations in the vernacular. These factors were age, education, and morphological composition. Stratton seeks to raise awareness of the important role of social factors in German variation and change, as previous research has historically focused predominantly on geography.

Chapter seven analyzes case syncretism in German-heritage varieties, specifically Indiana German. Karen Rösch's research with the Indiana German Dialect Project (IGDP) gathers data on several varieties of Indiana German. Her purpose is to document and preserve these endangered heritage varieties, collect sociolinguistic and historical data, and use the data to understand the linguistic features of these varieties.

Rösch's concern is the slow language death of Indiana German. Her data collection was limited to older heritage speakers because the younger generations had not learned the varieties. This challenge and that most of these last heritage speakers (the last fluent generation was born in the late 1940s) were not fluent in their heritage variety told her that these varieties were in the last stage of language death. Her study compared previous studies to see the changes in the heritage varieties, and she concludes that the observable case syncretism is "associated with the processes of a dying language."[29]

The effects of a dying language and its few remaining speakers have social and linguistic implications. With no one to learn these varieties, their death is inevitable, yet it gives linguists valuable insight into the life and death of languages. Approaches like this in current philological work provide an overview of the field's vibrancy in the twenty-first century.

The last chapter looks at the origin of philological work in the eighteenth and nineteenth centuries. Ulrike Wagner overviews philology's linguistic and philosophical sources and their "trajectory." She interlaces both with the trans-Atlantic exchange of liberal learning and what it meant to read philologically inside and outside academic institutions. Understanding the underlying philosophical currents that shaped English translations of German philological scholarship provides insight into the eighteenth and nineteenth-century American social significance of the translations. The cultural value attributed to philology at the time gave it a status, unlike other research disciplines.[30]

---

[29] See pg. 165.
[30] "Still, we are only beginning to recover how language study in its heyday formed the skeleton of modern erudition and gave us many disciplines that today make up the humanities and even social sciences. Historians have excavated philology's role in the origins of anthropology, of classics (as distinct from mere teaching of Greek and Latin), of comparative study of religions, of literary scholarship, indeed of certain kinds of legal

Approaches to philological research varied in the eighteenth and nineteenth centuries. From holistic approaches to strictly textual or linguistic analysis, debates between different scholars were lively and heated. For example, Wagner points to Herder and Wolf's differing opinions and accusations and Heyne and Winckelmann's divided approaches to reconstructing antiquity. The differences between the holistic and linguistic approaches were significant, and both had weaknesses. The first, trying to establish a contextual environment around the text, could rely too heavily on constructing imaginary ideals of the past, whereas the latter provided insight into critical linguistic facets of grammar, rhetoric, and etymology; however, it did not provide full context outside of the text. Since the latter approach succeeded in the nineteenth century and with the dawn of critical theory pushing philological and literary analysis to the side, a philological approach was no longer seen as it had been in the nineteenth century. As a result, the twenty-first century has inherited the problem of how to identify philology itself.

Wagner states that during the nineteenth century, Americans started studying at German universities, and some went on to teach at higher institutions of learning in the United States. They brought the European structure of philological research to the country that embraced it. Many other disciplines had gained inspiration and influence from philology, especially when it came to research practices.

Wagner analyses the translations of German works by translators George Ripley and James Marsh. She maintains that these texts bring "characteristics of what reading philologically implies" and "how critical techniques may generate new perspectives on matters of religion, culture, and individual Bildung."[31] *Bildung*, in terms of the romantic definition of "continuous self-development,"[32] is important to Wagner's analysis of American higher education, the process of open-ended learning, and the influence of critical work on the individual and their environment.

Looking back at the past, Wagner urges us to bring "the past in dialogue with today's debates."[33] The current critical position of the humanities and the

---

research. We have also become increasingly aware that two other learned activities, related in topics, method, and attitude, went alongside philology for most of its long history: rhetoric (the art of expressive speaking and writing) and antiquarianism (the study of physical and other relics of the past). Their traces, too, appears in scholarship today" Turner, *Philology: The Forgotten Origins of the Modern Humanities*, xii-xiii.
[31] See pg. 186.
[32] Ibid.
[33] See pg. 199.

precarious status of philology should remind us to look to the past with understanding and, with self-awareness, look to the future of philology.

The Future of Philology

The future of philology is a grandiose heading. We do not know the future, of course.[34] Therefore, we bookended the volume with the first and last chapters that looked at Germanic philology's "big" questions to frame the contributions. In essence, it is an attempt to open the conversation to give answers to the big questions. For example, Adam Oberlin provides a much-needed evaluation of the current periodization problems philologists have faced ever since the study of language change began. His call for including extralinguistic factors touches on one of the methodological foundations of philology. On the other hand, in the final chapter, Ulrike Wagner provides an in-depth look at philology's origin and how to read philologically in the eighteenth and nineteenth centuries, hence categorizing "philology" itself. Both chapters grapple with categories and help us look at language and texts, their changes, and how we, as scholars, categorize our work and the categories within which we work.

We optimistically propose that in the twenty-first century, we can use philology as a *Sammelbegriff* or an umbrella term under which various methods and approaches are welcome to evaluate texts and languages.[35] This

---

[34] In her editorial preface to *Shimmering Philology*, Michelle R. Warren presents an attempt to work with the past and speculate about the future of the discipline, stating "[i]n the end, philology is retrofuturist – simultaneously excavation, projection and fixing (in the present, but also for all time)," (*Postmedieval* 5, no. 4 (2014): 396). The edited volume provides, in both its diversity of world languages and breadth of different approaches, a possible way in which philology can develop in the future (389). While the volume looks at the big picture of world philology, our edition tackles the ideologically and ethically weighted Germanic branch. Since European philology owes some of its inheritance to German scholars, it is necessary to *aufarbeiten* or come to terms with how German scholars and Germanic philology shaped the academic discussion of the past centuries. If this tainted inheritance is not analyzed and processed, Germanic philology will become a fossil or at best a marginalized branch of linguistics, ignored by both language and linguistics departments. It is time to actively engage with the past and diversify our approaches to Germanic philology.

[35] Other than in *Shimmering Philology*, we are predominantly occupied with the linguistic approaches of the discipline and enhancing them. We share Sheldon Pollock's concern: "The core problem of philology today, as I see it, is whether it will survive at all; and it is philology's survival that I care about and how this might be secured" ("Future Philology? The Fate of a Soft Science in a Hard World," *Critical Inquiry* 35, no. 4 (2009): 931). His solution to that problem is three-fold, as he states: "Do not capitulate to others by uncritical acceptance, he seemed to tell us; instead, challenge and demand truth, for truth does exist. At the same time, work as hard as you can to try to see things their way,

edition provides a glimpse into these approaches. Philology is not only a linguistic discipline. To understand the linguistic changes scholars research, we need to look at extralinguistic factors (to borrow Oberlin's term). Philology has the potential to show a text in its different facets, including historical, theological, social, political, and linguistic factors. Truly understanding a text or a language means knowing it in these contexts.

However, this idea of philology as an umbrella term, an all-encompassing welcoming discipline with diverse approaches, also calls for processing its birth and past. Looking back to the beginnings of philological research at universities, one can see those philological techniques were influenced and even shaped by their academic, social, and political settings. Since universities in the eighteenth and nineteenth centuries consisted of a male-dominated environment and access to education was restricted for minorities, philology's methodologies and influence in academia began and existed in a highly controlled sphere.[36] The exclusion of the groups was to the detriment of the discipline. With that in mind, we need an expansion and inclusion of marginalized people, texts, and languages. Furthermore, the inward focus of Germanic philology has not served

---

be open to having your mind changed, search for a sharable interpretation, show to others the hospitality of 'friendly, respectful spirits trying to understand each other.' Last and most important, be reflective about the fact that your historicity shapes your interpretation and that problems of others touch your own being and have meaning for your life; be resolutely objective but passionately non- neutral" (961).

[36] Concerning the future of philology, Galt Harpham offers two choices, suggesting that scholars could become more careful not to fall into the same traps as their predecessors in centuries past. Still, he also maintains that: "If we are truly to assume the full burden of the history of philology, we must also allow ourselves to be instructed, inspired, and challenged by the genuine achievements of the greatest scholars of the philological tradition, who were intellectually curious and ambitious to a degree we can scarcely imagine. Their ambition was the germ of much of what today seems their errancy, but we cannot become virtuous simply by becoming small; nor does our abandonment of any pretense to methodology or any attempt to acquire comprehensive knowledge necessarily count in our favor. A revealing mirror, the history of philology combines in a single image scholarship's highest aspirations and darkest fears. The ongoing challenge is not which to choose, but how to tell them apart." ("Roots, Races, and the Return to Philology," *Representations* 106, no. 1 (2009): 56). We think that balance is necessary. Caution and deliberation in research do not stand against using the genuine achievements of the past and thinking expansively. The danger lies in romanticizing and idealizing the scholars of past centuries because with that comes the risk of thinking them greater than any who will follow. They were scholars, but they were also humans bound in a cultural web with all the preconceived notions and biases of their time. In this sense, we follow Pollock's advice that "historicity shapes your interpretation" (961).

it well in the last century. It has restricted an understanding of Germanic texts in a greater context outside the European lens.

Philology has not faded into the background. On the contrary, it adjusts to changes in time, embracing the new and innovative while maintaining the scientific principles of the past. There is no reason to fear that philology will disappear as long as philologists use old theories with proper respect to abuse in the past. This acknowledgment of philology in the wrong hands (ethically, morally, and scientifically) used for terrible purposes (ideologically, politically, socially) is essential in continuing the discipline. Much work must be done to rectify the mistakes of exclusion, racism, and misogyny to gain a fuller picture of our profession and its future.

Our model of philology inherited from male-dominated academies of the nineteenth century needs an influx of new approaches, among them anthropology and sociology, for example. Moving beyond linguistic analyses to see a bigger, more inclusive picture will help Germanic philology survive and thrive. With this expansion in mind, Pollock's words are essential to its success:

> [p]hilology enhances critical understanding and sharpens the demand for truth. At the same time, it enlarges the very domain of reality by enlarging our capacity to see things the way other people, people earlier than or otherwise different from us, have seen them.[37]

Furthermore, he states that philology "stimulates care for memory and helps shape a usable sense of the past, preserving memory from surrender to its enemies while opening the past to responsible, evidence-based critique."[38] These essential skills are at the heart of philological inquiry and will serve future philologists well. As a small part of this bigger picture, we hope our volume will contribute to the effort.

Bibliography

Enenkel, Karl, and Konrad Ottenheym. "Introduction - The Quest for an Appropriate Past: The Creation of National Identities in Early Modern Literature, Scholarship, Architecture, and Art." In *The Quest for an Appropriate Past in Literature, Art and Architecture*, 1–11. Leiden: Brill, 2018.

Featherstone, Mike, and Scott Lash. "Introduction." In *Spaces of Culture: City, Nation, World*, 1–13. London: Sage, 1999.

Harpham, Geoffrey Galt. "Roots, Races, and the Return to Philology." *Representations* 106, no. 1 (2009): 34–62.

---

[37] Sheldon Pollock, "Philology in Three Dimensions," *Postmedieval* 5, no. 4 (2014): 399.
[38] Ibid.

Kasten, Ingrid. "Einleitung." In *Transkulturalität Und Translation: Deutsche Literatur Des Mittelalters Im Europäischen Kontext*, 1–17. Berlin: De Gruyter, 2017.

Lakoff, George, and Mark Johnson. *Metaphors We Live By*. Chicago: University University Of Chicago Press, 1981.

Momma, Haruko. "Introduction: Where Is Philology?" In *From Philology to English Studies: Language and Culture in the Nineteenth Century*, 1–27. Cambridge: Cambridge University Press, 2012.

Pakis, Valentine A. *Perspectives on the Old Saxon Heliand: Introductory and Critical Essays, with an Edition of the Leipzig Fragment*. West Virginia University Press, 2010.

Pollock, Sheldon. "Future Philology? The Fate of a Soft Science in a Hard World." *Critical Inquiry* 35, no. 4 (2009): 931–61.

———. "Philology in Three Dimensions." *Postmedieval* 5, no. 4 (2014): 398–413.

Putnam, Michael T., and B. Richard Page, eds. *The Cambridge Handbook of Germanic Linguistics*. Cambridge Handbooks in Literature and Linguistics. Cambridge and New York: Cambridge University Press, 2020.

Turner, James. *Philology: The Forgotten Origins of the Modern Humanities*. Princeton, N.J.: Princeton University Press, 2014.

Warren, Michelle R. "Shimmering Philology." *Postmedieval* 5, no. 4 (2014): 389–97.

Wegmann, Nikolaus. "Philology - An Update." In *The Future of Philology: Proceedings of the 11th Annual Columbia University German Graduate Student Conference*, edited by Hannes Bajohr, Benjamin R. Dorvel, Vincent Hessling, and Tabea Weitz, 28–46. Newcastle-upon-Tyne, UK: Cambridge Scholars Publisher, 2014.

Welsch, Wolfgang. "Transculturality: The Puzzling Form of Cultures Today." In *Spaces of Culture: City, Nation, World*, edited by Mike Featherstone and Scott Lash, 2–28. London: Sage, 1999.

Chapter 1

On Language History and Extralinguistic Periodization in Germanic

Adam Oberlin
Princeton

"Any system of periodization is thus inevitably social, since our ability to envision the historical watersheds separating one conventional 'period' from another is basically a product of being socialized into specific *traditions* of carving the past. In other words, we need to be mnemonically socialized to regard certain historical events as 'turning points.'"[1]

Abstract: This chapter will not provide a novel argument for the organization of linguistic history in the Germanic languages, but rather seeks to contextualize current models and directions in linguistic and literary studies on the one hand and to emphasize the rationale for further consideration of the role of literary history and other factors in the linguistic periodization of the pre-modern Germanic languages on the other. One of the universally recognized hallmarks of language periodization is that it is as scientifically necessary as it is necessarily difficult to justify; there are indeed distinct periods and mechanisms of change, but as in other areas of historical research, the taxonomic and archeological methods and approaches in historical linguistics are neither uniform nor uncontested. Methodological concerns in language periodization begin with structural models according to criteria of interruption and/or consistency and their lack (e.g., interrupted and uniform change in a traditional step model or uninterrupted and irregular change in an erratic wave form) and proceed through sometimes-overlapping categories of extralinguistic

---

[1] Eviatar Zerubavel, *Time Maps: Collective Memory and the Social Shape of the Past* (Chicago: University of Chicago Press, 2003), 95.

and linguistic criteria. Instances of the former include linguistic-historically significant events and people, dominant groups or identities of speakers/writers, and media-historical developments, while the latter consists of the familiar categories of derivational and inflectional morphological, syntactic, lexical, orthographic, and phonological changes.

For example, while both the structural underpinnings and various attributes of language change offer significant challenges to periodization, perhaps the greatest point of contention belongs to the transitional stages between identifiable periods. According to current argumentation, which is uncontroversial in the broad strokes, there exist periods of relatively distinct phenomena along a diachronic linguistic continuum, between which are transition zones, e.g., in English the period between the Norman conquest and the Early Middle English texts of the second half of the twelfth century, and in German the partially typological restructuring of the language between late MHG and ENHG. Whether these periods exhibit epistemological consistency or fulfill sufficiently explanatory functions, however, remain unanswered questions. How one groups, defines, and understands periods through a linguistic lens is inseparable from other systems of temporal topography and methods from literary history, historiography, and the philosophy of history, which may offer useful insights when applied to linguistic periodization.

Keywords: Premodern Germanic; historical linguistics; periodization

***

Philological inquiry presupposes the pastness of all or, in the case of comparison with contemporary language stages, at least some of its subjects; it is fundamentally a diachronic pursuit, both an examination of and method of creating historical documentation. From this starting point, all philological study must grapple with temporal structures. Historical linguistics' methodological *terra firma*, although flecked with the quicksand of controversy, is surrounded by rather more fluid epistemological and ontological problems. Periodization ranks among the thorniest historical linguistic paradigms, provoking in every diachronic language survey various anxieties that lie beneath lists of common features or changes and occupy at least some space in literature on historical language stages. Among studies of the Germanic languages, as among many others, these anxieties are pronounced: to what extent is the traditional tripartite (old, middle, new) division of language history valid? What does it mean for a language to be at a particular stage? Which quanta lend themselves to analysis? What discriminatory means can one apply to chronologies or systems of chronology? Can a language be assigned to a stage asynchronously from generalized, cross-linguistically-defined periods?[2] The following account of issues and possibilities in Germanic language periodization stems from the insufficiency of a single disciplinary model, apparent in many theoretical discussions of periodization in which language is either the primary or secondary object of diachronic analysis. A more inclusive and, therefore, explanatory periodization requires an account that encompasses extralinguistic frameworks of temporal organization, not only extralinguistic factors in an otherwise strictly historical linguistic framework. Historiography and the philosophy of history, literary history, and social history provide additional epistemological foundations for the reorganization of linguistic periodization.

Problems in Periodization

One of the hallmarks of language periodization is that it is both scientifically necessary and difficult to justify: it is "ein wissenschaftlich notwendiger, aber nur mehr oder weniger begründbarer Versuch, die kontinuierliche diachronische Entwicklung nach bestimmten Kriterien des Sprachsystems zu unterteilen" ['a scientifically necessary, but only more or less justifiable attempt to subdivide continuous diachronic development according to particular criteria of the language system'].[3] There are indeed distinct periods and mechanisms of change, but as in other areas of historical research, the taxonomic and archeological methods and approaches of historical linguistics are neither uniform nor universally agreed upon. Methodological concerns in language periodization begin with motivations and originary assumptions, from *in principio erat verbum* and an eschatological/teleological analytical framework to the implications of phylogenetic metaphors and evolutionary *Ahnentafel/ Stammbaum* models. Later structural models adhere to criteria of interruption and/or consistency and their lack, e.g., interrupted and uniform change in a traditional step model or uninterrupted and irregular change in an erratic wave

---

[2] This question reveals the additional complications that arise when viewing language history from familial or areal perspectives. Even within the same language family, neighboring languages may fall under different periodization schemata or exhibit different breaks and transition zones between periods, resulting in a situation in which even closely related cross-linguistic periodizations are difficult to reconcile and require taking a methodological stance.

[3] Stefan Sonderegger, *Grundzüge deutscher Sprachgeschichte. Diachronie des Sprachsystems*, vol. 1 (Berlin: de Gruyter, 1979), 169. Despite such difficulties, the enduring consensus can be condensed as follows: "Still, dividing language history into periods is a valuable heuristic, a way of organizing things that allows us to develop better analyses." Joseph Salmons, *A History of German*, 2nd ed. (Oxford: OUP, 2018), 191.

form,[4] and proceed through sometimes-overlapping categories of extralinguistic and linguistic criteria. Examples of extralinguistic criteria include linguistic-historically significant events and people, dominant groups or identities of speakers/writers, and media-historical developments, while linguistic criteria consist of the familiar categories of derivational and inflectional morphological, syntactic, lexical, orthographic, and phonological changes.[5]

While both the structural underpinnings and various attributes of language change offer significant challenges to periodization, perhaps the greatest point of contention belongs to the transitional stages between more clearly identifiable periods. According to current scholarly consensus, there exist periods of relatively distinct phenomena along a diachronic linguistic continuum. Between periods of distinct phenomena lie transition zones, e.g., in English, the period between the Norman conquest and the Early Middle English texts of the second half of the twelfth century, and in German the partially typological restructuring of the language between late Middle High German and Early New High German–to use Thorsten Roelcke's metaphor, the *frühneuhochdeutsche Brücke*.[6] Stefan Sonderegger describes this phenomenon in terms of a continuum punctuated with distinct norms between which periods of indistinct properties form transitional phases.[7] In the case of the history of German, understanding the geographical-dialectal distinctions in the development of new language stages requires the denormalization of regional linguistic landscapes. However, as Sonderegger notes, the transitional period is not the only available paradigm to describe discrete points in diachronic language change: each primary division is likewise marked by a comprehensibility boundary, resulting in a tripartite scheme of boundaries separating Old High German from late common (West) Germanic, Middle High German from Old High German, and Early New High German from

---

[4] Thorsten Roelcke, "Die Periodisierung der deutschen Sprachgeschichte," in *Sprachgeschichte*, ed. Werner Besch et al., vol. 2.1 (Berlin: de Gruyter, 1998), 799.
[5] See Thorsten Roelcke, ed., *Periodisierung. Die zeitliche Gliederung der deutschen Sprachgeschichte*, Dokumentation Germanistischer Forschung 4 (Frankfurt: Peter Lang, 2001), 10-13; Thorsten Roelcke, *Periodisierung der deutschen Sprachgeschichte. Analysen und Tabellen*, Studia Linguistica Germania 40 (Berlin: de Gruyter, 1995), 29-31; Sonderegger, *Grundzüge*, 199-202; and C.J. Wells, *Deutsch: eine Sprachgeschichte bis 1945*, trans. Rainhild Wells, Reihe Germanistische Linguistik 93 (Tübingen: Niemeyer, 1990), 25-31.
[6] See Thorsten Roelcke, "Die frühneuhochdeutsche Brücke. Überlegungen zur sprachtypologischen Periodisierung der deutschen Sprachgeschichte," *Zeitschrift für deutsche Philologie* 119.3 (2000): 369-96.
[7] Sonderegger, *Grundzüge*, 169-72.

Middle High German.[8] While the resulting periods remain the same, in this paradigm, the grounds for division shift the focus from mechanisms and realizations of change to their effects on speakers or, perhaps better stated, readers. In terms of nomenclatural problems, the concept of 'middle' itself poses particular difficulties. While this is partially the legacy of triadomania among the neogrammarians and a logic problem in the form of ever-rightward shifting frames of reference, it is also indicative of a typology, albeit a 'fuzzy' one.[9]

Extralinguistic factors of the type previously mentioned expand our view of linguistic diachrony and help explain, for example, the extent and processes of contact phenomena in the engagement of the Anglo-Saxon kingdoms with the peoples of the Danelaw[10] or colonial/koinéization processes as in early modern Dano-Norwegian.[11] Additionally, from the perspective of historical materialism, East German linguists such as Joachim Schildt unsurprisingly championed historical-socioeconomic factors as drivers of language change.[12] Our view may be broadened further: counting among the language-external periodization criteria are certain literary-historical factors such as genre, text-type, the emergence of secular literature, and the transmission of foreign literatures. Textual grounds are the only available sources on which evidence for diachronic language change beyond the lifespan of living speakers can be established. On the example of German, the Middle High German language stage is inseparable from its literary production and the composition of its literary corpus. This involves not only linguistic phenomena such as cross-regional normalization from the perspective of developments from the Old

---

[8] Ibid., 185-93.
[9] See Roger Lass, "Language Periodization and the Concept 'Middle'," in *Placing Middle English in Context*, eds. Irma Taavitsainen et al., Topics in English Linguistics 35, 7-41 (Berlin: de Gruyter, 2000).
[10] For a recent study on morphological change, see Florian Dolberg, *Agreement in Language Contact: Gender Development in the Anglo-Saxon Chronicle*, Studies in Language Companion Series 208 (Amsterdam: John Benjamins, 2019), and on lexis Sara M. Ponz-Sanz, *The Lexical Effects of Anglo-Scandinavian Linguistic Contact on Old English*, Studies in the Early Middle Ages 1 (Turnhout: Brepols, 2013). Both studies are diachronic in scope.
[11] For example, political and social conflicts leading to linguistic policy-making strategies both as compromise and in identity-formation processes. See Oddmund L. Hoel, *Nasjonalisme i norsk målstrid 1848-1865*, KULTs skriftserie 51 (Oslo: Noregs forskingsråd, 1996).
[12] See Joachim Schildt, "Zum Verhältnis von Gesellschafts- und Sprachgeschichte: Periodisierungsprobleme," in *Zur Periodisierung der deutschen Sprachgeschichte: Prinzipien – Probleme – Aufgaben*, ed. Joachim Schildt, Linguistische Studien, Reihe A 88, Berlin: Akademie der Wissenschaften der DDR, 1982, 30-39.

High German period, but also extra-linguistic and inherently literary-historical phenomena such as the importation of French lexical items and phrases via the transmission of literary currents and core narrative traditions in the High Middle Ages.

This fundamental entanglement can be seen in the fact that lexical differences between Old High German and Middle High German cannot be removed from the literary-historical developments that account for the presence or absence of lexical items in various domains and in various text types (e.g., poetic archaisms or the constraints of *Stabreim*). This situation is more nuanced than can be explained by a religious-secular generic dichotomy. In languages with smaller, generically restricted, or otherwise interpretively difficult corpora, the same dynamic governs the lexical inventory: for example, Old Saxon, whose primary literary attestation the *Hêliand* also comprises the bulk of the surviving corpus, exhibits a high degree of interference of this type. Because of the style and form in which the *Hêliand* was written, regardless of the interpretive lens through which one views it, its lexical inventory contains an abundance of items from domains attributed to Germanic heroic legend despite the context and genre of the poem. Old Saxon is also chronologically narrow compared to the attested span of neighboring Old High German. However, this means neither that Old Saxon preserves an older or pre-Christian vocabulary better than other contemporary Germanic languages and dialects nor that it resists lexical developments introduced by Christianization, nor further that it was spoken for a shorter duration.[13] Instead these lexical characteristics are contingent, circumstantial and, in terms of causality, entirely extra-linguistic: the historical factors of Charlemagne's wars against the Saxons, their subsequent conversion, and whatever stylistic reasons or purpose it may have, the *Hêliand*'s form leave us with an extraordinary document, not a representative one, "[…] not written in a vacuum but was, as is everything, a

---

[13] Compare the standard OHG period of the eighth to eleventh centuries with the ninth to twelfth for OS. Lexical influence from within Germanic has long been the object of research in the field, from early handbooks to later, more detailed studies. See, for example, Ferdinand Holthausen, *Altsächsisches Elementarbuch*, Sammlung von Elementarbüchern der altgermanischen Dialekte 5 (Heidelberg: Winter, 1899) and Werner Simon, *Zur Sprachmischung im Heliand*, Philologische Studien und Quellen 27 (Berlin: Erich Schmidt, 1965).

product of its place and time."[14] Summarizing the *status quaestionis* made possible by G. Ronald Murphy in 1989,[15] Seiichi Suzuki writes:

> "Without deviating from the theological and dogmatic orthodoxy in the least, the poem reworks the Gospels by adapting to the traditional Germanic cultural world as fully as seems possible. The poet put to practice accommodating methods at all levels of composition, ranging from micro-linguistic units such as lexis and phraseology to macro-narrative devices such as stage setting, description of scenes, sequencing of events, and demarcation of narrative units (fitts or songs)[.]"[16]

Structurally and in terms of content, this depiction is correct. However, while appearing rhetorically extreme without the ameliorating context of the subsequent "dennoch," Johannes Rathofer's proclamation on the state of the poem's lexical-semantic and textual ambiguity also remains substantively accurate:

> "Erst wenn wir wissen, ob und in welchem Maße das aus der germanischen Dichtung stammende Wort- und Bildgut die ursprünglich mit ihm verbundenen Vorstellungen und Bedeutungen aufgegeben und einen inhaltlichen Wandel in Richtung auf die ganz neuen christlich religiösen Sinnzusammenhänge durchgemacht hat, die diese alten Wörter nunmehr ausdrücken sollten, und aus denen heraus sie dann mit ihrem neuen Gehalt zu verstehen waren und auch verstanden werden konnten, – erst dann werden wir bei einer gehaltlichen Interpretation des *Hêliand* nicht in die Irre gehen."

> ['Only when we know whether and to what extent the lexical and symbolic inventory originating from Germanic poetry has relinquished the ideas and meanings originally associated with it and has undergone a change in content in the direction of the completely new Christian-religious contexts of meaning that these old words should now signify, and from which they were to be understood with their new content and

---

[14] James E. Cathey, "The Historical Setting of the Heliand, the Poem, and the Manuscripts," in *Perspectives on the Old Saxon* Heliand: *Introductory and Critical Essays, with an Edition of the Leipzig Fragment*, ed. Valentine A. Pakis, Medieval European Studies XII (Morgantown: University of West Virginia Press, 2010), 3.

[15] G. Ronald Murphy, *The Saxon Savior: The Germanic Transformation of the Gospel in the Ninth-Century Heliand* (Oxford: OUP, 1989).

[16] Seiichi Suzuki, *The Metre of Old Saxon Poetry: The Remaking of an Alliterative Tradition* (Cambridge: D.S. Brewer, 2004), 2.

also could be understood - only then will we not go astray in an interpretation of the content of the *Hêliand.*']¹⁷

A formidable task as articulated here, but normatively indicative of the contingency of language history in social history and political history. Rathofer's project *in toto* reflects another consequence of small corpora, namely a baroque interpretation inversely proportional to the extent of the text(s). Although the meaning, form, and composition of the Old Saxon gospel harmony will continue to provoke in this manner, most often on the basis of lexicography, the study of Old Saxon lexis, much like Gothic, benefits from comparative treatment in standard lexica in order to cover perceived gaps and enhance the relatively restricted corpus from which they are derived.[18] That this does not occur with, for example, Middle High German and Middle Dutch is as much a function of corpus, and therefore reference work, size as it is of national language status.

Analogous claims may be made about the status of both the chronology and the lexical inventory of Old Frisian, e.g., in the context of alliterative word pairs, which are not uncontested markers of old Germanic oral literature.[19] Attested in a relatively small number of texts primarily from the legal sphere, Old Frisian in its widest sense spans the sixth through the sixteenth centuries, the first half

---

[17] Johannes Rathofer, *Der Heliand,. Theologischer Sinn als tektonische Form. Vorbereitung und Grundlegung der Interpretation*, Niederdeutsche Studien 9 (Cologne: Böhlau, 1962), 18-19.

[18] A recent Old Saxon dictionary relies on comparison with words from Anglo-Saxon and Old High German sources relating to Old Saxon, Heinrich Tiefenbach, *Altsächsisches Handwörterbuch. A Concise Old Saxon Dictionary* (Berlin: de Gruyter, 2010), vii-viii, while the standard Gothic reference is fundamentally centered on comparative Germanic and Indo-European organizational principles, Sigmund Feist, *Vergleichendes Wörterbuch der Gotischen Sprache Mit Einschluss des Krimgotischen und sonstiger zerstreuter Überreste des Gotischen*, 3rd rev. ed. (Leiden: Brill, 1939).

[19] "Although the technique dates back to the common Germanic period, as is demonstrated by the many binomial phrases which Old Frisian shares with other Germanic languages and by obsolete words petrified in alliterative word pairs, this revered age need not imply that the Frisian laws themselves, too, date back to long before the coming of literacy to Frisia, at a time when law was allegedly recited as verse during ceremonial court sessions of the people. Nor is the presence of alliteration to be seen as a mnemonic device that facilitated the mental storage of laws before the introduction of literacy. Rather, the use of alliterative phrases was stimulated by the example set by ecclesiastical and administrative Latin prose and was a shared phenomenon in Western Europe, well into the Renaissance." Rolf H. Bremmer, "Dealing Dooms: Alliteration in the Old Frisian Laws," in *Alliteration in Culture*, ed. Jonathan Roper (Basingstoke: Palgrave Macmillan, 2011), 88.

of which is subsumed also under Proto-Frisian periods. In written documents, however, it extends only from the thirteenth through the sixteenth centuries[20] and is thus contemporary with other 'middle' languages such as Middle English, Middle Dutch, Middle Low German, and Middle High German. This period also overlaps partially the slightly later Old/Middle transition in East and West Norse languages while fully encompassing the middle period (for example, Middle Norwegian is entirely within the Old Frisian period). While it has been argued by Arjen Versloot and others that Old Frisian is typologically an 'old' Germanic language according to numerous criteria of syntax, inflection, word-formation, lexicon, negation, numeral declension, orthography, etc., the old argument that the "great age of content of the Old Frisian texts [is] to be distinguished from the age of the actual manuscripts containing the texts" still deserves attention.[21] Chronology and state languages seem to exhibit an epistemological symbiosis; for Old Frisian, the diachronic trajectory toward dispersal, fragmentation and non-standard status can occlude synchronic knowledge with immediate political effect. On the example of toponyms in the present, "[t]he consequence [of this opaque diachronic process of borrowing and layering] is that the synchronic perception of what is a Frisian endonym and what an exonym from a neighboring language does often not match the linguistic derivation," exposing that the root of the problem is inextricable from extralinguistic factors. "Even when onomastics can provide background knowledge on the origin of names, the core of this debate is subject to disciplines such as mass-psychology, rather than to onomastics[,]"[22] highlighting the extralinguistic factors that contribute to the interpretation of otherwise strictly linguistic data.

Perhaps further from the previous two examples, and yet from a bird's eye view also falling under similar taxonomic, evidential, and lexical difficulties, is the situation of Gothic; although the East Germanic languages generally suffer from extraordinarily poor attestation, Gothic presents enough evidence of the language during Wulfila's time and in bits and scraps from later centuries to imagine Old and Middle stages, if not further, by the time of de Busbecq's reporting of Crimean Gothic in the sixteenth century. Such an experiment would address the generic overrepresentation of New Testament vocabulary and numerous points of syntactic and other types of interference from Koiné

---

[20] Rolf H. Bremmer, *An Introduction to Old Frisian: History, Grammar, Reader, Glossary* (Amsterdam: John Benjamins, 2009), xii.
[21] Arjen Versloot, "Why Old Frisian is Still Quite Old," *Folia Linguistica Historica* 25 (2004): 264. The author also proposes a Middle Frisian period from ca. 1400-1550.
[22] Arjen Versloot, "Frisian Place-Names and Place Names in Friesland," *Onoma* 46 (2011): 146.

Greek in the two primary mss., *Codex Argenteus* and *Codex Ambrosianus*, and other fragmentary sources, which are made clearer by the comparative evidence afforded by the chance survival of the native *Skeireins*. One could imagine a genealogy of Gothic complicating the tripartite scheme in a similar manner to Old Frisian, a taxonomy whose 'middle' branch would undoubtedly more closely resemble the 'old' forms of West and North Germanic languages. But we need not rely on speculation alone for the duration of the 'old' period, however, slight as the available evidence may be: the discovery in 2015 of the graffiti in Mangup, Crimea, offers at least tentative support for the continuation of Wulfila's Gothic into the ninth and tenth centuries, not only as a colloquial spoken language alongside liturgical Greek, but also as a written liturgical and commemorative language among clerics and the laity, whose form is likely not a frozen archaic remnant.[23] Extant late antique and medieval textual sources of Wulfila's Gothic suggest that the language had not undergone any perceptible diachronic change. Crimean Gothic, on the other hand, presents in the current discussion a different sort of challenge than the usual question of genealogical descent. From de Busbecq to Adelung's citation of a report asserting similarity between a Germanic Tatar language and "Plattdeutsch"[24] to later reports and copies of the glossary, names, and 'song,' Crimean Gothic has always been represented at several levels of remove.[25] Whether Crimean Gothic is, as Stearns argues, an East Germanic language not descended from Wulfila's Gothic, or, as Grønvik and others have argued, a West Germanic language under the influence of East Germanic forms and phonology,[26] its questionable dialect-geographical status and minute corpus render it of little use as comparative evidence for the later development of Gothic as preserved in the biblical corpus, if such a stage ever existed. Language death is never apolitical or caused by 'natural,' intralinguistic, forces; whatever the corpus size or availability of textual evidence after the tenth century, the hindrance to periodization in Gothic is extralinguistically contingent on the defeat of Arianism, the conversion of various peoples to other forms of Christianity, or integration into Greek and other language communities from Iberia to the Black Sea. For Crimean Gothic, regardless of typology, not only had contact

---

[23] See Maksim Korobov and Andrey Vinogradov, "Gotische Graffito-Inschriften aus der Bergkrim," *Zeitschrift für deutsches Altertum und Literatur* 145.2 (2016): 141-57.
[24] Johan Christoph Adelung, *Mithridates oder allgemeine Sprachenkunde*, vol. 4 (Berlin: Vossische Buchhandlung, 1817), 168.
[25] Patrick Stiles, "A Textual Note of Busbecq's "Crimean Gothic" *Cantilena*," *Neophilologus* 68 (1984): 637-39.
[26] See the summary in MacDonald Stearns, "Das Krimgotische," in *Germanische Rest- und Trümmersprachen*, ed. Heinrich Beck, Ergänzungsbände zum RGA 3, 175-94 (Berlin: de Gruyter, 1989), 181-85.

broken off with other Gothic-speaking peoples in the Early Middle Ages and they had assimilated to some degree with Tatar culture centuries later, "[s]chon immer fanden sich die Krimgoten umgeben von den Sprachen anderer Völker wie Hunnen, Avaren, Bulgaren, Utiguren, Alanen, Griechen, Tataren, Chasaren, Mongolen, Armenier, Genuesen, Venezianer, Türken" ['the Crimean Goths always found themselves surrounded by the languages of other peoples, such as Huns, Avars, Bulgars, Utigurs, Alans, Greeks, Tatars, Khazars, Mongols, Armenians, Genoese, Venetians, Turks'].[27]

At the nexus of periodization, language history, and literary history lies the Old English and Old Norse pairing, as notable for its discontinuities as for its utility. Mentioned previously in the context of Old Frisian, the designation of a Germanic language as 'old' is determined relatively, not statically, and attested Old Norse does not overlap OE in any substantial way, particularly if one looks at the bulk of manuscript production. That Old Norse is 'old' linguistically is not only uncontroversial, but also the very diachronic conservatism of Icelandic renders certain arguments in periodization more difficult by extension, to say nothing of typological and extralinguistic conditional similarities between Old English and Old Norse.[28] And yet the contemporary of Old Norse is not Old English but Middle English, despite centuries of 'old stage' coexistence in the British Isles leading to the significant influence of North Germanic on the history of English.[29] As with the example of Old Frisian, it is the assumed or demonstrable age of textual content rather than the date of composition or copying that facilitates such common comparison with Old English literary monuments in service to both literary and linguistic arguments. Ubiquitous literary anthologies for students and the name of the ASNAC program at Cambridge offer two examples of this intertwining. This (admittedly mostly

---

[27] Stearns, "Das Krimgotische," 186
[28] For example, Hans Frede Nielsen, "The Vowel Systems of Old English, Old Norse and Old High German Compared," in *Early Germanic Languages in Contact*, eds. John Ole Askedal and Hans Frede Nielsen, Nowele Supplement Series 27, 261-76 (Amsterdam: John Benjamins, 2015)
[29] For example, Dolberg, *Agreement in Language Change*, and Pons-Sanz, *The Lexical Effects of Anglo-Scandinavian Linguistic Contact*, cited in n. 9 above; research on the diachrony of Norse influence has been extended into the ME period in terms of attestation, see Angelika Lutz, "Norse Loans in Middle English and their Influence on Late Medieval London English," *Anglia* 135 (2017): 317-57. It is also worth noting that the presence of similar or different features cross-linguistically are contingent on many forces other than contact, including historical processes than remain unclear, for example, Anatoly Liberman, "Some Unsolved (and Probably Insoluble) Aspects of Initial Fricative Voicing in Early English: Voicing in Early English Viewed as Part of the Great Germanic Lenition," in *Early Germanic Languages in Contact*, 245-60.

defensible and beneficial) approach had for generations dominated not only comparative work in Old English but also the backwards-glancing focus in Old Norse scholarship. Given that the manuscript evidence of Old Norse texts is generally not only late but sometimes no longer even medieval in a strict sense, and that the body of Old Norse literature comprises so much more than the *Íslendingasögur*, *Fornaldarsögur*, and mythological texts, it is no surprise that recent decades have seen a shift in priorities. This shift has led toward examining streams of common medieval European literary tradition in the North and the history of Nordic manuscript culture synchronically, as well as its reception history, not only comparative-diachronically from the quasi-legendary time of actual narratives or putative *Urlegende* and *-texte*.[30] In part informed by the New Philology and comparative literature and philology (e.g., with French or Latin), this outward and forward turn in Old Norse studies has produced a more nuanced and accurate picture of the late medieval realities of both the non-normalized Old Norse language and its literary history.[31] It is only in the context of a small number of texts, albeit canonical and therefore widely discussed, that the triangulation of Old Norse onomastic or other evidence bears on the interpretation of texts such as *Beowulf*, whether proposed or refuted.[32] Likewise, the chronological near-monomania that characterizes a significant body of comparative scholarship on the Nibelung and Tristan legends, one example from epic and the other from romance, across the Old Norse-continental divide illustrates the anachronistic, stemmatic triangulation of *Urtext* from which current research has somewhat distanced itself. 'Old Norse' can be viewed in the historical context of Old and Middle Icelandic, Middle Norwegian, Middle Swedish, and Middle Danish in order to trace the

---

[30] To name only a few very recent examples, see Margaret Clunies Ross, ed., *The Pre-Christian Religions of the North: Research and Reception*, 2 vols. (Turnhout: Brepols, 2018); Mikael Males, *The Poetic Genesis of Old Icelandic Literature*, Ergänzungsbände zum RGA 113 (Berlin: de Gruyter, 2019); and Amy C. Mulligan and Else Mundal, eds., *Moving Words in the Nordic Middle Ages: Tracing Literacies, Texts, and Verbal Communities*, Acta Scandinavica 8 (Turnhout: Brepols, 2019).

[31] Inwardly, too, periodization has both fractured and expanded according to linguistic and extralinguistic criteria for individual languages and among the Nordic languages. See Oskar Bandle, et al., eds., *The Nordic Languages: An International Handbook of the History of the North Germanic Languages*, 2 vols. (Berlin: de Gruyter, 2002), particularly the chapters on previous periodization models and literary historical background for each language.

[32] For an example of the former, see Paul Beekman Taylor, "*Searoniðas*: Old Norse Magic and Old English Verse," *Studies in Philology* 80.2 (1983): 109-25, and for the latter, a recent article strongly refuting any Norse influence in the poem: Leonard Neidorf and Rafael J. Pascual, "Old Norse Influence on the Language of Beowulf: A Reassessment," *Journal of Germanic Linguistics* 31.3 (2019): 298-322.

growth and dissemination of its textual evidence, which is likewise categorically extensive. Old Norse literary history is generically broad, both transnational in geographical scope and, in evidential terms, chronologically distributed across the High and Late Middle Ages and into the Renaissance and early modern period.

Collected and discussed thoroughly by Thorsten Roelcke in 1995, there have been in the intervening years few new periodizations of German to add to the core models of linguistic chronology proposed earlier, notwithstanding various arguments for (dis)continuities and literary historical approaches, such as John M. Jeep's extralinguistic case for the role and depiction of women in vernacular literature as a potential bridge between the OHG and MHG periods.[33] For the Nordic languages, a general cross-linguistic division of ancient-old-modern,[34] which correspond to prehistoric, runic-medieval, and literary-early modern and modern periods of linguistic-literary history, exists alongside other divisions for individual languages. These divisions have been normalized and aligned with traditional tripartite models of old-middle-new, as in Danish, whose periodization once held multiple 'old' designations (cf. *old-, gammel-, ældre middle-*),[35] and in Icelandic, in which the great shift in the middle period is phonological rather than inflectional or lexical.[36] Boundaries shift, periods are further partitioned, and in some proposals, extralinguistic factors play a role in nomenclature, but the basic divisions persist. This is unsurprising given the empirical and theoretical phenomena that undergird diachrony in the Germanic languages–changes in typology, morphology, phonology, and lexis– and no flirtation with radically different approaches seems likely to topple the dominant linguistic paradigm. Language history, however, also remains within the disciplinary and philosophical horizon of history and is itself part of the

---

[33] John M. Jeep, "Women in the Vernacular and the Periodization of Medieval German Literature," *Medieval Feminist Newsletter* 23 (1997): 37-47, and elaborated in terms of the OHG evidence in John M. Jeep, "The Roles of Women in Old High German Literature," *Mediaevistik* 14 (2001): 95-123. Jeep's work in alliterating word-pairs also charts continuities and discontinuities in linguistic periodization on the basis of phraseological units; see *Alliterating Word-Pairs in Old High German*, Studien zur Phraseologie und Parömiologie 3 (Bochum: Brockmeyer, 1995), and *Alliterating Word- Pairs in Early Middle High German*, Phraseologie und Parömiologie 21, (Baltmannsweiler: Schneider Verlag Hohengehren, 2006).

[34] For example, part of the organizational basis of Bandle et al., eds., *The Nordic Languages*.

[35] Bent Jørgensen, "Sproghistoriske perioder," in *Dansk Sproghistorie 1: Dansk tager form*, eds. Ebba Hjorth et al., 79-83 (Copenhagen and Aarhus: Det Danske Sprog- og Litteraturselskab and Aarhus Universitetsforlag, 2016).

[36] Kristján Árnason, *The Phonology of Icelandic and Faroese* (Oxford: OUP, 2011), 11-23.

historical sciences as an object of discursive significance. In the next section, several possible ways of conceptualizing periodization and linguistic diachrony provide a bridge between historical linguistics and other disciplines.

Interventions

In the fourth edition of the *Encyclopaedia Brittanica* published in 1810, the entry "Germany" in vol. 9 spans 20 pages (673-93), highlighting the temporally unstable and difficult-to-define borders of a state, the *Rheinbund*, just over halfway through its short-lived existence between the cessation of the War of the Third Coalition and the Treaty of Paris.[37] After a discussion of the borders primarily via the territories of neighboring states, the entry further describes a historical chronology from the third century BCE onward, as well as the contemporary political structure of Germany with a few statistical charts of the military strengths of the various German polities and their revenues. One map can be found near the end of the entry. A century later, after the rise and consolidation of modern universities, academic disciplines, and the first united German state, the eleventh edition of the *Encyclopedia Brittanica* reflects significant changes both in the objects of its entries and in its editorial practices, contributors, motivations, and scale.[38] After separate articles on the German language and its history, German literary history, and German colonial history, which was separated into two articles on German South West Africa and German East Africa, the updated entry "Germany" in vol. 11 spans nearly one hundred pages (804-901). It contains, among other information, a detailed statistical survey of Germany's physical and human geography: time zones (both observation and a painstakingly exact mention of the 1 hour 8 minute span from east to west), degrees of latitude and longitude, the distance between extreme points, the lengths of various coastlines and total coastlines in miles, the lengths of various borders and total borders in miles, the land area excluding bodies of water, population, commerce, railways, and so on. Clearly, more than a shift in scope has occurred. We have moved from one period to another, not simply moved one hundred years forward in time.[39]

---

[37] "Germany," in *Encyclopaedia Brittanica*, ed. James Millar, 4th ed., vol. 9 (Edinburgh: A. Bell, 1810).
[38] Arthur William Holland, "Germany," in *Encyclopaedia Brittanica*, ed. Hugh Chisholm, 11th ed., vol. 11 (Cambridge: CUP, 1911).
[39] The developments and discontinuities that provoked these encyclopedic, statistical, and citational differences are themselves contested markers of periodization within the long nineteenth century. See Jürgen Osterhammel, *Die Verwandlung der Welt: eine Geschichte des 19. Jahrhunderts* (Munich: C.H. Beck, 2009), 84-128 for a historiographical overview of temporality, and Martin Hewitt, "Introduction: Victorian Milestones," In *The*

While historical linguistics has moved beyond narratives of progress and decline, nonlinear or other non-traditional approaches have been argued in literary periodization longer and in greater depth than for language. Analogous to the ways in which the encyclopedic description of a state changes not only with its march through time, but also with the ways that history is divided, measured, and presented, language history and periodization have in some ways already escaped their linguistic boundaries. Revisions to language history need not only encompass periodization–as the entire multidisciplinary field of PIE migration studies[40] and Theo Vennemann's career as a revisionist of prehistoric contact phenomena in Europe attest–but nevertheless cannot be detached from the concerns of periodization wherever chronological, linguistic, or extralinguistic factors are concerned. Moreover, the politics of linguistic periodization reflect similar concerns in historiography; for example, much in the way that the ubiquitous cartographic representation of *Kleinstaaterei* in the Holy Roman Empire alongside neat borders for larger polities elsewhere in Europe obscures a persistent history of 'feudal' entanglements and ruptures in France or Spain, the construction of periods and transitional zones in one language can elide the same phenomena in another that shares types of phonological and grammatical changes, but whose disciplinary argumentation have diverged. An analogy with state history is not entirely coincidental: one handbook of Germanic languages notes three primary ways of dividing Germanic, namely the genetic, the typological or areal, and the distinction between state and non-state languages.[41] The final

---

Victorian World, ed. Martin Hewitt, 1-54 (New York: Routledge, 2012), on debates in periodization and the merits of watershed years as markers of subdivisions in the Victorian Era.

[40] As a disciplinary apologetic for relative chronology in historical linguistics against biologized phylogenetic statistical models of language change, see Ch. 8, "Why linguists don't do dates – Or do they?," in Asya Pereltsvaig and Martin W. Lewis, *The Indo-European Controversy: Facts and Fallacies in Historical Linguistics* (Cambridge: CUP: 2015), 159-181. As a culmination of decades of suggestive but controversial arguments for revising the linguistic strata and contact history of Germanic in particular, see Robert Mailhammer and Theo Vennemann, *The Carthaginian North: Semitic Influence on Early Germanic. A Linguistic and Cultural Study*, NOWELE Supplement Series 32 (Amsterdam: John Benjamins, 2019).

[41] Wayne Harbert, *The Germanic Languages* (Cambridge: CUP, 2007), 6-14. "The GMC languages, relative to other language families of the world, include a high proportion of national languages. [...] This accidental distinction between state and non-state languages is not unconnected with the internal shape of the language, since official recognition as a standard for public purposes usually brings with it greater normalization and regulation, the development of varying degrees of stylistic divergence between

division encompasses the essential truth of the quip, often misattributed to Max Weinreich rather than his retelling, 'a language is a dialect with an army and navy,' in its full extent a call to address politics that has itself been abused toward political ends.[42]

A language is a rather amorphous object: contingent, composite, mutable, existing along continua in space and time, receiving meaning from the community of its speakers, but also shaping those communities, subject to laws and tendencies (often towards simplicity, but also including grammaticalization and the contest between constraints under Optimality Theory). Capturing these and other dimensions through conceptual metaphor is often necessary to describe diachronic change coherently, but metaphor is not always consistent: 'development' has in the past suggested evolution, teleology, and positive growth, while 'loss' often still evokes entropy and devolution, alongside a more neutral concept of reduction. In terms of periodization, the 'archaic,' the 'old,' or in other eras the 'primitive' stage implies qualities one might associate with half-formed, inchoate, emergent systems, rather than the often-baroque morphology typical of PIE and its early-stage daughter language families and languages.

Turning to literary-historical engagement with historiography, one finds both promise and defeat in the acknowledgement that old paradigms and conceptual metaphors may still best serve various needs. In the introduction to an edited volume on the interface between literary studies and historiographical theories of chronology, Lawrence Besserman concedes that despite "our post-Freudian, neo-Marxist, deconstructionist, and Foucauldian postmodern insights,"[43] the structural model proposed by Marc Bloch and others of the *Annales* school, whose fundamental intervention not only centers duration and continuity but also simultaneous, punctuated change, remains a forceful argument for the heuristic value of older periodization schemes. In the same volume, another contributor notes regarding the medieval period that "[…] to dispense with diachronic periodization is to run another risk. If the Middle Ages is to become part of a usable past, it must take its place in the

---

written and spoken varieties, and the articulation of the vocabulary in certain domains (e.g., technology and bureaucracy)" 14.

[42] And consistently and fascinatingly incorrectly cited. See Alexander Maxwell, "When Theory is a Joke: The Weinreich Witticism in Linguistics," *Beiträge zur Geschichte der Sprachwissenschaft* 28.2 (2018): 263-92.

[43] Lawrence Besserman, ed., *The Challenge of Periodization: Old Paradigms and New Perspectives* (New York: Garland, 1996), 13.

teleological story we constantly retell ourselves."[44] Indeed, thinking about disrupting chronological and temporal discourses disguised as heuristics has an essentially ludic, conjectural nature; the more one challenges dominant structures, often the weaker the resulting model's explanatory force in light of the prior model's hegemony in the epistemology of academic disciplines such as history or linguistics, but value remains in testing not only the substance of linguistic periodization, but also its underlying assumptions.

Stefan Tanaka, in the provocatively titled *History without Chronology*, promotes thinking about the advent of chronological, Newtonian absolute time as a rupture in previous modes of time, including the mythical and cyclical. As Tanaka rightly notes, "[p]rior to the modern period, and [still today] in places not dominated by abstract time, time is episodic, local, uneven, and irregular."[45] Tanaka's proposition, that chronology, history, geology, and the measuring of the world conspire to hide the epistemological foundation of progression narratives in these disciplines, is a condensed variation on many modern and postmodern discussions of duration in historiography–Braudel, Le Goff, Koselleck and many others have challenged 'traditional' models: the *longue durée*, merged periods, sediments of time, a collapse of natural and chronological history in the Anthropocene, etc.[46] attest to the widespread interest in disrupting what may be termed an already historicized paradigm, whose own history is unstable. If literary history and political history offer room to think alternative orders but ultimately seem to require paradigmatic concessions, periodization through the lens of social history and the mnemonics of social time may present another way forward.

In *Memory, History, and Forgetting*, Paul Ricoeur writes on calendar time as a mode of extrinsic temporal inscription and suggests that, on analogy of the lived body in geographical-cartographical space, a temporal symmetry with memory can be expressed in the future: "Every noteworthy coincidence refers in the final analysis to those events, in chronological time, between some social event and an astrally based cosmic configuration."[47] The coincidence of mnemonic weight informs the peaks of memory and the valleys of forgetting, explaining why some events become overburdened with significance and

---

[44] Lee Patterson, "The Place of the Modern in the Late Middle Ages," in *The Challenge of Periodization*, 54.
[45] Stefan Tanaka, *History without Chronology* (Amherst: Lever Press, 2019), 24, a substantial expansion of a previous article, Stefan Tanaka, "History without Chronology," *Public Culture* 28 (2016): 161-86.
[46] Tanaka, *History without Chronology*, 94-100.
[47] Paul Ricoeur, *Memory, History, Forgetting*, trans. Kathleen Blamey and David Pellauer (Chicago: University of Chicago Press, 2004), 154-55.

others fade into obscurity.[48] In recognizing the fundamental multidisciplinarity of the critical-historical mode, or more accurately the historical-philological mode, in bridging these concepts, Reinhart Koselleck, pioneer of *Begriffsgeschichte* and an adroit connector of the epistemology of history to other disciplines, deserves a central place in any discussion of social history, time, and language:

> "Daß eine historische Klärung der jeweils verwendeten Begriffe nicht nur auf die Sprachgeschichte, sondern ebenso auf sozialgeschichtliche Daten zurückgreifen muß, ist selbstverständlich, denn jede Semantik hat es als solche mit außersprachlichen Inhalten zu tun. Darin gründet ja ihre prekäre Randlage in den Sprachwissenschaften, darin ihre vorzügliche Hilfeleistung für die Historie"
>
> ['It is a matter of course that a historical clarification of the terms used must not only refer to the history of language, but also to social-historical data, because every semantics as such has to do with extralinguistic contents. Therein lies its precarious marginal position in linguistics, and therein its excellent support for history.']⁴⁹

An irreducibly basic component of this entanglement is the relationship, indeed fraught as Koselleck notes, between language, social structures, social history, events, and historical time. Within his concept of *Wiederholungsstrukturen* two critical mediations, namely the simultaneous interdependence and necessary separation of event and structure, lead to the "proposition [...] that events can never be fully explained by assumed structures, just as structures cannot only be explained by events. There is an epistemological aporia involving the two levels so that one can never entirely deduce one thing from another."[50] Although not novel in historical linguistics, various 'turns' to the cyclical, i.e., to the repetitive structural level of historical processes, have surfaced again through newer lenses.[51] Koselleck has addressed language in the general sense, noting despite the interdependence of language and history that earlier-later,

---

[48] Zerubavel, *Time Maps*, 25-34.
[49] Reinhart Koselleck, "Begriffsgeschichte und Sozialgeschichte," in *Soziologie und Sozialgeschichte: Aspekte und Probleme*, ed. Peter Christian Ludz, 116-31 (Opladen: Westdeutscher Verlag, 1972), 120-21.
[50] Reinhart Koselleck, *The Practice of Conceptual History: Timing, History, Spacing Concepts* (Stanford: Stanford University Press, 2002), 125.
[51] For example, in a generative framework in Miriam Bouzouita et al., eds., *Cycles in Language Change*, Oxford Studies in Diachronic and Historical Linguistics 37 (Oxford: OUP, 2019).

inside-outside, and above-below dichotomies are pre-linguistic conditions of history,[52] but also in a more specific sense, remarking that syntax, grammar, and pragmatics are relatively stable in comparison to other linguistic phenomena such as semantics; furthermore, he notes that these separate domains are analogous to structures and events, even if language change tends to move languorously compared to event-driven historical change– "[... der] Hiatus, der zwischen Sach- und Sprachgeschichte immer wieder aufklafft" ['(... the) hiatus that time and again erupts between language history and narrative history'][53] that can also never be bridged.[54] What structures of repetition and the discrete points of exceptionality in them offer is a break with the fundamentally teleological mode of some historiographies, whether a linear model of progression or the same programmatic progression narrative repackaged in cyclical theories (*Kreislauflehre*): "Dann ließen sich auch, je nach Mischungsverhältnissen von Wiederholung und Einmaligkeit, die Zeitalter pluralisieren, ohne auf die wenig oder nichtssagende Periodenbestimmung zu verfallen, sie seien 'alt,' 'mittel' oder 'neu'" ['Then, depending on the ratio of the mixture of repetition and uniqueness, the ages could be pluralized without resorting to the definition of periods as being 'old,' 'middle,' or 'new,' which says little or nothing at all.'][55] German linguists, among others, have embraced some of these insights in recent decades with an unsurprising emphasis on applications in modernity and reassessments of modern linguistic science.[56]

---

[52] It should be noted, however, that the assumption of a people possessing a history is not immediately contingent on possessing a language, but first filtered through political, social, and anthropological discourses. In his description of the Iroquois demonym *Ongoue-onoue* 'men of forever' (*les hommes toujours*) in *Voyage en Amérique*, which seemingly places them outside of chronological, absolute time, Chateaubriand remarks on the manner in which indigenous peoples are described by Europeans, occupying a correlative *either/or* or *both/and* space within dichotomies of civilized-savage, Roman-"ape," and prelinguistic-linguistic consciousness and self-reflection. François Hartog, *Regimes of Historicity: Presentation and Experiences of Time*, trans. Saskia Brown, European Perspectives (New York: Columbia University Press, 2015), 83-84, citing François René de Chateaubriand, *Voyage en Amérique*, in *Œuvres complètes de Chateaubriand*, ed. Henri Rossi (Paris: Honoré Champion, 2008), 359.
[53] See Reinhart Koselleck, "Sprachwandel und Ereignisgeschichte," *Merkur* 486 (1989): 657-73 and "Wiederholungsstrukturen," 13.
[54] "Die Differenz zwischen der vergangenen Wirklichkeit und ihrer sprachlichen Aufbereitung wird nie geschlossen werden." Koselleck, "Sprachwandel," 673.
[55] Koselleck, "Wiederholungsstrukturen," 3.
[56] For example, the essays in Dieter Cherubin, Karlheinz Jakob, and Angelika Linke, eds., *Neue deutsche Sprachgeschichte: Mentalitäts-, kultur- und sozialgeschichtliche Zusammenhänge*, Studia Linguistica Germanica 64 (Berlin: de Gruyter, 2002).

What remains of heuristic value for linguistic periodization at the nexus of other disciplines? Certainly, for premodern (or pre-print) language stages, literary studies and new-philological approaches have provided in the form of the material turn new ways of thinking about canon, archive, corpus, and the political and social dimensions of their taxonomic uses. While traces of linguistic periodization are never uniformly inscribed, whether geographically or diachronically, in the archive of language in a broader sense, through the lens of a certain type of literary history, they can illustrate the structural, repetitive continuities that may serve as potential frameworks. One example is paradoxically nearly synchronic, or at least only briefly diachronic from a linguistic perspective: David Wallace's monumental *Europe: A Literary History, 1348-1418*, which surveys a cross-linguistic, transnational body of texts via itineraries or 'sequences,' routes of transmission and loci of production that eschew both national literature models and monolingualism.[57] The result is effectively a synchronic approach with diachronic consequences: extended fluidly to the before and after of its event-driven 'period,' such an approach can contain both repetitive structures and ruptures. Examples of the former include the literary and linguistic forms of Christianity and French literary and lexical influences in the form of romance, while the latter includes any number of events (the Norman Conquest) or developments (the emergence of literary prose). The mixture of French influence and Christian texts in Germanic-speaking areas in the thirteenth century, for instance, is one possible point of convergence from this perspective: Hákon Hákonarson and Sturla Þórðarson, Henry III and the two Edwards after him, and the Hohenstaufen dynasty supported, commissioned, and fostered a culture of literary works that from the standpoint of national language traditions resulted in an efflorescence of West Norse (Old Norwegian and Old Icelandic), Early Middle English, and Middle High German texts.[58] As much as this common development can be explained by exchange and currents of intellectual culture, it can also be challenged in terms of linguistic and political boundaries. Middle Low German and Middle Dutch are synchronic witnesses to and participants in these developments, as are East Norse (Old Danish and Old Swedish) and Old Yiddish, whose entry into the vernacular adaptation of French literary currents

---

[57] David Wallace, ed., *Europe: A Literary History, 1348-1418*, 2 vols. (Oxford: OUP, 2016).
[58] Admittedly, such a characterization fails partially for Middle English in comparison with the abundance of textual creativity in the fourteenth century, but the thirteenth century nevertheless stands out as the period of renewal in vernacular literary production, not coincidentally in verse via French influence. R. M. Wilson, *Early Middle English Literature*, Repr. 3rd ed. 1968, Routledge Library Editions: The Medieval World 53 (Oxford: Routledge, 2020), 19-20.

lingered until the early fourteenth and sixteenth centuries respectively. Such a literary-historical period can exercise great explanatory power across space and linguistic boundaries: it foregrounds common phenomena in literature, such as generic conventions and shared storyworlds, and in language, such as developments in lexical inventories. It would admittedly not fully encompass phenomena such as the weakening of unstressed vowels in 'middle' West Germanic or the development of aspiration and preaspiration in Middle Icelandic, but it would incorporate certain cross-linguistic lexical-semantic developments. Significantly, it would not require special pleading for misaligned periods across languages and allow for a wider array of analytical perspectives for describing 'transitional' periods. Social historical lenses, paradigmatic for 'extralinguistic' modes of organizing linguistic history, are advantageous not because they best describe the diachrony of social processes *in addition to* grammatical, syntactic, phonological or other processes, but because they are able to be expressed in configurations that embrace multiplicity and simultaneity.

Koselleck emphasizes these properties when he notes that "[social history] can be likened to a rubber band, that is to say it is flexible enough to embrace several more or less heterogenous areas."[59] This view requires acknowledging that historical language stages, no matter how far removed or recent in time, are only comprehensible via the contingent material witnesses produced by certain speakers in particular conditions, whether in the service of literary-philological, textual study or of the historical linguistic reconstruction of spoken language, not simply recognizing that diachrony and synchrony are interrelated.[60] It is thus an essential task in philology to continually question not only extant paradigms of periodization but also the relevant criteria that undergird them, on the grounds that restrictive conditions produce restricted models. A perfect model likely does not exist, but a model that incorporates comparative criteria from within, beyond, and between languages and the peoples that produced and used them would advance the periodization question beyond the functional stalemate of the status quo.

---

[59] Koselleck, *The Practice of Conceptual History*, 115.
[60] While this may appear as a simplification of positions in the philosophy of history, it was nevertheless a relatively hard-won debate in the Prague School contra de Saussure. For an example of this type of argumentation in a later structuralist/functionalist paradigm, see E.H. Raidt, "Oor die Skeiding van die Sinchroniese en die Diachroniese Taalstudie," *Taalfasette* 3 (1967): 20-33 on theory and application in Afrikaans.

Bibliography

Adelung, Johan Christoph. *Mithridates oder allgemeine Sprachenkunde*. Vol. 4. Berlin: Vossische Buchhandlung, 1817.

Árnason, Kristján. *The Phonology of Icelandic and Faroese*. Oxford: Oxford University Press, 2011.

Bandle, Oskar, et al., eds. *The Nordic Languages: An International Handbook of the History of the North Germanic Languages*. 2 vols. Berlin: de Gruyter, 2002.

Besserman, Lawrence, ed. *The Challenge of Periodization: Old Paradigms and New Perspectives*. New York: Garland, 1996.

Bremmer, Rolf H. "Dealing Dooms: Alliteration in the Old Frisian Laws." In *Alliteration in Culture*. Ed. Jonathan Roper. 74-92. Basingstoke: Palgrave Macmillan, 2011.

———. *An Introduction to Old Frisian: History, Grammar, Reader, Glossary*. Amsterdam: John Benjamins, 2009.

Cathey, James E. "The Historical Setting of the Hêliand, the Poem, and the Manuscripts." In *Perspectives on the Old Saxon* Hêliand: *Introductory and Critical Essays, with an Edition of the Leipzig Fragment*. Ed. Valentine A. Pakis. Medieval European Studies XII. 3-33. Morgantown: University of West Virginia Press, 2010.

Chateaubriand, François René de. *Voyage en Amérique*. In *Œuvres complètes de Chateaubriand*. Ed. Henri Rossi. Paris: Honoré Champion, 2008.

Dolberg, Florian. *Agreement in Language Contact: Gender Development in the Anglo-Saxon Chronicle*. Studies in Language Companion Series 208. Amsterdam: John Benjamins, 2019.

"Germany." In *Encyclopaedia Brittanica*. Ed. James Millar. 4th ed. Vol. 9. Edinburgh: A. Bell, 1810.

Harbert, Wayne. *The Germanic Languages*. Cambridge: Cambridge University Press, 2007.

Hartog, François. *Regimes of Historicity: Presentation and Experiences of Time*. Trans. Saskia Brown. European Perspectives. New York: Columbia University Press, 2015.

Holland, Arthur William. "Germany." In *Encyclopaedia Brittanica*. Ed. Hugh Chisholm. 11th ed. Vol. 11. Cambridge: Cambridge University Press, 1911.

Jeep, John M. *Alliterating Word- Pairs in Early Middle High German*. Phraseologie und Parömiologie 21. Baltmannsweiler: Schneider Verlag Hohengehren, 2006.

———. "The Roles of Women in Old High German Literature." *Mediaevistik* 14 (2001): 95-123.

———. "Women in the Vernacular and the Periodization of Medieval German Literature." *Medieval Feminist Newsletter* 23 (1997): 37-47.

———. *Alliterating Word-Pairs in Old High German*. Studien zur Phraseologie und Parömiologie 3. Bochum: Brockmeyer, 1995.

Jørgensen, Bent. "Sproghistoriske perioder." In *Dansk Sproghistorie 1: Dansk tager form*. Eds. Ebba Hjorth et al. 79-83. Copenhagen and Aarhus: Det Danske Sprog- og Litteraturselskab and Aarhus Universitetsforlag, 2016.

Korobov, Maksim, and Andrey Vinogradov. "Gotische Graffito-Inschriften aus der Bergkrim." *Zeitschrift für deutsches Altertum und Literatur* 145.2 (2016): 141-57.

Koselleck, Reinhart. "Wiederholungsstrukturen in Sprache und Geschichte," *Saeculum* 57 (2006): 1-15.

———. *The Practice of Conceptual History: Timing, History, Spacing Concepts.* Stanford: Stanford University Press, 2002.

———. "Sprachwandel und Ereignisgeschichte." *Merkur* 486 (1989): 657-73.

———. "Begriffsgeschichte und Sozialgeschichte." In *Soziologie und Sozialgeschichte: Aspekte und Probleme.* Ed. Peter Christian Ludz. 116-31. Opladen: Westdeutscher Verlag, 1972.

Lass, Roger. "Language Periodization and the Concept 'Middle.'" In *Placing Middle English in Context.* Eds. Irma Taavitsainen et al. Topics in English Linguistics 35. 7-41. Berlin: de Gruyter, 2000.

Liberman, Anatoly. "Some Unsolved (and Probably Insoluble) Aspects of Initial Fricative Voicing in Early English: Voicing in Early English Viewed as Part of the Great Germanic Lenition." In *Early Germanic Languages in Contact.* Eds. John Ole Askedal and Hans Frede Nielsen. Nowele Supplement Series 27. 245-60. Amsterdam: John Benjamins, 2015.

Lutz, Angelika. "Norse Loans in Middle English and their Influence on Late Medieval London English." *Anglia* 135 (2017): 317-57.

Mailhammer, Robert, and Theo Vennemann. *The Carthaginian North: Semitic Influence on Early Germanic. A Linguistic and Cultural Study.* NOWELE Supplement Series 32. Amsterdam: John Benjamins, 2019.

Males, Mikael. *The Poetic Genesis of Old Icelandic Literature.* Ergänzungsbände zum RGA 113. Berlin: de Gruyter, 2019.

Maxwell, Alexander. "When Theory is a Joke: The Weinreich Witticism in Linguistics." *Beitrage zur Geschichte der Sprachwissenschaft* 28.2 (2018): 263-92.

Mulligan, Amy C., and Else Mundal, eds. *Moving Words in the Nordic Middle Ages: Tracing Literacies, Texts, and Verbal Communities.* Acta Scandinavica 8. Turnhout: Brepols, 2019.

Murphy, G. Ronald. *The Saxon Savior: The Germanic Transformation of the Gospel in the Ninth-Century Hêliand.* Oxford: Oxford University Press, 1989.

Neidorf, Leonard, and Rafael J. Pascual. "Old Norse Influence on the Language of Beowulf: A Reassessment." *Journal of Germanic Linguistics* 31.3 (2019): 298-322.

Nielsen, Hans Frede "The Vowel Systems of Old English, Old Norse and Old High German Compared." In *Early Germanic Languages in Contact.* Eds. John Ole Askedal and Hans Frede Nielsen. Nowele Supplement Series 27. 261-76. Amsterdam: John Benjamins, 2015.

Osterhammel, Jürgen. *Die Verwandlung der Welt: eine Geschichte des 19. Jahrhunderts.* Munich: C.H. Beck, 2009.

Patterson, Lee. "The Place of the Modern in the Late Middle Ages." In *The Challenge of Periodization: Old Paradigms and New Perspectives.* Ed. Lawrence Besserman. 51-66. New York: Garland, 1996.

Pereltsvaig, Asya, and Martin W. Lewis. *The Indo-European Controversy: Facts and Fallacies in Historical Linguistics.* Cambridge: Cambridge University Press, 2015.

Ponz-Sanz, Sara M. *The Lexical Effects of Anglo-Scandinavian Linguistic Contact on Old English.* Studies in the Early Middle Ages 1. Turnhout: Brepols, 2013.

Raidt, E.H. "Oor die Skeiding van die Sinchroniese en die Diachroniese Taalstudie." *Taalfasette* 3 (1967): 20-33.

Rathofer, Johannes. *Der Hêliand. Theologischer Sinn als tektonische Form. Vorbereitung und Grundlegung der Interpretation.* Niederdeutsche Studien 9. Cologne: Böhlau, 1962.

Ricoeur, Paul. *Memory, History, Forgetting.* Trans. Kathleen Blamey and David Pellauer. Chicago: University of Chicago Press, 2004.

Roelcke, Thorsten, ed. *Periodisierung. Die zeitliche Gliederung der deutschen Sprachgeschichte.* Dokumentation Germanistischer Forschung 4. Frankfurt: Peter Lang, 2001.

———. "Die frühneuhochdeutsche Brücke. Überlegungen zur sprachtypologischen Periodisierung der deutschen Sprachgeschichte." *Zeitschrift für deutsche Philologie* 119.3 (2000): 369-96.

———. "Die Periodisierung der deutschen Sprachgeschichte." In *Sprachgeschichte.* Ed. Werner Besch et al. Vol. 2.1. Berlin: de Gruyter, 1998.

———. *Periodisierung der deutschen Sprachgeschichte. Analysen und Tabellen.* Studia Linguistica Germania 40. Berlin: de Gruyter, 1995.

Salmons, Joseph. *A History of German.* 2nd ed. Oxford: Oxford University Press, 2018.

Schildt, Joachim. "Zum Verhältnis von Gesellschafts- und Sprachgeschichte: Periodisierungsprobleme." In *Zur Periodisierung der deutschen Sprachgeschichte: Prinzipien – Probleme – Aufgaben.* Ed. Joachim Schildt. Linguistische Studien, Reihe A 88. 30-39. Berlin: Akademie der Wissenschaften der DDR, 1982.

Simon, Werner. *Zur Sprachmischung im Hêliand,* Philologische Studien und Quellen 27. Berlin: Erich Schmidt, 1965.

Sonderegger, Stefan. *Grundzüge deutscher Sprachgeschichte. Diachronie des Sprachsystems.* Vol. 1. Berlin: de Gruyter, 1979.

Stearns, MacDonald. "Das Krimgotische." In *Germanische Rest- und Trümmersprachen.* Ed. Heinrich Beck. Ergänzungsbände zum RGA 3. 175-94. Berlin: de Gruyter, 1989.

Stiles, Patrick. "A Textual Note of Busbecq's "Crimean Gothic" *Cantilena. Neophilologus* 68 (1984): 637-39.

Suzuki, Seiichi. *The Metre of Old Saxon Poetry: The Remaking of an Alliterative Tradition.* Cambridge: D.S. Brewer, 2004.

Tanaka, Stefan. *History without Chronology.* Amherst: Lever Press, 2019.

———. "History without Chronology." *Public Culture* 28 (2016): 161-86.

Taylor, Paul Beekman. "*Searoniðas:* Old Norse Magic and Old English Verse." *Studies in Philology* 80.2 (1983): 109-25.

Tiefenbach, Heinrich. *Altsächsisches Handwörterbuch. A Concise Old Saxon Dictionary.* Berlin: de Gruyter, 2010.

Versloot, Arjen. "Frisian Place-Names and Place Names in Friesland." *Onoma* 46 (2011): 127-50.

———. "Why Old Frisian is Still Quite Old." *Folia Linguistica Historica* 25 (2004): 259-302.

Wallace, David, ed. *Europe: A Literary History, 1348-1418*. 2 vols. Oxford: Oxford University Press, 2016.

Wells, C.J. *Deutsch: eine Sprachgeschichte bis 1945*. Trans. Rainhild Wells. Reihe Germanistische Linguistik 93. Tübingen: Niemeyer 1990.

Wilson, R. M. *Early Middle English Literature*. Repr. 3rd ed. 1968. Routledge Library Editions: The Medieval World 53. Oxford: Routledge, 2020.

Zerubavel, Eviatar. *Time Maps: Collective Memory and the Social Shape of the Past*. Chicago: University of Chicago Press, 2003.

Chapter 2

Metaphor and Metonymy in Germanic Noun Periphrasis

John Paul Ewing
Indiana University Bloomington

Abstract: Scholarly consensus has held that the anonymous poet of the Old Saxon *Hêliand* composes poetic variations and circumlocutions that are rather mundane and literalistic compared to the more colorful rhetorical figures of Old English noun periphrases. Moreover, the construction types that occur within Old Saxon poetic circumlocutions are mostly limited to synonymic simplices, endocentric compounds, and two-part genitive periphrases; this tendency contrasts starkly with the tortuous, puzzle-like metaphors present in skaldic *rékit* kennings.

In addition to fulfilling metrical and alliterative demands, many periphrases and nominal appositions employed in *Hêliand* and *Beowulf* engage their contemporaneous audiences by utilizing recurrent typologies and construction types that evoke heroic oral traditions. In the case of *Hêliand*, these poetic variations simultaneously catechize listeners by describing biblical referents in familiar, analogical terms that are accessible within the 9th century Saxon context. However, many circumlocutory noun structures employed by the *Hêliand*-poet have no clear parallels in the alliterative verse corpora of Old English or Old Norse. I contend that this is due to the *Hêliand*-poet's fruitful synthesis of traditions, including the use of metaphorical and metonymic devices identified within ancient and medieval rhetorical commentaries.

My goal for this contribution is to employ recent and historic rhetorical research to articulate the types of metaphor and metonymy present in Germanic noun periphrasis to provide a basis for comparing rhetorical figures among the early Germanic alliterative verse corpora. I employ modern scholarship on metaphor and metonymy, as well as classical commentaries, to provide a taxonomical schema for the metaphorical and metonymic devices employed in Germanic noun periphrasis. Using this framework, I show that Old English and Old Saxon noun periphrases make use of many of the same categories of rhetorical figuration as Old Norse skaldic kennings, and they are by no means 'mundane' or intrinsically of lesser quality.

Keywords: Old English; Old Norse; Old Saxon; periphrasis; rhetorical analysis; metaphor; metonymy; kennings

***

Objectives

Early twentieth-century researchers of skaldic kennings and similar forms of poetic circumlocution in Germanic verse observed that nominal periphrases follow recurring semantic and rhetorical patterns that often employ various forms of metaphor and metonymy.[1] However, since much of the terminology pertaining to figurative trope has been bequeathed to modern scholarship through classical rhetorical tradition, many of those inherited figurative categories, or 'tropes,' imperfectly reflect the modes of semantic transfer that occur in nominal periphrases within Old English, Old Saxon, and Old Norse verse.[2] While this lack of precise correspondence does not in itself negate the usefulness of the traditional terminology for describing modes of semantic transfer and other figurative processes that occur within Germanic periphrasis, it will be beneficial to qualify several of these categories and to adjust their definitions to reflect the contributions of contemporary semantic and rhetorical research.

In this chapter, I identify and define the categories of metaphor and metonymy that occur in Germanic noun periphrases within early Germanic alliterative verse corpora. Iprovide several examples of these rhetorical categories and analyze the linguistic means of implementation. In doing so, I

---

[1] In twentieth-century discourse, scholars have contended with the issue of metaphor and other tropic categories primarily within the area of skaldic kennings. See Rudolf Meissner, *Die Kenningar der Skalden: Ein Beitrag zur skaldischen Poetik* (Bonn: Kurt Schroeder, 1921); Andreas Heusler, Review of "Die kenningar der skalden. Ein beitrag zur skaldischen poetik," by Rudolf Meissner. *Anzeiger für deutsches Altertum und deutsche Literatur* 41 (Leipzig: S. Hirzel Verlag, 1922), 127–34; and Edith Marold, *Kenningkunst: Ein Beitrag zu einer Poetik der Skaldendichtung* (Berlin: W. de Gruyter, 1983). In connection with Old English circumlocutions, Arthur Brodeur distinguishes strongly between metaphorical kennings and similar non-metaphorical periphrases. See Arthur Gilchrist Brodeur *The Art of Beowulf,* (Berkeley: U of California P, 1960), 251.

[2] See especially ancient and medieval rhetorical commentaries such as Tryphon's *De Tropis*, the anonymous *Rhetorica ad Herennium*, Bede's *De Schematis et Tropis Sacræ Scripturæ Liber*, and Isidore of Seville's *Etymologiae*.

present counterevidence to the consensus view that Old English[3] and especially Old Saxon[4] periphrasis avoid colorful figurative expressions, as well as the view that poetic noun expressions in those corpora contrast fundamentally with Old Norse skaldic kennings as regards the use of metaphor and metonymy. This will provide the scholarship with a fuller perspective on the varying uses of tropic rhetorical categories in Old English and Old Saxon periphrasis as compared to Old Norse skaldic kennings.

Arthur Brodeur contends that Old English poetic periphrases are essentially compatible with the various categories of skaldic kennings and similar constructions as described by Snorri Sturluson, known as 'Snorri's categories.'[5] Brodeur states,

> Old English poetic appellations fall, in general, into the same categories as those of Old Norse poetry. In practice, however, we observe two major differences: (1) the Old English poetic periphrases are much less esoteric and far-fetched than the Norse; and (2) whereas, in Icelandic poetry, the periphrasis, or the traditional poetic simplex, for a given concept, functions most frequently as substitution for the direct, literal term, in

---

[3] For critiques of the term 'kenning' as applied to Old English periphrasis, see Thomas Gardner, "The Old English Kenning: A Characteristic Feature of Germanic Poetical Diction?" *Modern Philology* 67.2 (1969): 109-117 and Thomas Gardner, "The Application of the Term Kenning," *Neophilologus* 56 (1972): 464-468.

[4] For variations on the contention that Old Saxon periphrasis is poetically bland, see Richard Heinzel, *Über den Stil der germanischen Poesie* (Strasbourg: K.J. Trübner, 1875), 19; James W. Rankin, "A Study of the Kennings in Anglo-Saxon Poetry," *JEGP* 9 (1910): 80-82; Wolfgang Mohr, *Kenningstudien: Beiträge zur Stilgeschichte der altgermanischen Dichtung* (Verlag W. Kohlhammer, 1933), 27.

[5] (*The Art of Beowulf*, 247). Snorri Sturluson was an early thirteenth-century Icelandic poet and commentator, as well as the composer of the *Prose Edda*. Snorri's categories are elucidated in his works *Háttatal* and *Skáldskaparmál*, and they include numerous figurative and literal circumlocution types, as well as descriptions of kennings of various length and complexity. See Anthony Faulkes, ed., *Snorri Stuluson. Edda: Skáldskaparmál* (London: Viking Society for Northern Research; University College London, 1998); *Snorri Sturluson. Edda: Prologue and Gylfaginning*, 2nd edition (London: Viking Society for Northern Research; University College London, 2005); *Snorri Sturluson. Edda: Háttatal*, 2nd edition (London: Viking Society for Northern Research; University College London, 2007). For interpretations of Snorri's categories, see Arthur Brodeur, "The Meaning of Snorri's Categories," *University of California Publications in Modern Philology*, vol. 36, U of California P (1952): 129-147 and Anthony Faulkes, "Snorri's rhetorical categories," in *Sagnaþing helgað Jónasi Kristjánssyni sjötugum 10. Apríl 1994* (Reykjavík: Hið íslenska bókmenntafélag, 1994), 167-176.

Old English substitution is somewhat less common than the use of the poetic appellation as a variation of an *expressed* literal term, or as a variation of a transparent equivalent for the literal word.[6]

The characteristic 'esotericism' of skaldic kennings to which Brodeur refers is primarily linked to skaldic poetic diction, which is composed of *heiti* (mostly figurative, substantival, simplex 'terms'). This skaldic poetic diction functions as a figurative code frequently employed as base-words in skaldic kennings.[7] Brodeur's 'esotericism' thus seems to describe the same general phenomenon that Heusler refers to when he defines the kenning as "Metapher mit Ablenkung" ('metaphor with deviation,' or 'deflection'), meaning that the tropic modalities employed in the kenning base-word cause puzzlement or otherwise distract from the referent term rather than clarifying it through logical comparisons or associations.[8] In general, Brodeur's observations regarding the relatively sober nature of Old English periphrasis may be extended to analogous expressions in Old Saxon in the sense that both tend to lack the 'Ablenkung' phenomenon present in typical skaldic kennings. Yet, many expressions are comparable among all three corpora in terms of the presence of metaphor and metonymy. I demonstrate in the following that both Old English and Old Saxon periphrasis regularly feature metaphor and metonymy, even if the use of figurative trope is commonly less dramatic or 'far-fetched' due to the absence of an esoteric poetic diction comparable to skaldic *heiti*. Thus, the distinction between the typical skaldic kenning and other forms of Germanic periphrasis lies not in the presence or absence of figurative speech modalities as such, but in the obscurity or 'esotericism' of the figurative comparison posited in the expression.

---

[6] Ibid.
[7] For instance, common skaldic *heiti* for the referent 'man' include various expressions relating to trees (Kálf *Kátr* 40[VII] *lundr hjörva*, 'tree of swords' = MAN); see explanation below under metaphorical subcategory a2.2 [section 3]. Also, *heiti* for 'poetry' include expressions relating to 'mead' (Þblǫnd Frag 1[III] *mjǫðr burar Bors*, 'the mead of the son of Borr [→ Odin]' = POETRY; Bragi Frag 5[III] *drykkja Fjǫlnis fjalla*, 'drink of the Fjǫlnir [i.e., a mythological king] of the mountains [→ the giant Suttungr]' = POETRY), based on the Norse myth of the Mead of Poetry.
[8] Heusler, Review of "Die kenningar der skalden. Ein beitrag zur skaldischen poetik," by Rudolf Meissner, 130.

Three Problems in Rhetorical Discourse

In order to isolate the figurative modalities related to metaphor and metonymy that are operative within Germanic circumlocutions, one must address three principal difficulties. The first and perhaps most conspicuous of these is that numerous historical and contemporary rhetorical commentators have conceptualized metaphor and metonymy quite variously. Definitions for the diverse categories of figurative trope are not uniform even among pre-modern rhetorical commentaries operating within a mostly consistent tradition of discourse. Additionally, terms pertaining to figurative modes of expression are frequently defined quite differently in modern strains of discourse as compared to ancient and medieval sources, and this is particularly true of the subtypes of metaphor and metonymy. Notably, Aristotle's conceptualization of metaphor diverged considerably even from those of subsequent classical commentators, as illustrated by Tryphon's essay *De Tropis*.[9] Moreover, contemporary commentators have understood several figurative terms and categories as existing in subordinate or superordinate taxonomical relationships to other tropic categories, which has yielded numerous discrepancies between the various historical and contemporary rhetorical schemes.[10] For this reason, I articulate in the subsequent sections a terminological and organizational framework that applies specifically to the figurative modalities that occur in Germanic noun periphrasis; this framework is informed by contemporary rhetorical research, yet it utilizes many of the received terms and categories from classical commentaries.

---

[9] Aristotle, *Poetics* 1.21, 1457b and in contrast, M. L. West,. "Tryphon *De Tropis*." *The Classical Quarterly*, 15, no. 2 (Cambridge: Cambridge UP, 1965), 237.

[10] Particularly, classical approaches to figurative expression differ greatly from those of twentieth-century scholars such as Roman Jakobson and Morris Halle, *Fundamentals of Language* (The Hague: Mouton & Co., 1956), 76-82; and George Lakoff and Mark Johnson, *Metaphors We Live By* (Chicago: U of Chicago P, 1980). Both works trace the various figurative categories identified by historical commentators to metaphorical and metonymic cognitive processes. Moreover, classical commentators such as Bede and Isidore discuss synecdoche separately from metonymy, while Lausberg identifies synecdoche as a subcategory of metonymy. See Heinrich Lausberg, *Handbook of Literary Rhetoric: A Foundation for Literary Study* (Leiden: Brill, 1998), § 572. Similarly, Aristotle (*Poetics* 1.21, 1457b) understands analogy as a form of reciprocal metaphor, though the term is interpreted by post-Aristotelian classical writers as a protracted expression that draws explicit comparisons. On the other hand, Marold has argued for the use of the term 'analogy' as a subtype of metaphor based upon relationships of functional similarity, as opposed to similarity of characteristic. See Marold, *Kenningkunst: Ein Beitrag zu einer Poetik der Skaldendichtung*, 30.

A second difficulty with classical rhetorical categories concerns the divergent opinions of commentators regarding the linguistic structures that are able to convey a given category of semantic transfer. Since nominal periphrasis in Germanic is mostly limited to nominal compounds and constructions featuring an independent noun plus a limiting, dependent genitive,[11] figurative categories that consist of protracted expressions or narrative modes of comparison, perhaps most notably allegory and simile, are plainly incompatible with kennings and other forms of noun periphrasis.[12] Instead, nominal periphrasis concerns the so-called *brevitas*-form of tropic comparison which consists of direct semantic transfer between two words without explicit narrative comparison or clarification (for example, by the use of 'like' or 'as' in a protracted simile).[13] Yet, ancient and medieval commentators provide greatly divergent examples of metaphor and metonymy as regards formal structure; these range from conventional, *brevitas*-form noun substitutions to various forms of conceit, verbal metaphors, and implausible adjectival attributions that obliquely postulate figurative comparisons. This formal variability suggests that classical rhetorical commentators do not distinguish strongly between the different linguistic means for expressing figurative trope, as the conceptual processes

---

[11] Compounding and the use of limiting genitives are the most common means of nominal determination in early Germanic verse, and these morphological structures lend themselves to colorful poetic expression due to their ability to supply a sphere of reference for interpreting metaphorical and otherwise figurative compound heads and base-words. It is also possible for adjectives (Þfagr *Sveinn* 5[II] *rauðu vápnlauðr*, 'red weapon-foam' = BLOOD), adverbs (*Beo* 2346, 2830 *se wīdfloga*, 'the far-flyer' = DRAGON), and certain other word combinations such as prepositional phrases (*Hel* 3657 *lioht an theson lībe*, 'light in the body' = EYESIGHT) to supply sphere of reference or qualification for base-words, but such examples do not represent standard compositional conventions.

[12] Protracted and narrative forms of comparison occur in the classical tropic categories of *allegory* and *homoeosis*. Lausberg explains the sustained nature of *allegory* as follows: "the allegory is to an idea what the metaphor [...] is to a single word; so allegory stands in a close relationship of comparison to the intended serious idea. The relation of allegory to metaphor is quantitative; an allegory is a metaphor sustained for the length of a whole sentence (and beyond)." See Lausberg, *Handbook of Literary Rhetoric: A Foundation for Literary Study*, § 895. On the other hand, Isidore renders the term *homoeosis* into Latin as *similitudo*, which he defines as "that by which the description of some less known thing is made clear by something better known which is similar to it" (*Etym* 1.37.31). Isidore's examples suggest that homoeosis is always an explicit, protracted comparison in which both the notion being described and the term to which it is likened are present.

[13] This is achieved by substituting the referent term (*verbum proprium*) with the notion to which the poet compares it (*immutatio*). The *immutatio* occurs in the base-word of a nominal periphrase, while a determinant element contextualizes the base-word metaphor (or other expression) by delimiting its semantic field.

involved in formulating semantic transfer are generally considered identical.[14] Thus, the varying linguistic means for expressing metaphor and metonymy remain largely unaddressed in ancient and medieval rhetorical commentaries. This lack of formal distinction poses a problem for describing how figurative categories operate within Germanic periphrasis, because the methods for generating semantic transfer are at least as diverse as the formal implementations thereof.

For instance, while metaphor ordinarily involves the substitution of one appellative for another non-synonymic appellative, significantly more oblique comparisons result from the attribution of an implausible verbal action or an adjectival characteristic to a given substantival term. By way of these adjectival or verbal attributions, the *verbum proprium* (i.e., the referent term or 'proper term') is circuitously compared to an unexpressed substantival notion that the audience must infer. Bede provides an example of metaphorical adjective attribution from Ezekiel 11:19, rendered in the Vulgate as "et auferam cor lapideum de carne eorum, et dabo eis cor carneum" ['and I will take away the stony heart out of their flesh, and will give them a heart of flesh,'].[15] Here, *cor* ['heart'] is metaphorically compared to a stone by means of the attributive adjective *lapideum* ['stony'] without resorting to metaphorical substitution. While the comparison between 'heart' and 'stone' is essentially the same regardless of the lexical means, the process for comparison is quite different from metaphorical noun substitution.[16] Hence, verbal and adjectival metaphors postulate comparisons between nominal concepts without explicitly supplying an *immutatio* (i.e., a substitutive term or 'replacement') as in the more typical noun metaphors. Yet, metaphorical comparisons may take any of these structural forms. Since the linguistic means for manifesting a given category of semantic transfer are quite numerous, an accurate representation of semantic transfer within nominal periphrasis should draw sharp distinctions between the raw language components of an expression and the rhetorical modalities used within those expressions to draw comparisons and generate semantic transfer. Despite the convenience of describing a given language formulation as 'a metaphor' or 'a metonym,'[17] it is more accurate to state that

---

[14] Cf. Lausberg, *Handbook of Literary Rhetoric: A Foundation for Literary Study*, § 560.

[15] "*The Vulgate*, Ezekiel 11:19," *Latin Vulgate*, February 1, 2024, http://www.latinvulgate.com/. Further Biblical words or quotes, also taken from the *Vulgate*.

[16] See Bede, "Concerning Figures and Tropes," in *Readings in Medieval Rhetoric*, eds. Joseph M. Miller et al., trans. Gussie Hecht Tannenhaus (Bloomington: Indiana UP, 1973), 106.

[17] This approach runs contrary to Heusler's definition of the kenning as 'Metapher mit Ablenkung,' as well as the taxonomical framework of Marold, who considers metaphor, metonymy, and synecdoche to constitute categories of kennings. See Heusler, Review of "Die kenningar der skalden. Ein beitrag zur skaldischen poetik," by Rudolf Meissner, 130; Marold, *Kenningkunst: Ein Beitrag zu einer Poetik der Skaldendichtung*, 30-31.

such expressions 'implement' rhetorical modalities when they suggest semantic transfer between two disparate notions. This principle is assumed in the ensuing analyses of figurative expression in Germanic periphrasis.

The third and final difficulty in need of address is that ancient commentators did not distinguish starkly between truly figurative expressions[18] and several literal-descriptive devices[19] that inhabit the proverbial 'big-tent' of rhetorical trope. The classical rhetorical categories of epithet, onomatopoeia, and hyperbaton, for example, do not technically concern transferred meaning between semantically incongruent notions, yet these categories are almost universally included in classical commentators 'catalogues of 'trope.' Bede, for instance, states that hyperbaton involves "a kind of transposition of words which upsets their natural order." Thus, hyperbaton represents a departure from the conceptualization of trope as involving semantic transfer, as it pertains foremost to syntax. An indiscriminate approach to figurative and literal rhetorical modalities as regards 'poetic' or 'rhetorical' expression leads to potential conflation of tropic categories, which would prevent meaningful semantic observations concerning both kennings and other forms of poetic expression and circumlocution. Therefore, precise demarcations are necessary between figurative modes of expression and other rhetorical and poetic categories that are either literal-descriptive in nature or which exist outside of the figurative-literal paradigm. In order to avoid peripheral or dubious instances of figurative categories, this chapter focuses strictly on tropic modes of expression within Germanic noun periphrasis that plainly fall within the interpretive range of metaphor and metonymy.

In an effort to avoid the three major difficulties highlighted above, the approach of this study is to consider the base-word and the determinant (or multiple determinants) of each noun periphrase as semantically distinct entities, as each component relates differently to the referent term of the expression. If each periphrase component is considered singly for its independent rhetorical properties, it becomes possible to identify the various tropic categories simultaneously at play within a single expression and thus to gain a more precise understanding of the semantic properties at play therein. This focused approach to rhetorical modality functions as a viable remedy to classical commentators' unspecified methods for identifying rhetorical devices within structurally complex expressions. Out of concern for length, this chapter concentrates on subcategories of metaphor and metonymy that describe

---

[18] That is, poetical devices that involve transfer of meaning between semantically incongruent lexemes.
[19] Such devices may employ hypernymic or synonymic language, as is the case with patronyms and circumlocutory expressions which feature *nomina agentis*.

semantic transfer between a tropically used substantive in the base-word position and the apparent *verbum proprium* of the whole periphrase as deduced from narrative context.[20]

Since the rhetorical terminology employed in this study is conceptualized in various ways by ancient and modern rhetorical scholars, I formulate a tailored model for analyzing categories of rhetorical expression as they pertain to Germanic noun periphrasis specifically. The paradigm suggested in the following sections assimilates suitable concepts and terms from classical rhetorical tradition. I then incorporate elements of more recent rhetorical and philological analysis to help describe the semantic conventions of figurative noun periphrasis within the early Germanic verse corpora.

Metaphor in Base-Words

The following figure illustrates the various permutations of metaphor that occur within base-words in Germanic noun periphrasis:

Figure 2.1: Subtypes of Metaphor in Germanic Noun Periphrasis

a) Metaphor
    a1) Analogical Metaphor
        a1.1) Analogical Personification
        a1.2) Analogical Objectification
        a1.3) Analogical Animate-to-Animate Transfer
        a1.4) Analogical Inanimate-to-Inanimate Transfer
    a2) Qualitative Metaphor
        a2.1) Qualitative Personification
        a2.2) Qualitative Objectification
        a2.3) Qualitative Animate-to-Animate Transfer
        a2.4) Qualitative Inanimate-to-Inanimate Transfer

Fundamentally, metaphor draws a comparison between two semantically unrelated noun terms based either upon *function* or *characteristic*. In Figure 2.1, therefore, metaphor is subdivided into the categories of a1) Analogical Metaphor and a2) Qualitative Metaphor, reflecting these two types of operative

---

[20] Examples of additional categories of semantic transfer and poetic expression are pervasive in Germanic verse corpora and may even occur within some of the examples provided in this examination. See the concluding section of this essay for a brief discussion of tropic categories other than metaphor and metonymy. While this study focuses on tropic base-words, the rhetorical properties of determiner words comprise a logical next step in this line of inquiry.

comparisons.[21] While analogical metaphor asks the question, "What does it do?" (i.e., function), qualitative metaphor asks, "What is it like?" (i.e., quality, characteristic). Both analogical metaphor and qualitative metaphor may feature the subcategories of personification, objectification, or species-to-species transfer (in which semantic transfer occurs between two animate notions or two inanimate notions).[22]

Subtype a1) Analogical Metaphor consists of a functional comparison between two notions that exist within different referential contexts. More precisely, analogical metaphor compares a figuratively used term to its intended referent based on similarity of action, agency, or essential function within disparate spheres of reference. Clear examples of analogical personification (subtype a1.1) are pervasive in Old English periphrasis and Old Norse kennings. Examples of this subtype represent several semantic patterns, as may be observed in connection with kennings for the referent 'sword.' The expression *gūðwine* (*Beo* 1810, 2735, 'war-friend' = SWORD)[23] is a strong instance of imputing a human relationship to an inanimate object, whereby a sword functions as a companion and 'helper' within the context of battle. Likewise, compare the skaldic examples *dolglinnr* (Anon *Pl* 10[VII], 'battle-serpent' = SWORD) and *ormr*

---

[21] Qualitative metaphor is sometimes referred to as *simile*. However, rather than the common meaning of 'protracted comparison,' this term can be used to indicate a lexical substitution based on similarity of characteristic. I have avoided the term *simile* in an effort to avoid confusion on this point. Marold makes a similar distinction between metaphors based on quality and those based on function, yet she uses the term 'analogy' in a different sense from that of Aristotle or other classical rhetorical commentators. See Marold, *Kenningkunst: Ein Beitrag zu einer Poetik der Skaldendichtung*, 30; Aristotle, *Poetics* 1.21, 1457b. Bede equates analogy with *parabole* (Gk. παραβολή), which he defines as "a comparison of things which differ in kind." Bede considers this a subtype of *homoeosis*, which is an explicit, protracted comparison rather than a *brevitas*-form substitutive metaphor. See Bede, "Concerning Figures and Tropes," 122.

[22] Bede succinctly defines metaphor as "a transference of qualities and words" which may feature any combination of animate creatures or inanimate objects (Bede, "Concerning Figures and Tropes," 106). More specifically, he contends that semantic transfer of the strictly metaphorical type may be manifest in four ways: 1) transfer occurs between two different animate creatures; 2) transfer occurs between two different inanimate objects; 3) the comparison may cross these categories, such that an inanimate object is represented as an animate creature; 4) conversely, an animate creature may be represented as an inanimate object. Based on classical definitions, Lanham defines metaphor somewhat more vividly as "changing a word from its literal meaning to one not properly applicable but analogous to it." See Richard A Lanham, *A Handlist of Rhetorical Terms* 2nd Edition. (Berkeley: U of California P, 1991), 100.

[23] All text citations of *Beowulf* are from *Klaeber's Beowulf: And the Fight at Finnsburg*. 4th Edition. Toronto: University of Toronto Press, 2008.

vals (SnSt *Ht* 6^(III), 'reptile of corpses' = SWORD).²⁴ In these instances, the threat of a serpent or a reptile is analogous to that of a sword in the sense that both are understood to 'bite' or wound prey; thus, a sword acts as a serpent in 'battle' in the former example and with regard to the 'corpse' it produces in the latter. The fact that both swords and snakes are long and slender in form also suggests that the comparison has simultaneously a qualitative basis in addition to the analogical, which demonstrates that rhetorical categories are not rigidly exclusive.²⁵

Additionally, several periphrases from *Beowulf* appear classifiable as an oblique form of analogical personification: *billes bite* (*Beo* 2060, 'bite of the sword' = WOUND) and *hiorodrynċ* (*Beo* 2358, 'sword-drink' = WOUND). In addition to sharing a referent term, these expressions also utilize similar semantic patterns whereby the base-word notions 'bite' and 'drink' attribute animate capacities to the determinant 'sword.' The basis of the analogy is therefore that a sword wounds in battle much as a predator bites while on the hunt. This is quite distinctive from the examples of analogical personification suggested above, in which animate comparisons are made between the base-word and the referent notion. Skaldic kennings for the referent 'wound[s]' may follow similar patterns, as in *spor eggja sverðs* (ÞKolb *Eirdr* 15^I, 'tracks of the edges of the sword' = WOUND). Here, 'tracks' are conceptualized as being left on flesh by the determinant 'sword' much as an animal or a human leaves prints on terrain.

Somewhat differently, an oblique example of analogical personification from Old English, *merehrægl* (*Beo* 1905, 'sea-garment' = SAIL), technically compares the base-word 'garment' to a ship's sail. The comparison between 'garment' and 'sail' is not functional or analogical, as a sail does not function primarily as a covering in the way a garment does, but rather as a means of propelling a ship. The comparison between base-word and referent notion seems more likely founded upon the similarity of the material out of which both items are made; both sails and garments are made of fabric, though perhaps of different sorts. Clearly, the relationship between the base-word 'garment' and the referent notion 'sail' is not one of personification, but rather a transfer between two

---

²⁴ All Skaldic text citations are taken from Kari Ellen Gade and Edith Marold, eds.. *Skaldic Poetry of the Scandinavian Middle Ages*, volumes 2 and 3.
²⁵ The example *hestr grœðis* (ÞKolb *Eirdr* 14^I, 'horse of the sea' = SHIP) would be an instance of analogical personification only, as a horse does not share any qualitative attributes with a ship; both function as means of transportation, but in different contextual spheres. In contrast, the example *seiðr sóknar* (Anon *Pl* 37^(VII), 'fish of attack' = SWORD) is more viably understood as an instance of qualitative personification (a2.1) alone, based on the similarity of shape and of reflectiveness between a sword's blade and a fish (i.e., fish do not stereotypically 'bite' or wound as does a sword).

inanimate notions. Yet, an interpretation of this example merely as inanimate-to-inanimate transfer would be inadequate. The implication that a ship 'wears clothing' imputes personified qualities to the unspoken ship upon which the sail is hoisted. In this manner of thinking, the boat 'wears a sail' much as a person wears a garment, hence the analogical connection. Similar Old Norse kennings exist, namely *ript vinda* (Ólhvít *Hryn* 9^{II} 'cloth of wind' = SAIL) and *skikkja byrjar* (Grett Lv 4^V 'cloak of wind' = SAIL). Considered next to the Old English example, the kenning *ript vinda* suggests that the material ('cloth') prompts this semantic pattern, hence it comprises a form of material synecdoche (see below). On the other hand, the example *skikkja byrjar* references a specific item of clothing ('cloak'), and in combination with the determinant 'wind,' it evokes an image of a cloak flapping in the wind much as a sail might. This seems to indicate that the personification is secondary and implicit.

Instances of analogical personification (a1.1) specifically are rare or non-existent in Old Saxon verse, but a soft example of analogical personification from *Hêliand* may be inferred from verbal expressions such as *that herta sterkian* (*Hel* 55, 5049, 'to strengthen [bolster] the heart' = TO GIVE COURAGE), where courage or determination are made 'animate' by mapping these inanimate notions onto the body.[26] To be clear, this is not an occurrence of nominal periphrasis properly understood, but of a verbal metaphor. Moreover, this example could be read, perhaps even more plausibly, as a metonymic physical association (subtype b1.2) with the heart's reaction to fear and distress.

On the other hand, a strong instance of analogical objectification (subtype a1.2) from *Hêliand* may be found in the example *lioht mikil allun elithiodun* (*Hel* 487-488, 'great light to all heathen peoples' = CHRIST). Here, Christ is analogically compared to the notion 'light'; Christ is to the human spirit as light is to the eye. Thus, Christ is conceptualized as providing spiritual illumination to pagans, such that both Christ and light allow those in 'darkness' to 'see.' Although light is not classifiable as an 'object' in the most ordinary sense,

---

[26] All text citations of the *Hêliand* are from Otto Behagel, 10th edition. Marold classifies personification in kennings as comprising a subset of "abgeleitete Kenningar" (i.e., 'derived kennings'); see Marold, *Kenningkunst: Ein Beitrag zu einer Poetik der Skaldendichtung*, 32. Kennings featuring personification require the recipient to posit an action suggested by the base word, which is typically uniquely human in nature. Marold's understanding of personification as a subtype of "abgeleitete Kenningar" involves a conflation of personification with other forms of contextually derived meaning. This lacks sufficient justification in my view, since comparison based on human-like activity suggests the presence of analogical metaphor rather than a meaning derived from other elements in the kenning. I therefore understand personification, in accordance with Lakoff and Johnson, as a distinct figurative category that qualifies as a subtype of metaphor. See Lakoff and Johnson, *Metaphors We Live By*, 33.

objectification accurately describes the semantic transfer from the animate 'Christ' to the inanimate visual manifestation 'light,' which justifies this classification. One may be tempted to interpret this as a conceptual metonymy,[27] but the physicality of light and the compared functionality of 'Christ' and 'light' in their separate functional spheres seem sufficient cause to favor an analogical interpretation. While analogical objectification rarely appears in Old English periphrasis, skaldic kennings for 'horse' such as *lung váfaðar Gungnis* (Bragi Frag 4[III], 'longship of the swinger of Gungnir [= Odin's spear]' = HORSE) constitute a reciprocal pattern alongside the noted skaldic kenning for 'ship.'[28]

Analogical metaphors may also feature semantic transfer between two taxonomically unrelated notions, either between two unrelated animate categories or between two unrelated inanimate categories. The Old English example *brimwylf* (*Beo* 1506, 1599, 'she-wolf of the lake' = GRENDEL'S MOTHER) is a sharp example of animate-to-animate metaphorical transference (a1.3) based on an analogical relationship; Grendel's mother is to human beings as a she-wolf is to her prey (or, perhaps, to any threat to her progeny).[29] Examples also include frequent depictions within *Hêliand* of Christ as 'king' (*Hel* 598, 973, etc. *cuning*, 'king' = CHRIST) or 'lord' (*Hel* 264, 401, etc. *drohtin*, 'lord' [or 'prince,' 'ruler,' 'master,' 'king'] = CHRIST; *Hel* 917, 932, etc. *herro*, 'lord' = CHRIST; *Hel* 269 *mâri* **theodan**, 'famous lord' [or 'prince,' 'ruler,'] = CHRIST).[30] These are examples of taxonomically lateral analogies in which an animate person is analogically represented by another animate term, in this case, a socio-political title. One should not mistake these terms for Christ as literal or hyponymic categories, because worldly titles do not accurately describe Christ's relationship

---

[27] Cp. *friðu uuið fiundun* (*Hel* 1011, 'peace against enemies' = CHRIST). See *Abstract or Conceptual Association* below in § 3 (b1.1).

[28] I.e., *hestr græðis* (ÞKolb *Eirdr* 14[I], 'horse of the sea' = SHIP).

[29] Of course, this does not preclude that Grendel's mother may share physical characteristics or other qualities with a 'she-wolf,' in which case this example could be read as a qualitative metaphor (a2.3).

[30] Owing to the traditional nature of these titles as they relate to God and Christ, as well as the transparency of their metaphorical connection to the referent, such expressions are interpretable as instances of *catachresis*. Lausberg describes catachresis as a form of 'necessary' tropic expression that occurs when there is no term that is adequate to the *voluntas* ('will,' 'signification'; i.e., the intended meaning of the poet); see Lausberg, *Handbook of Literary Rhetoric: A Foundation for Literary Study*, § 562. Bede moreover states that catachresis "differs from metaphor in that metaphor bestows another name to an object which already has a name; catachresis makes use of another name because the object lacks a specific name;" see Bede, "Concerning Figures and Tropes," 108. This figure also helps to account for terms such as 'father' and 'son' as relates to God and Christ respectively, as these terms express mystical relationships rather than earthly, biological ones.

to other persons, even by Christ's own measure.[31] The use of the expressions 'king,' 'chieftain,' and 'lord' analogically compare Christ to a 'worldly political leader' in the conventional sense of that phrase. In literally accurate and earthly terms, Christ could be described more accurately as 'son of Mary of Nazareth,' 'adopted son of Joseph of Nazareth,' 'rabbi,' 'teacher,' 'messiah,' and so on. While the biblical theme of Christ's spiritual kingship renders the terms of rulership apt, the nature of the metaphorical analogy exists along the following lines: Christ relates to all of humanity and the universe just as a worldly king relates to his subjects, namely with ruling authority. On the other hand, instances of terms such as 'king' and 'lord' do not express metaphor in instances where they accurately describe the referent term.[32]

Analogical semantic transfer between two distinctive inanimate categories (a1.4) occurs in several Old English examples such as *woruldcandel* (*Beo* 1965, 'world-candle' = SUN) and the prominent expression *hronrād* (*Beo* 10, 'whale-road' = SEA). The former example could be understood as expressing a qualitative comparison, since both the sun and a candle are 'bright.' However, the qualification of 'candle' by the determinant 'world' indicates a reanalysis and semantic displacement of the base-word founded upon similar functionality, which is characteristic of analogical metaphor. The sun thus illuminates the 'world' as a 'candle' illuminates a room. As for *hronrād*, both the referent term 'sea' and the base-word 'road' are likewise inanimate categories that analogize to different semantic spheres. There is no conceivable attribute or characteristic common to both 'sea' and 'road,' only an analogous function; as a whale travels through the sea, so travels a human or a horse upon a road. The expression *wælrāp* (*Beo* 1610, 'water-fetter' = ICE) likewise draws a functional analogy based upon the ability of ice to bind or confine. Instances of inanimate category transfer in Old Saxon are rare, but the type is nonetheless represented in the examples *galgo* (*Hel* 5532 'gallows' = CROSS), *niuwi galgo* (*Hel* 5553 'new gallows' = CROSS) and *niuwi rôda* (*Hel* 5732 'new gallows' = CROSS).[33] In all three examples, the analogy is based upon the function of the

---

[31] One recalls Christ's words from John 18:36 to this effect, "my kingdom is not of this world. If my kingdom were of this world, my servants would certainly strive that I should not be delivered to the Jews: but now my kingdom is not from hence" (trans. Douay-Rheims 1899).

[32] Literal-descriptive and hypernymic examples of these titles are pervasive in *Beowulf*, as in *Deniġa frēa* (*Beo* 271, 'lord of the Danes' = HROTHGAR), *þēoden Scyldinga* (*Beo* 1675, 1871, 'lord of the Scyldings' = HROTHGAR), and *dryhten Ġēata* (*Beo* 2402, 2560, etc., 'lord of the Geats' = BEOWULF [*Beo* 2991 = HYGELAC].

[33] Other readings of OE *rôda* include 'rod' and 'pole.'

cross as an instrument of capital punishment, although the cross clearly possesses a different physical form than the standard mental image of a 'gallows.'

A spatial metaphor for 'heaven' that belongs to the category of analogical animate-to-animate transference may be found in examples such as *êuuig rîki* (*Hel* 947, 'eternal kingdom' = HEAVEN), *iuuues uualdandes rîki* (*Hel* 1554, 'your Lord's kingdom' = HEAVEN), *drohtines rîki* (*Hel* 1366, 'Lord's kingdom' = HEAVEN), and *that hôha himila rîki* (*Hel* 1601, 1606, etc., 'that high kingdom of heaven' = HEAVEN). In these examples, God's rule in heaven is analogized to a secular king's rule over his lands. The expression *uuîdbrêd uuelo* (*Hel* 1840, 'infinite estate [or 'property']' = HEAVEN) functions similarly, though emphasizing God's ownership of the heavenly realm as a human landowner possesses a tract of land.[34] Slightly different instances such as *thie mârion erðe* (*Hel* 1305, 'the renowned land' = HEAVEN) *upôdes hêm* (*Hel* 947, 2798, 'home of heavenly bliss' = HEAVEN),[35] *thiu mârie erða* (*Hel* 1305 'the glorious land' = HEAVEN), *thiu berhte bû* (*Hel* 3654, 'the bright dwelling' = HEAVEN), and *fadero ̂ ðil* (*Hel* 4497, 'fatherland' [lit. 'father's homeland'] = HEAVEN) also analogize heaven in terms of earthly spaces based upon their shared function as places of habitation; heaven functions as the abode of God, angels, and saints much as the land of the earth, a home, or a homeland are abodes of living human beings upon the earth.

An inversion of the pattern in these spatial metaphors occurs in certain base-word references to the world as a 'kingdom,' such as *erðrîki* (*Hel* 376, 'earth-kingdom' = WORLD) and *uueroldrîki* (*Hel* 1290, 'world-kingdom' = WORLD). Here, the base-word *rîki* ('kingdom') suggests the presence of a 'lord' or 'king' to rule over it, either emphasizing the secular monarchical order or obliquely implying the pervasive biblical metaphor of God as 'king' over the earth. The presence of the terms 'earth' and 'world' in the determinant positions of these examples, which are themselves effectively identical with the referent terms of both periphrases, suggests that the base-word primarily emphasizes God's rule over the entire world; God's rule is analogized once again to that of a secular king. These examples of analogical metaphor feature lateral, species-to-species transfer between two inanimate spatial terms.

In contrast to the comparisons of function or agency in analogical metaphor, qualitative metaphor (subcategory a2 in figure 2.1) consists in a comparison based upon essential qualities, features, or characteristics. Thus, this category is a strictly 'qualitative' comparison akin to the classical conceptualization of

---

[34] Contrast these with examples like *godes uuang* (*Hel* 1323, 1865, etc., 'God's meadow' = HEAVEN), examined below under subcategory a2.4.

[35] Compare the example *gramono hêm* (*Hel* 3359, 'home[-land] of devils' = HELL).

the *brevitas*-form of simile. Qualitative personification (a2.1) seems rare both among Old Saxon and among Old English periphrases, but it is pervasive in skaldic kennings, as one observes from a prominent semantic pattern for the referent term 'axe': *gífr sóknar* (Sturl *Hryn* 8[II], 'troll-woman of battle' = AXE); *vargr unda* (Anon [*FoGT*] 33[III], 'wolf of wounds' = AXE); *galkn hlífa* (Hfr *ErfÓl* 8[I], 'monsters of shields' = AXES). These examples compare the inanimate referent 'axe' to animate monsters or predators based on shared characteristics; both the referent notion and the base-word notions in these examples fall into the category of 'potentially dangerous things' and thus pose a lethal threat to human beings or other prey.

Poets frequently favor qualitative objectification (a2.2) in skaldic kennings for the referent terms 'man' and 'warrior,' as in the oft-occurring semantic pattern represented in the examples *borr seims* (Anon *Pl* 4[VII], 'tree of gold' = MAN) and *lundr ógnar* (Anon *Pl* 41[VII], 'tree of battle' = WARRIOR). Here, a 'man' is conceptualized as a tree, possibly due to vague physical similarities (both stand upright and bear 'limbs'), but certainly not because of analogous function or agency.[36] Also, the common Old English poetic expression *frumgār* (*Beo* 2856, lit. 'first spear' = LORD [or RULER; here: BEOWULF]) may be understood as an example of qualitative objectification, albeit somewhat problematically.[37] Ostensibly, the inanimate base-word notion 'spear' substitutes for the animate referent term 'Beowulf,' suggesting a clear instance of objectification. Furthermore, one may infer that the comparison between 'spear' and 'lord' (or any other martial figure) is based upon the lethal and threatening qualities of both notions. However, there is also an unmistakable metonymic component to this expression, whereby the character Beowulf is referred to by the object with which a warrior is archetypally associated. Therefore, Beowulf is the 'first spear' in the sense that he leads in battle, together with the weapon he carries. Qualitative objectification thus coexists with the metonymic reading, and both processes appear to be operative in this expression.

---

[36] The origin of the base-words relating to trees in skaldic kennings is unclear. According to *Völuspá* 17-18 and *Gylfaginning* 9, the first human beings, Askr ['ash'] and Embla ['elm' or 'vine'], were created from logs, and this may have influenced the emergence of these base-words in skaldic kennings. Evidence for this proposed origin may exist in kennings such as *askr rimmu* (Refr *Giz* 1[III], 'ash [tree] of battle' = WARRIOR) and *álmdrós* (SnSt *Ht* 60[III], 'elm-bow woman' = VALKYRIE). However, metaphorical *heiti* drawing comparisons between trees and human beings could have predated and inspired the myth of Askr and Embla. For tree-names as base-words, see Meissner, *Die Kenningar der Skalden: Ein Beitrag zur skaldischen Poetik*, 245; 266-72.

[37] OE *frumgār* is likely a transliteration of Lat. *primipilus*. See Hans Kuhn, "Das römische Kriegswesen im germanischen Wortschatz," *Zeitschrift für deutsches Altertum und Literatur* 101 (1972): 25-26.

As one may observe from certain periphrases that feature qualitative animate-to-animate transfer (a2.3), such as the traditional title *lamb godes* (*Hel* 1131, 'lamb of God' = CHRIST), even the fundamental distinction between 'analogical' and 'qualitative' metaphor is not strict. When one considers this example within the original context of John 1:29 (lat. *agnus dei*), this biblical metaphor is perhaps best classified as a form of analogical personification, whereby Christ 'functions' as a sacrificial lamb, slaughtered as propitiation for sin. This is precisely how Christ is characterized in the verse surrounding the above example from *Hêliand*:

'thit is that lamb godes,   that thar lôsean scal

af thesaro uuîdon uuerold   uurêða sundae,

mancunneas mên,   mâri drohtin,

cuningo craftigost.'

(*Hel* 1131a-1134b)

Separated from this context, which echoes the biblical rationale for the traditional expression, one might mistakenly presume that the comparison of Christ to a lamb is based merely on the shared characteristics of innocence, purity, meekness, or gentleness. If these shared characteristics are granted, the expression could also be reasonably interpreted as qualitative metaphor. Similarly, skaldic kennings for 'snake' or 'serpent' regularly employ various words for 'fish' as base-words, often to unintentionally comical effect, as in *ins døkkva hrøkkviseiðr lyngs* (Esk *Geisl* 16[VII] 'the dark coiling fish of the heather' = SNAKE), *myrkaurriði markar* (Ill *Har* 1[II] 'dark trout of the forest' = SERPENT [= FÁFNIR]), and *lax urðar* (RvHbreiðm *Hl* 7[III] 'salmon of the rocky slope' = SERPENT).

Multiple examples of semantic transfer between two inanimate notions based on qualitative similarity (a2.4) occur in Old Saxon periphrases for the referent 'heaven' (*Hel* 1323, 1865, etc. *godes uuang*, 'God's meadow' = HEAVEN;[38] *Hel* 3082 *grôni godes uuang*, 'God's green meadow' = HEAVEN). Here, the referent term 'heaven' is compared to earthly spaces and locales, apparently based on the shared qualities of beauty, magnificence, and serenity. Of course, it is entirely possible that the poet imagined heaven in precisely this manner (i.e., as a picturesque, green meadow), but the qualitative basis for this comparison is present regardless.[39] Similarly, certain representations of hell

---

[38] Cf. *wlitebeorhtne wang* (*Beo* 93, 'beautiful plain' [lit. 'beauty-bright plain'] = EARTH).
[39] As a contrast, recall here the analogical example *êuuig rîki* (*Hel* 947, 'eternal kingdom' = HEAVEN), etc. under subcategory a1.4.

also make use of natural imagery, as in *dalu thiustri* (*Hel* 2140, 'dark valleys' = HELL) and *diap dôdes dalu* (*Hel* 5170, 'deep valleys of death' = HELL).[40]

Examples of inanimate-to-inanimate qualitative transfer other than spatial metaphors are rare in *Hêliand*, but they are pervasive in Old English and especially in skaldic verse. The expression *heofones ġim* (*Beo* 2072, 'heaven's gem' = SUN) is founded upon the quality of illumination shared by the sun and gems, while the example *heofones hwealf* (*Beo* 576, 2015, 'heaven's vault' = SKY, FIRMAMENT) invokes the architectural element of the 'vault' based on height and its expansive nature. Likewise, qualitative transfer between inanimate categories occurs in several skaldic kennings for 'sword,' such as *blóðíss* (Anon *Lið*s 8, 'blood-ice' = SWORD) and *hrækerti* (*HjQ* 7, 'corpse-candle' = SWORD).[41] The first example compares a sword to ice based either upon the coldness of metal or upon the similarity in shape to an icicle. The second example compares a sword to a candle, probably based upon a visual comparison between the lighted tip of a candle and the point of a sword (or the brightness of a sword's reflection, perhaps at the point). The fact that both swords and candlesticks are long and thin in shape possibly aids the metaphor, but these qualities appear secondary considering certain skaldic *heiti* for 'sword' that denote 'fire,' such as *eldr* (Anon *Pl* 14[VII] *eldr ulfvíns*, 'fire of wolf-wine [→ BLOOD]' = SWORD) and *hyrr* (Anon *Pl* 49[VII] *hravnvíns hyrr*, 'fire of raven-wine' = SWORD).[42]

Metonymy in Base-Words

Distinctions between the various forms of metonymy that occur in Germanic periphrasis are shown in the following figure:

---

[40] In these cases, 'valley' is a mild euphemistic analogue for the referent 'hell' (both are pictorially depicted as 'dark' and 'deep,' in the sense that hell is understood as being located vaguely 'below'). Yet, it is clearly not the case that the *Heliand*-poet has an aversion to using the *verbum proprium* 'hel,' as numerous examples demonstrate (*Hel* 2511, 3357, etc.). Thus, euphemism traverses into the realm of authorial intent, requiring subjective judgment calls that can only be validated by context. Because other modes of semantic transfer are always present in euphemism, and since euphemism is to some degree dependent upon the *voluntas* of the poet, this should not be classified as an independent mode of semantic transfer in itself. However, it undoubtedly co-exists with other categories in *Heliand*.
[41] Cf. *rækyndill* (Anon *Krm* 7[VIII] 'corpse-candle' = SWORD) *hjaldrkyndill* (RvHbreiðm *Hl* 68[III] 'battle-candle' = SWORD).
[42] Moreover, OE *brond* and ON *brandr* ('fire,' 'sword') may be used prosaically. See respective entries in Angus Cameron et al., eds. *Dictionary of Old English* [currently A-I] (Toronto: U of Toronto P, 1986) and Geir T. Zoëga, *A Concise Dictionary of Old Icelandic* (Toronto: U of Toronto P, 2004).

Figure 2.2: Subtypes of Metonymy in Germanic Noun Periphrasis

b) Metonymy
    b1) Metonymic Association
        b1.1) Abstract-Conceptual Association
        b1.2) Physical-Spatial Association
    b2) Synecdoche
        b2.1) *pars pro toto* Synecdoche
        b2.2) *totem pro parte* Synecdoche
    b3) Antonomasia

Whereas metaphor involves substituting a referent notion with another semantically dissimilar notion, typically based on comparisons of agency or attributes, the various forms of metonymy rename the *verbum proprium* by invoking a plausible association, connotation, material substance, context, cause, or effect that is directly related to that notion.[43] Under the general classification of metonymy, three subcategories have been included in Figure 2.2: *Metonymic Association* (b1), *Synecdoche* (b2), and *Antonomasia* (b3). Each of these subcategories in turn has its own distinctive subtypes, which are addressed under the applicable headings.

The subcategory *Metonymic Association* (b1) may be understood as 'metonymy proper' in the sense that ancient and medieval rhetorical commentators gave the remaining two categories associated with metonymy more exacting designations and definitions, namely *synecdoche* and *antonomasia*. This is due to the higher degree of specificity in the kinds of 'real-world' relationships indicated by these latter categories as compared to the broader criteria and definition of standard metonymy. I have designated the present subcategory 'metonymic association' because the relationship between *verbum proprium* and *immutatio* is typically founded upon a conceptual or physical relationship that is somewhat remote or peripheral to the referent notion but nonetheless plausibly associated with it. As it occurs in Germanic periphrasis, associative metonymy may be subdivided into a conceptual subtype and a material subtype.

---

[43] Thus, this study assumes Lausberg's understanding of metonymy as involving a 'real' semantic relationship between immutatio and verbum proprium. Lausberg argues that metonymy involves the "replacement of the verbum proprium by another word whose actual meaning stands in a real relationship [...] to the intended meaning in the particular instance – not in a comparative relationship [...] as in the metaphor. [...] Thus metonymy employs a word in the meaning of another word which stands in a real semantic relationship to the word employed." See Lausberg, *Handbook of Literary Rhetoric: A Foundation for Literary Study*, § 565.

As the designation suggests, *Abstract-Conceptual Association* (b1.1) replaces the *verbum proprium* with a concept or abstract notion with which the referent is closely associated. Due to the high level of dependence on a shared set of conceptual associations between poet and audience, this subtype is possibly more dependent on cultural presumptions and motifs than any other category. Abstract-conceptual association typically replaces a concrete common noun referent with an abstract concept. For example, periphrases of this subtype may feature a referent term which comprises an inanimate object, location, or other notion. In an almost riddling manner, the Old English examples *homera lāf* (*Beo* 2829, 'remains of hammers' = SWORD) and *fēla lāf* (*Beo* 1032, 'remains of files' = SWORD) conceptualize swords as the product of the forging process; thus a sword is that which 'remains' after hammers and files have performed their work on the raw material.[44] Another 'sword' example, *mægenfultum* (*Beo* 1455 'strength-help'[45] = SWORD), conceptualizes the referent term according to the assistance it provides in battle. Whereas *manno drôm* (*Hel* 763, 3349, 'joy of men' = WORLD)[46] associates the world with the joys that one may experience in it, the example *hêlagaro handgiuuerk* (*Hel* 531, 'holy handiwork' [or 'holy creation'] = SCRIPTURE) substitutes one abstraction for another based on the concept of divine revelation, thus scripture is the 'work' of God's hand. Somewhat differently, in the example *friðu uuið fiundun* (*Hel* 1011, 'peace against enemies' = CHRIST), the metonymic base-word *friðu* ostensibly signifies Christ by the peace he teaches in the face of enemies and persecution. Here, Christ is not metaphorically compared to the abstract noun 'peace' – this would be nonsensical, as the concrete notion 'Christ' cannot share abstract attributes or function with 'peace.' Rather, Christ is associated with a reoccurring theme of his preaching, most notably in the Sermon on the Mount ('blessed are the peacemakers,' 'love your enemies,' 'turn the other cheek,' etc.).

Physical-Spatial Association (b1.2) describes metonymic associations between material objects and other physical realities or manifestations in one of two ways. The substitutive term either 1) physically or spatially attends the referent term, or it 2) draws a connection to a material reality or a physical

---

[44] Old English *lāf* may also mean 'relic' or 'heirloom,' giving resulting in a play on words; a sword is both an inherited (or inheritable) heirloom and the iron that remains after the forging process. Compare *yrfelāf* (*Beo* 1053, 1903, 'inheritance-relic' = SWORD).
[45] Or 'powerful help.'
[46] Importantly, the expression *manno drôm* does not indicate 'world' in *Hel* 1126b, where it simply means 'joy of men' in terms of social company. Yet, *manno drôm* varies the directly preceding expressions *erlo gemang* (*Hel* 1125b) and *mâri meginthiode* (*Hel* 1126a), and it alliterates with the latter. This represents a context-dependent shift in meaning, yet the metonymic association between 'joy' and 'social company' is comparable to that between 'joy' and 'world.'

manifestation that characterizes or exemplifies the referent. This may be seen in two examples from *Hêliand* that employ the notion 'light,' the most common notion associated with this subtype, to indicate various concrete common nouns. In the example *lioht an thesumu lîbe* (*Hel* 3657, 'light in the body' = EYESIGHT), the eye is signified by the light that enters it. Thus, light is a manifestation that metonymically attends the eye in the sense that its very function is to detect light. Light is therefore closely associated with the eye, and it even spatially attends the eye without being a physical component of the eye itself. Similarly, the example *liudeo lioht* (*Hel* 199, 5268, 'light of people' = EARTH) substitutes the light that shines upon the surface of the earth for the earth itself. The determinant notion 'people' appears to express the preconception that both the light and the earth it shines upon serve primarily the needs of human beings; the earth and the cosmos provide both an abode for human beings and the illumination necessary for human flourishing.[47]

Similarly, the Old English examples *lēoma* (*Beo* 1570, 'light' = SWORD) *hildelēoma* (*Beo* 1143, 'battle-light' = SWORD) and *beadolēoma* (*Beo* 1523, 'battle-light' = SWORD) characterize the referent 'sword' by means of the light that reflects off polished steel. Once again, the physical manifestation 'light' attends the physical object referenced without constituting a material component of that object.[48] The same must be said of the expression *flōda ġenipu* (*Beo* 2808, 'mists of the floods' = SEA), where the base-word notion *ġenipu* ('mists') tends to physically accompany the sea without comprising part of the sea as such – rather, mist may hover above the sea. Likewise, in the example *wīġheafola* (*Beo* 2661, 'war-head' = HELMET), the base-word *heafola* ('head') indicates not only the physical proximity of a helmet to the head when worn in battle; rather, since the helmet presumably encloses the head and face completely in conformity with the style of the period, it effectively 'becomes' the head that the warrior presents before the enemy.[49] Much as mist may cover

---

[47] The use of the notion 'light' in these examples stands in stark contrast to its use in the example *lioht mikil allun elithiodun* (*Hel* 487-488, 'great light to all heathen peoples' = CHRIST). See subcategory a1.2.

[48] This example differs from the previously cited metaphorical example *hrækerti* (*HjǪ* 7, 'corpse-candle' = SWORD) because the base-word 'candle' bears only an unrealistic resemblance to a sword, probably conceived upon the image of reflective light at the tip of a sword. Whereas 'light' is a realistic metonymic association with a sword, the notion 'candle' is an unrealistic comparison.

[49] Compare *beadogrīma* (*Beo* 2257 'war-mask' = HELMET) and *heregrīma* (*Beo* 396, 2049, 2605 'war-mask' = HELMET). In contrast with *wīġheafola*, those examples could plausibly be interpreted as instances of analogical metaphor (a1.4) or as a literal expression, given that at least some Anglo-Saxon helmets incorporated protective face shields resembling masks. Given the semantic closeness of the notions, this may also be interpreted as an

and perhaps visually obscure the sea, a helmet covers and obscures the head that bears it.

In agreement with Lakoff and Johnson (1980, 36), I categorize *Synecdoche* (subcategory b2) as an additional subcategory of metonymy, since both implement a closely associated term to refer to a person or some other object. More particularly, however, synecdoche signifies the *verbum proprium* by means of a material or object which contains, is contained, physically composes, is physically adjacent to, or is contiguous with the referent notion. There are two varieties of synecdoche: *pars pro toto* ('part for the whole') and *totum pro parte* ('whole for the part').[50] The pars pro toto variety (b2.1) occurs frequently in *Hêliand*; this subtype represents the entirety of the referent notion by substituting it for a compositional material or some other component or constituent element. This occurs in periphrases such as *ordos endi eggia* (*Hel* 3697, 'points and edges' = SWORDS), *hôh uuall* (*Hel* 3116 'high wall' [or 'high face'] = MOUNTAIN), and *grôni uuang* (*Hel* 757 'green meadow' = EGYPT).[51]

---

instance of catachresis. Since catachresis is a form of semantic imprecision, this device is interrelated with other relationships of semantic transfer, especially metonymy and analogical metaphor. See Lausberg, *Handbook of Literary Rhetoric: A Foundation for Literary Study*, §§ 562, 577.

[50] Alternatively, Henry describes synecdoche as involving semantic transfer between the referent term and another word that has greater or lesser semantic 'extension'; see Albert Henry, *Métonymie et métaphore* (Paris: Klincksieck, 1971), 18. Henry's notion of 'extension' appears to acknowledge somewhat the classical subtypes of synecdoche, *totum pro parte* and *pars pro toto*. Yet, Henry's understanding differs in at least one important manner: if *totum pro parte* could be seen as consisting of general categorical substitutions that carry greater semantic range than the referent term (i.e., they are more general than the referent term), then, logically, words used in a *pars pro toto* manner should express a narrower semantic range than the referent term (i.e., they are more specific than the referent term). However, *pars pro toto* substitutions usually consist of a constituent physical element of the referent notion, as when one refers to an automobile colloquially as a 'set of wheels.' It is unclear what constituent elements or substances have to do with narrow semantic extension or taxonomic specificity. Fidjestøl also questions the usefulness of Henry's paradigm for the skaldic kenning, as the distinction between synecdoche (understood in terms of 'extension') and metaphor is unclear, and "the structures of language are in constant movement with no stable hierarchy among the semantic units;" see Bjarne Fidjestøl, "The Kenning System: An Attempt at a Linguistic Analysis," in *Selected Papers*, ed. Odd Einar Haugen and Else Mundal, trans. Peter Foote (Odense: Odense UP, 1997), 26. I tend to agree with Fidjestøl's evaluation. Henry's notion of 'semantic extension' seems more clearly articulated by the classical categories of semantic transfer and the linguistic notions of hyponymy and hypernymy.

[51] The poet's topographical knowledge of far-away Egypt was perhaps lacking if he thought this was a representative synecdoche. There are no indications of intentional irony in the verse context. Compare *grôni godes uuang* (*Hel* 3082, 'God's green meadow' = HEAVEN). On a separate note, the expression *lêhni fehu* (*Hel* 1548, 'fleeting cattle i.e.,

Similarly, the examples *eðili sprâca, ârundi godes* (*Hel* 2455, 'noble speech, message of God' = GOSPEL) and *hêlag himilisc uuord* (*Hel* 15, 'holy, heavenly word' = GOSPEL) refer to the whole 'gospel' by employing an abstract element that constitutes the referent ('speech,' 'message,' 'word'). In this sense, these examples could be understood as a conceptual form of *pars pro toto* synecdoche, but one that is clearly not based in physical composition since the referent term itself is also an abstraction.

Examples of base-words that indicate their referents by means of material composition do not appear to occur in *Hêliand*, but this particular form of *pars pro toto* synecdoche is common in *Beowulf*. These instances seem exclusively to consist of inanimate referent terms, such as *īren* (*Beo* 673, 802, etc. 'iron' = SWORD) and *gleobeam* (*Beo* 2263 'glee-wood' = HARP), as well as several periphrases for 'ship' such as *sǣwudu* (*Beo* 226 'sea-wood' = SHIP), and *sundwudu* (*Beo* 208, 1906 'voyage-wood' = SHIP). Other examples for the referent notion 'ship' represent the whole by means of a smaller component rather than material composition as such, e.g., *wundenstefna* (*Beo* 220 'curved prow' = SHIP) and *hringedstefna* (*Beo* 32, 1131, 1897 'ringed prow' = SHIP).

Synecdoche of the *totum pro parte* subtype (b2.2), in which a larger whole represents a part, occurs in *Hêliand* in connection with periphrases for 'cross,' such as *bôm* (*Hel* 5534, 5592, 5608 'tree' = CROSS), *bômin treo* (*Hel* 5554 'wooden tree' = CROSS), and *uuaragtreo* (*Hel* 5563 'criminal[52] tree' = CROSS). Similarly, limited examples from *Beowulf* may be interpreted as *totum pro parte* synecdoche, but not without qualification. The expressions *æsc* (*Beo* 1772 'ash' = SPEAR) and *lind* (*Beo* 2341, 2365, 2610 'linden' = SHIELD) could conceivably be interpreted so that 'spear' and 'shield' are described in terms of the respective trees they were taken from in their entirety. Under this interpretation, the spear and the shield are 'parts' of the trees they were taken from, suggesting that *totum pro parte* synecdoche is the most logical label for these examples. An alternate reading would conceptualize 'ash' and 'linden' as the materials (i.e., the types of wood) that compose the objects in question, rendering these further instances of *pars pro toto* synecdoche.

Although it does not appear to occur in Old Saxon or in Old English verse, a peculiar type of antonomasia (subcategory b3) occurs in skaldic kennings. The term 'antonomasia' is often used in rhetorical literature to refer to all forms of circumlocutory substitution for a person's proper name; thus, the referent term in instances of antonomasia is consistently a named, living being (typically human). Ancient rhetorical commentaries suggest that antonomasia consists

---

[property, money]' = WEALTH) is probably also a synecdoche in its etymology. *Fehu* and its Germanic cognates are found as expressions for 'property' or 'money,' indicating that it is clearly not a poetic figure here, but rather a habitualized synecdoche inherited from Proto-Germanic.

[52] Or 'evildoer,' 'sinner.'

of a purely descriptive epithet that replaces a proper name.[53] Under this definition, antonomasia would be considered a literal device rather than a figurative one. However, Lausberg suggests that what has been referred to as 'Vossian antonomasia' is, in fact, a form of metonymy.[54] Examples of Vossian antonomasia appear quite frequently in kennings for human persons (Gamlkan *Has* 25[VII] *hring-Þrótt*, 'ring-Þróttr [= ODIN]' = MAN) and 'woman' (Anon [*FoGT*] 33[III] *öl-Gefn*, 'ale-Gefn [= FREYJA]' = WOMAN).[55]

Conclusion and Research Trajectory

One may conclude from the categories and examples presented here that there exists a schema of metaphorical and metonymic speech modalities that are primarily expressed through the base-words of Germanic noun periphrases. These figurative modalities occur both in typical skaldic kennings and in the less convoluted (and less 'esoteric') poetic expressions that occur in Old English and Old Saxon verse. Despite various scholarly assertions that kenning-like expressions in Old English verse tend to favor patronymics and accurate description over figurative trope, as well as the observation that Old Saxon periphrasis tends to employ less colorful language than skaldic kennings, periphrases with metaphorical and metonymic base-words occur in all three verse corpora. Yet, the subcategories of metaphor and metonymy specified above undoubtedly constitute only a small portion of the rhetorical modalities and devices that occur in the base-words of Germanic noun periphrasis. Therefore, this study can only serve as a starting point for further examination of figurative language in Germanic noun periphrasis. Furthermore, the examples of metaphor and metonymy presented here represent only a limited array of compositional patterns and poetic conventions for the use of these figures.

The figurative categories explored in this study can serve as a foundation for determining how poets employ those categories within Germanic periphrasis to achieve additional rhetorical devices and effects such as overstatement, understatement, and irony among others. Obscurer categories of rhetorical trope, as well as literal-descriptive devices, occur with great frequency in Germanic periphrasis, and many of these figurative categories and poetic figures are in some way based upon or related to the forms of metaphor and

---

[53] See Bede, "Concerning Figures and Tropes," 109; Isidore, *Etym* 1.37.11; Lausberg, *Handbook of Literary Rhetoric: A Foundation for Literary Study*, § 580.

[54] This inversion of the standard form of antonomasia is named after the Dutch humanist Gerardus Vossius (b. 1577, d. 1649).

[55] Moreover, it occurs as well in the Christian tradition in a biblical title for Christ, *novissimus Adam* (1 Corinthians 15:45, 'new Adam' [or 'last Adam']), and in the early Christian title for Mary, *nova Eva* ('new Eve'). Marold used the term 'antonomasia' to denote what is in fact the strictly Vossian type of antonomasia found in skaldic kennings. See Marold, *Kenningkunst: Ein Beitrag zu einer Poetik der Skaldendichtung*, 57-8.

metonymy discussed above. These include antiphrasis,[56] euphemism,[57] hyperbole,[58] litotes,[59] and patronym[60] to name a few. Likewise, literal-descriptive epithets based upon characteristic activity or personal qualities abound in Germanic periphrasis, as well as examples of hypernymy and hyponymy in basewords (i.e., more generic, and more specific synonyms, respectively).[61]

Further identification of these various devices and speech modalities within Germanic noun periphrasis promises to reveal the rich semantic processes

---

[56] Bede defines *antiphrasis* as "irony expressed in one word […] [A]ntiphrasis does not express a contrary thought through the vocal intonation, but merely through words used with a meaning contrary to their true, original meaning;" see Bede, "Concerning Figures and Tropes," 116-117. An example of this would be the designation of Grendel as *gĩst* (*Beo* 1522 'guest,' or 'visitor' = GRENDEL) when in fact he is an unwelcomed invader at Heorot. The example *lēðaro drôm* (*Hel* 946 'joy of [the] evil [ones]' = HELL) represents an ironic manipulation of the previously cited expression *manno drôm* (*Hel* 763, 1126, etc., 'joy of men' = WORLD, though both fundamentally employ a metonymic association with an abstract notion, 'joy.'

[57] E.g., *dalu thiustri* (*Hel* 2140, 'dark valleys' = HELL) and *diap dôdes dalu* (*Hel* 5170, 'deep valleys of death' = HELL). For explanation of euphemism according to classical rhetorical commentators, see Lausberg, *Handbook of Literary Rhetoric: A Foundation for Literary Study*, §§ 587, 905-908, 1246.

[58] An example of non-metaphorical hyperbole may be found in *helið hardmôdig* (*Hel* 3137 'bold hero' = PETER), where *helið* has the primary meaning of 'hero.' However, *helið* may also be used in a broader sense to denote a 'man,' though implying exceptional vitality and virility. Thus, the semantic incongruity does not result from taxonomical distinction, but rather from exaggeration of degree. The example *snel suerdthegan* (*Hel* 4866 'brave sword-thane' = PETER) is quite similar in this regard.

[59] Though focusing on Old Norse examples, Hollander contends that litotes is a vital component of Germanic verse composition in general, and numerous instances in *Beowulf* and *Heliand* support this assertion; see Lee M. Hollander, "Litotes in Old Norse," *PMLA* LIII (1938): 2. The *Beowulf*-poet is especially fond of litotes, e.g., "nalas for fæhðe mearn" (*Beo* 1537-1538 'he was not sorrowful for the hostility,' i.e., Beowulf is enthusiastic for the fight). For a short overview of litotes in Beowulf, see Roberta Frank, "Conversational Skills for Heroes," in *Narration and Hero: Recounting the Deeds of Heroes in Literature and Art of the Early Medieval Period*, ed. Victor Millet and Heike Sahm (Berlin: Walter de Gruyter, 2014), 25-28. Examples of litotes in *Heliand* are comparatively rare, but the device may occur within noun variations, as in the following adjectival example: "flêsk is unc antfallan, fel unscôni" (*Hel* 153 '[the] flesh has fallen down from us, [the] skin [is] unlovely'). While this example demonstrates that litotes and nominal periphrasis are conceptually compatible, the two devices occur only rarely in conjunction with one another.

[60] E.g., *sunu Healfdenes* (*Beo* 268, 344, etc. 'son of Healfdene' = HROTHGAR); *Scyldes eafera* (*Beo* 19 'Scyld's heir' = BEOW), *mæg Hyġelāces* (*Beo* 737, 758, etc. 'kinsman of Hygelac' = BEOWULF).

[61] See Lausberg, *Handbook of Literary Rhetoric: A Foundation for Literary Study*, § 676.

behind a device that was foundational to the pre-ecclesiastical poetic traditions of Germanic peoples. More importantly, continued work in this area promises to uncover general compositional patterns based on poetic figuration, some of which may be unique to or particularly prominent within certain works or corpora, while others could represent universal, cross-Germanic patterns. For example, a logical inconsistency between a kenning determinant and its far-fetched, metaphorical base-word[62] frequently sets skaldic kennings apart from other forms of nominal periphrasis. This difference is especially true for non-kenning circumlocutions that employ conventional titles and monikers in the base-word position rather than figurative expressions. Although many periphrases in Old English and Old Saxon verse feature metaphor and metonymy, the tropic devices employed in *Beowulf* and *Hêliand* typically present the audience with comparatively little interpretive difficulty. Proceeding forward with this line of inquiry, attestation rates of the metaphorical and metonymic subtypes identified here could help determine whether this is due to a relative lack of certain tropic categories, or if the discrepancy is due to a familiarity with the tropic conventions in those works[63] as opposed to the strange *heiti* that comprise skaldic diction.[64] Identification of compositional patterns could also aid the detection of influence, attribution, common Germanic inheritance of certain expressions, or other conventions of poetic diction within each early Germanic language. Knowledge of the frequency of attestation for the various devices and categories identified here and in classical rhetorical sources would help meet these objectives.

Lastly, let us consider once again the scholarly consensus that literal-descriptive modalities are more common among Old English and Old Saxon circumlocutions than they are among skaldic kennings. Scholars have quite reasonably hypothesized that the *Hêliand*-poet seems especially inclined to utilize noun periphrasis to provide literal, theologically accurate descriptions of biblical personages, while the *Beowulf*-poet employs similar circumlocutions to establish ancestry, ethnic extraction, and historical verisimilitude. Identification of figurative modalities in base-words and calculation of their respective attestation rates could serve to test these and similar perceptions in the discourse, thus revealing and clarifying general aspects of authorial intent. Also, high attestation rates of figurative modalities among Old Saxon and Old English

---

[62] Understood in accordance with the Aristotelian manner of thinking about metaphor, this perceived incompatibility between poetic term and referent in the skaldic kenning, as well as the resulting perplexing quality, is due to transfer of meaning between terms belonging to dissimilar semantic genera.
[63] E.g., *lamb godes* (*Hel* 1131, 'lamb of God' = CHRIST).
[64] E.g., *borr seims* (Anon *Pl* 4[VII], 'tree of gold' = MAN).

periphrases would help challenge the prior scholarly consensus concerning the relative lack of semantic transfer in Old English and Old Saxon noun periphrasis. Future collection of quantitative evidence regarding figurative modalities in nominal periphrasis thus has the potential to clarify the historical and philological relationships between the various Germanic poetic corpora regarding these devices.

Bibliography

Aristotle. *Poetics and Rhetoric*. Edited by George Stade, translated by S. H. Butcher (*Poetics*) and W. Rhys Roberts (*Rhetoric*). New York: Barnes & Noble Books, 2005.

Bede. "Concerning Figures and Tropes." In *Readings in Medieval Rhetoric*, edited by Joseph M. Miller et al., translated by Gussie Hecht Tannenhaus, 96-122. Bloomington: Indiana UP, 1973.

Behaghel, Otto, ed. *Hêliand und Genesis*. 10th edition. Tübingen: Max Niemeyer Verlag, 1996.

Brodeur, Gilchrist. *The Art of Beowulf*. Berkeley: U of California P, 1960.

Fidjestøl, Bjarne. "The Kenning System: An Attempt at a Linguistic Analysis." In *Selected Papers*, edited by Odd Einar Haugen and Else Mundal, translated by Peter Foote, 16-67. Odense: Odense UP, 1997.

Frank, Roberta. "Conversational Skills for Heroes." In *Narration and Hero: Recounting the Deeds of Heroes in Literature and Art of the Early Medieval Period*, edited by Victor Millet and Heike Sahm, 19-43. Berlin: Walter de Gruyter, 2014.

Gade, Kari Ellen, ed. *Poetry from the Kings' Sagas 2: From c. 1035 to c. 1300*. Vol. 2, *Skaldic Poetry of the Scandinavian Middle Ages*. Turnhout: Brepols, 2009.

———, and Edith Marold, eds. *Poetry from Treatises on Poetics*. Vol. 3, *Skaldic Poetry of the Scandinavian Middle Ages*. Turnhout: Brepols, 2017.

Gardner, Thomas. "The Old English Kenning: A Characteristic Feature of Germanic Poetical Diction?" *Modern Philology* 67, no. 2 (1969): 109-117.

———. "The Application of the Term Kenning." *Neophilologus* 56 (1972): 464-468.

Heinzel, Richard. *Über den Stil der germanischen Poesie*. Strasbourg: K.J. Trübner, 1875.

Henry, Albert. *Métonymie et métaphore*. Paris: Klincksieck, 1971.

Heusler, Andreas. Review of "Die kenningar der skalden. Ein beitrag zur skaldischen poetik," by Rudolf Meissner. *Anzeiger für deutsches Altertum und deutsche Literatur* 41 (1922): 127–34.

Hollander, Lee M. "Litotes in Old Norse." *PMLA*, LIII (1938): 1-33.

Jakobson, Roman, and Morris Halle. *Fundamentals of Language*. The Hague: Mouton & Co., 1956.

Klaeber, Friedrich, et al., eds. *Klaeber's Beowulf: And the Fight at Finnsburg*. 4th Edition. Toronto: University of Toronto Press, 2008.

Kuhn, Hans. "Das römische Kriegswesen im germanischen Wortschatz." *Zeitschrift für deutsches Altertum und Literatur* 101 (1972): 13-53.

Lakoff, George, and Mark Johnson. *Metaphors We Live By*. Chicago: U of Chicago P, 1980.

Lanham, Richard A. *A Handlist of Rhetorical Terms*. 2nd edition. Berkeley: U of California P, 1991.

Lausberg, Heinrich. *Handbook of Literary Rhetoric: A Foundation for Literary Study*. Leiden: Brill, 1998.

Latin Vulgate. "The Vulgate, Ezekiel 11:19," February 1, 2024. http://www.latinvulgate.com/.

Marold, Edith. *Kenningkunst: Ein Beitrag zu einer Poetik der Skaldendichtung*. Berlin: W. de Gruyter, 1983.

Meissner, Rudolf. *Die Kenningar der Skalden: Ein Beitrag zur skaldischen Poetik*. Bonn: Kurt Schroeder, 1921.

Mohr, Wolfgang. *Kenningstudien: Beiträge zur Stilgeschichte der altgermanischen Dichtung*. Verlag W. Kohlhammer, 1933.

Rankin, James W. "A Study of the Kennings in Anglo-Saxon Poetry." *JEGP* 8 (1909): 357-422.

———. "A Study of the Kennings in Anglo-Saxon Poetry." *JEGP* 9 (1910): 49-84.

West, M. L. "Tryphon De Tropis." *The Classical Quarterly* 15, no. 2 (1965): 230-248.

Chapter 3

Scribal Errors and Peculiarities in the *Hildebrandslied*

Robin Cummins
University of Wisconsin Madison

Abstract: The writing of the *Hildebrandslied* (Kassel 2° Ms. theol. 54) shows that the two scribes had largely different levels of experience, based on the number and types of corrections made by each scribe and by the types of letters each uses. While many scholars have addressed these errors in the *Hildebrandslied*, only one philologist attempts to catalog all the manuscript's errors (Danielowski 1919). Despite Danielowski's thoroughness, her work still contains its own share of flaws.

This study is an analysis of a number of scribal errors and habits in the *Hildebrandslied*. It assumes there are two scribes and investigates differences between the two. It also assumes that this manuscript had an exemplar and that the original language of composition was Old High German. The data, then, clarifies the text's transmission history. By examining each letter, this paper catalogues the scribal errors and atypical letters in the manuscript and sorts them into categories, including *calamo currente* errors, erasures, and instances of wynn.

Although both scribes made the same amount of *calamo currente* errors, the second scribe writes less than a fifth of the number of letters the first scribe writes. The first scribe favors erasures to *calamo currente*. These corrections also imply that certain errors must have existed in a previous copy (e.g. an <h> corrected from an <n> in "hiltibraht"). The data also suggests that both scribes were unfamiliar with the text because of errors such as <puas> (line 22 of the first folio) and punctuated wynn. Based on the frequency of certain variations of letters used by the first scribe in the last part of the manuscript, the second scribe's writing appears to have influenced the first scribe. Furthermore, both scribes' numbers of letters written per line demonstrate their skill and tendencies.

Keywords: OHG; scribal analysis; paleography

***

Digitalization has dramatically expanded the possibilities available for modern philologists, as digitized manuscripts allow for studying their texts without travel to the libraries where they are housed. The *Hildebrandslied* is one such manuscript, and, despite its age, its paleography demonstrates significant parallels to modern philology. In the process of making sense of the text they copied, the scribes drew on a large knowledge base to create the manuscript that survives today. Now, digital philology allows modern scholars to draw on another large knowledge base to analyze the text these two scribes left behind over a millenium ago.

The *Hildebrandslied* is perhaps the most mysterious text in the Old High German corpus: the language the lay was originally composed in, the purpose of the text's partial translation into Old Saxon, and the cause of the survival of the text all remain unanswered questions, which frame the core of current discussions. Yet the manuscript's paleography often remains unaddressed, the most recent being Helmich van der Kolk's overview of the *Hildebrandslied*[1] and a very brief mention of insular features in Brian Murdoch's overview of the text.[2] With only one surviving manuscript, paleography is a vital clue to the lay's transmission and history because the scribal practices demonstrated in the text offer clues about both the exemplar and the scribes themselves. The frequency of scribal errors and the patterns of different letter forms and sizes hint that the second scribe of the text influenced the first and that they likely had two different levels and types of experience, one being more experienced than the other. These written characters also show that many of these atypical features existed in the exemplar, meaning that they were transmitted intentionally.[3] Therefore, this project assumes that the text was copied from an exemplar because of the improbability that the manuscript contains the first instance of its written form due to the scribal errors and practices demonstrated in the manuscript. The second assumption is that two scribes wrote the text and that the original lay was composed in Old High German.

---

[1] See Helmich van der Kolk, *Das Hildebrandlied: Eine forschungsgeschichtliche Darstellung* (Amsterdam: Scheltma & Holkema N. V., 1967).

[2] See Brian Murdoch, "Das Hildebrandslied," in *German Writers and Works of the Early Middle Ages, 800-1170*, edited by Will Hasty and James N. Hardin. Dictionary of Literary Biography Vol. 148. (Detroit, MI: Gale, 1995). Gale Literature Resource Center (accessed February 11, 2022). https://link.gale.com/apps/doc/H1220000434/LitRC?u=wisc_madison&sid=bookmark-LitRC&xid=1523f3ac.

[3] For an overview of this recent scholarship on the *Hildebrandslied*, see Stammler, Wolfgang, and Karl Langosch, *Die deutsche Literatur des Mittelalters, Verfasserlexikon*, 2nd ed., vol. 3, edited by Kurt Ruh et al (Berlin: De Gruyter, 1981). It contains several of the works referenced in this article, for example those by Lühr and van der Kolk.

Three major facsimiles of the text exist: one from Wilhelm Grimm, one from Magda Enneccerus, and one digitized by the Universität Kassel. Grimm's facsimile is the oldest and depicts the original manuscript before reagents damaged it.[4] However, Grimm's text was copied by hand, adding another layer of scribal interpretation.[5] Although this facsimile demonstrates what the text most likely looked like before it was damaged, it cannot be used without skepticism because it is not the original manuscript and could have been influenced by the copier's interpretation. Magda Enneccerus created her facsimile by using early photograph technology in the late nineteenth century. The images accurately show the text but are limited by technology and the manuscript's damaged condition.[6] Over one hundred years later, the Universität Kassel digitized the manuscript, housed at the Murhardsche Bibliothek in Kassel, in 2011.[7] Not only does it show the text, but it can also be downloaded and digitally manipulated to examine the script more closely. Although some details are challenging to see digitally, investigation of the *Hildebrandslied* without travel to the physical manuscript is possible and enables the present research.

Other scholarship of the *Hildebrandslied* predates digitalization, beginning in the nineteenth century. Franz Saran and Hermann Pongs wrote overviews of the text in the nineteenth century that discuss the manuscript's language, history, and paleography.[8] Their studies demonstrate not only that many of these questions and topics have interested scholars for a long time or that many modern assumptions about the text are rather old (such as the number of scribes and the existence of an Old High German original) but they also demonstrate that the questions about the paleography of the text have long existed and been only partially answered.

More recent studies on the *Hildebrandslied* were important for this project as well. Helmich van der Kolk wrote about the history of the lay, the history of

---

[4] These markings made by nineteenth-century philologists are necessary to note, as they make a portion of the first folio nearly illegible, affecting the data. I collected data on these reagent stains, but even with editing software, I was unable to see finer paleographic detail. These markings need more investigation in the future.

[5] See Wilhelm Grimm, *De Hildebrando: Antiquissimi Carminis Teutonici Fragmentum* (Gottingae Sumtibus Editoris, 1830).

[6] See Magda Enneccerus, *Die ältesten deutschen Sprach-Denkmäler in Lichtdrucken herausgegeben* (Frankfurt am Main: Verlag von F. Enneccerus, 1897).

[7] Universität Kassel, *Hildebrandlied. Origenes, lat. Liber Sapientiae. Liber Iesu filii Sirach* (2011, https://orka.bibliothek.uni-kassel.de/viewer/image/1296741113093/169/).

[8] See Franz Saran, *Das Hildebrandslied* (Halle: Max Niemeyer, 1915). See Hermann Pongs, *Das Hildebrandslied, Ueberlieferung und Lautstand im Rahmen der ahd. Literatur* (Marburg: W. Hütter, 1913).

research on the text, and the text itself. He describes the text's paleography and gives an overview of paleographic research. These chapters also contain data on the number of corrections and erasures in the text, though these numbers do not match the numbers of this project.[9]

Any study of the paleography of the *Hildebrandslied* is insufficient without discussing the written language of the text. There are four major hypotheses for a language of origin: Langobardic, Gothic, Old Saxon, and Old High German. Willy Krogmann and Georg Baesecke supported a Langobardic original. Baesecke even went so far as to write a hypothetical Langobardic version of the text, even though little evidence of the Langobardic language survives to this day, namely, only a few glosses.[10] More recently, Maria Molinari argues that, although the story contains Langobardic elements, like the characters' names, the lay was more likely written in Old High German and then translated into Old Saxon. She writes that one should not confuse the Langobardic story elements with the overall language of the text.[11] There is otherwise no evidence that the original was Langobardic. Therefore, a Langobardic original is highly unlikely.

In contrast, Richard Lawson theorizes the possibility of a Gothic source, though he is not entirely convinced of its existence. He argues that, although much of the evidence points toward another language of origin, a Gothic original cannot be completely rejected. However, according to Lawson, the name element "-brand" is not known to have existed in Gothic, and the story has more Langobardic than Gothic elements.[12] Linguistic data also calls a hypothetical Gothic origin into question. Although, Lawson compares the classes of weak verbs in the text to patterns of weak verbs used in Gothic and argues that the patterns displayed in the *Hildebrandslied* are closer to those of Gothic than those of Old High German. First and second-class verbs arise in the text with unequal frequency. Lawson writes that the first class appears more

---

[9] See Helmich van der Kolk, *Das Hildebrandlied: Eine forschungsgeschichtliche Darstellung* (Amsterdam: Scheltma & Holkema N. V., 1967). The first two chapters, "Die Handschrift" and "Sprache und Heimat des Liedes" were particularly helpful for this project.

[10] See Willy Krogmann, *Das Hildebrandslied in der langobardischen Urfassung hergestellt* (Berlin: Erich Schmidt Verlag, 1959). See Georg Baesecke, *Das Hildebrandlied: Eine geschichtliche Einleitung für Laien, mit Lichtbildern der Handschrift, alt- und neuhochdeutschen Texten* (Halle: Max Niemeyer Verlag, 1945).

[11] Maria Vittoria Molinari, "Appunti Sulla Lingua Del Hildebrandslied," *Incontri Linguistici* 1 (1974): 91.

[12] Richard Lawson, "The Hildebrandslied Originally Gothic? Some Morphological and Syntactical Considerations," *Neuphilologische Mitteilungen: Bulletin De La Société Neophilologique/Bulletin of the Modern Language Society* 74 (1973): 334.

often in Gothic, hinting at the possibility of a Gothic original.[13] This argument lacks support, however. If the lay was translated from Gothic, the classes of verbs used in a translation to Old High German may not be the same. Furthermore, no Gothic poetry has survived to this day. Therefore, this argument can be rejected as *obscurum per obscurius*: without knowledge of other Gothic linguistic art forms and without a comparison of the frequency of weak verbs in other Old High German orally transmitted poems, we cannot begin to argue fully for a Gothic original. Even if this argument had more support, it would not confirm that the *Urtext* was Gothic. These factors rule out Gothic as the original.

These rejections leave Old High German and Old Saxon as the two most likely languages of original composition, and some evidence for both languages exist. Rosemarie Lühr's article, "Zum Hildebrandslied," demonstrates the high probability that the original text was in Old High German. Although the lay has elements of each language, it is most likely not originally Langobardic, Gothic, or Old Saxon. Lühr describes the elements of each language in the text and concludes that the original was in Old High German and then partially translated into Old Saxon, as Molinari argues as well.[14] In contrast, D'Alquen and Trevers argue that the original was written in Low German rejecting Lühr's hypothesis.[15] However, as Lühr notes, an Old Saxon original is unlikely: "[man kann] also nur von einem oberflächlichen sächsischen Einfluss sprechen." ["(one can) therefore only speak of a superficial Saxon influence,"][16] D'Alquen and Trevers, despite their support for an Old Saxon original, agree with Lühr that a Low German version would not rhyme. For example, "reccheo" in Old High German would be "wrekkio" in Low German and must alliterate with "riche."[17] The text was most likely originally in Old High German. Then an unknown translator began translating it into Old Saxon. This partial translation of the text is worth noting, as it is incomplete and inaccurate, and the reason for it is unknown. Most of the text remains in Old High German, and the Old Saxon beginning is mistranslated based on what appears to be a medieval understanding of the Second Sound Shift. This interpretation remains dominant in current scholarship: for example, Brian Murdoch, in his overview of the text, adopts this understanding. Thus, the project rejects an Old Saxon

---

[13] Lawson, 336-7.
[14] Rosemarie Lühr, "Zum Hildebrandslied," *Sprachwissenschaft* 38, no. 2 (2013): 147-170.
[15] R. D'Alquen and H. G. Trevers, "The Lay of Hildebrand: The Case for a Low-German Original," *Amsterdamer Beiträge zur älteren Germanistik* 22 (1984): 11-72.
[16] Lühr, 156, translation my own.
[17] D'Alquen and Trevers, 12.

original and assumes that the original text was Old High German and later partially translated into Old Saxon.

The number of scribes is also important and, much like the language of the lay, is a point of contention in scholarship. Previous research on the lay mostly indicates that two scribes wrote the text, though this is not the only opinion. Emma Danielowski believed that the text had only one scribe whom she called "der Angelsachse," [the Anglo-Saxon].[18] While the text contains many insular paleographic elements, this theory is improbable because an Old English scribe would have recognized the runic letters in the text. Richard Lawson notes that as many as five scribes have been posited on the opposite end of the spectrum.[19] Most scholars, however, believe that two scribes wrote the text (for example, Pongs, Saran, Van der Kolk), and this project also observed two key sets of scribal behaviors in the manuscript.

Methodology and Data

The methods for this project were largely drawn from Bernard Muir's study on paleography in the *Exeter Book*, which provides a method for looking at the *Hildebrandslied* as well. His article, Issues for Editors of Anglo-Saxon Poetry in Manuscript Form," describes how the transmission of Old English texts, particularly the *Exeter Book*, affected their reading. He points out that those who copied and read medieval texts were not passive transmitters of the writing but engaged with the text through corrections, notes, and other interactions. Most notably, for this analysis of the *Hildebrandslied,* Muir documents some of the *Exeter Book* manuscript's scribal errors and describes possible reasons for these mistakes. Both readers and scribes corrected many of the errors in the text; however, some errors remained unchanged, possibly because these errors did not hinder a reader's understanding of the text, according to Muir.[20] These ideas also apply to the *Hildebrandslied*: the manuscript's paleographic data gives information on how the text was likely transmitted and could demonstrate how later readers and scribes received the text.

Some of the technological aspects of this project come from the work of Timothy Price, who used picture editing software to investigate the L-fragment

---

[18] Emma Danielowski, *Das Hiltibrantlied: Beitrag zur Überlieferungsgeschichte auf paläographischer Grundlage* (Berlin: Mayer & Müller, 1919), 53-9.
[19] Lawson, 333.
[20] Bernard J. Muir, "Issues for Editors of Anglo-Saxon Poetry in Manuscript Form," *Inside Old English: Essays in Honour of Bruce Mitchell,* Edited by John Walmsley, 181-202 (Hoboken: Blackwell Publishing, 2006).

Scribal Errors and Peculiarities in the Hildebrandslied   61

of the *Hêliand*.[21] Emma Danielowski also performed a similar project using photography to look at details of the *Hildebrandslied* manuscript, albeit with the technological limitations of the 1910s. She photographed and enlarged portions of the text to investigate individual words and letters and provide closer details of some scribal features. Price and Danielowski, serve as the technological inspiration for this project. Although, she put forth some likely false hypotheses (for example, the idea of one English scribe copying the text), Danielowski's documentation of errors, erasures, and peculiarities are comprehensive. She notes some errors that are not visible in the text, but her lists are useful for the project.[22]

Using the digital facsimile provided by the Bayerische Staatsbibliothek, I used digital editing software to take images of each scribal error and variant letter and to store and organize them in a database. This database contains ten categories: additions, instances of name forms containing "braht," *calamo currente* corrections, digraphs, double-footed <m>, erasures, ligatures, stains, variations of letters, and miscellaneous. [23] I used the software GIMP to collect these images and to examine color contrasts to view smaller details more closely. To further understand the frequency of errors, corrections, and variations of letters, I also counted all the written characters in the text. The rules for this count were as follows: first, ligatures were counted as two characters, while digraphs were counted as one. Also, erasures were not counted because no exact number of letters can be gleaned from them, as well as marginalia. The line denoting a nasal was also not counted because it played no positive role in the length of a line and because it is not a complete letter. In contrast, insertions were counted, even though they did not add to the line length, as they were complete characters written by the scribes.

The manuscript's characters contain several variations, errors, and corrections that show how each scribe approached the writing process. The manuscript contains 2117 characters: 1790 that appear to be written by the first scribe and 327 that appear to be from the second. Among these characters, each scribe used five *calamo currente* corrections. While the exact proportions remain unclear, the number of *calamo currente* errors for the first scribe is a much higher percentage of the number of total letters than those of the second scribe. In

---

[21] Timothy Blaine Price, *Luther's "Heliand": Resurrection of the Old Saxon Epic in Leipzig*. Berkeley Insights in Linguistics and Semiotics: 80 (Pieterlen: Peter Lang Inc., 2011).
[22] See Danielowski.
[23] *Calamo currente* errors are those corrected "with the pen running," or those corrected as the scribe writes rather than being erased later with a penknife. I attempted to do a Chi-Square test of the *calamo currente* data, but unfortunately the numbers did not appear to function in the equation. In the future, a better statistician could test these numbers to see if these differences are statistically significant.

addition, the first scribe made seven erasures with the penknife, while the second scribe did not appear to use any. While extremely helpful, a digital facsimile makes it challenging to see which parts of the text have been erased with the penknife. Because they had access to the physical manuscript, previous scholars have more detailed numbers and analyses on erasures in the text, though these numbers still differ. For example, Emma Danielowski counts 15 erasures for the first scribe, while Helmich van der Kolk counts 20, but it is difficult to say which number, if either, is correct.[24] I only observed seven erasures in the digital facsimile, so I can only thoroughly discuss these seven. While the first scribe made all seven erasures, the second scribe could have some, but none were observable digitally.

However, *calamo currente* and erasures are not the only two types of corrections. Perhaps the most notable are the only two instances of insertions in the text, and the first scribe wrote both. The first is the correction of <hilt\i/u> from <hiltu> in the fifth line of the first folio (Figure 3.1.).[25] The form of the <i> here is worth noting, as it seems to be less carefully written than the letters around it, judging by the rounder base of the letter. The second addition occurs at the end of the text where the scribe inserts a <v> in <he\v/pun> (Figure 3.2.). Not only is this <v> significant as a correction in its own right, but it is also a correction that did not need to be made. The runic letter wynn is already represented here by <v>. This hints at two possibilities: first, that a <v> or <u> was written in the exemplar to clarify the rune *wynn*, and second, that the scribe felt the need to include this clarifying letter, either because the *Hildebrandslied* manuscript would be used for a similar purpose as its exemplar or because the scribe was unaware that this letter was unnecessary as part of the word.

Figure 3.1: Manuscript Evidence[26]

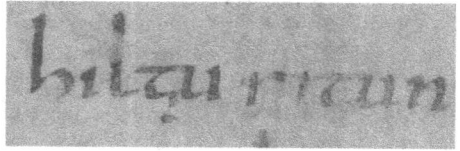

---

[24] Danielowski, 63-70. Van der Kolk, 10.

[25] See the digital facsimile by the Universitätsbibliothek Kassel, Landesbibliothek und Murhardsche Bibliothek der Stadt Kassel, 2° Ms. theol. 54, 1 recto and 76 verso. Reproduced in part under Creative Commons Attribution-ShareAlike 4.0 International Public License.

[26] Source of all figures: Universitätsbibliothek Kassel, Landesbibliothek und Murhardsche Bibliothek der Stadt Kassel, 2° Ms. theol. 54, 1 recto and 76 verso. Reproduced in part under Creative Commons Attribution-ShareAlike 4.0 International Public License.

Scribal Errors and Peculiarities in the Hildebrandslied

Figure 3.2: Manuscript Evidence

The runic letter *wynn* also appears elsewhere in the text, and these cases tend to be regular, with a few notable exceptions. The form of the character is sometimes miswritten (for example, as in Figure 3.2.), but the character always stands for the bilabial glide. The case of the erroneous word "puas" is therefore interesting because it showed that the scribe did not recognize *wynn*, and instead of it, wrote the letter combination <pu> (Figure 3.3.). Emma Danielowski noted this error and described it as a correction, but that may not be true.[27] The exemplar likely had a <u> written next to *wynn* for clarification of the pronunciation, and the scribe wrote this clarifying <u> alongside <p> by mistake. This does not explain why the scribe did not recognize it as a nonexistent word. The error occurs in the 22nd line of the text, after several other instances of the rune, so this sudden error is unusual within the manuscript. External to the manuscript, the monastery at Fulda received much of its scribal tradition from English sources, so it seems unlikely that experienced scribes at this monastery would be unfamiliar with *wynn*.[28] While this error offers no hints to the original language of the text, it does introduce the possibility that the scribe may not have fully understood what they were copying: the scribe did not recognize this word nor this character and chose to copy both to create an accurate visual copy, regardless of any linguistic comprehensibility. In other words, the scribe may have prioritized what they saw as adherence to the exemplar.

Figure 3.3: Manuscript Evidence

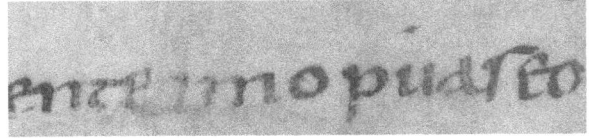

---

[27] Danielowski, 48.
[28] See Murdoch.

A mistake like this demonstrates what may have been the low contemporary value of this text. With a Latin text, particularly one with religious value, another scribe would have likely caught such errors and corrected them. The *Hildebrandslied*, being both in the vernacular and largely (if not entirely) pagan, did not receive the same level of care. This realization further complicates any possible explanation of why the Fulda scribes chose to copy the lay.

Another notable correction occurs in an instance of the name element "braht," which appears several times in the text. The reason for this alternate name spelling is unclear, though this correction sheds some light on what Heinz Klingenberg write was an intentional artistic decision by the poet.[29] While the original poet's artistic intentions are unclear, both scribes use this name variation, and the use of <h> instead of <n> appears intentional. Notably, none of these <h>s appears to have been corrected to <n>. Instead, the first case of "-braht" in the second line confirms that this <h> is not a repeated error because it was corrected from an <n>, based on the small stroke at the foot of the ascender that does not appear in other instances of this letter in the text. Therefore, it is highly likely that <h> appeared in the exemplar (Figure 3.4.) and was corrected *calamo currente*.

Figure 3.4: Manuscript Evidence

Including "braht" the text contains ten *calamo currente* errors. Although the numbers of *calamo currente* corrections made by both scribes are equal, these numbers are far from equal when considered proportionally. The second scribe made five corrections in 327 characters, while the second scribe made five in 1790 characters. The first scribe appears to have preferred using the penknife to erase mistakes rather than correcting them with a pen stroke or two. This preference for the penknife may demonstrate a higher level of care by the first scribe (they chose to completely correct a mistake rather than partially), but it

---

[29] Heinz Klingenberg, "Braht Und Brand: Zum Althochdeutschen Hildebrandlied". In *Comparative-Historical Linguistics: Indo-European and Finno-Ugric: Papers in Honor of Oswald Szemerényi, III*, edited by Bela Brogyanyi and Reiner Lipp, 407-467, (Amsterdam: John Benjamins, 1993), 411.

Scribal Errors and Peculiarities in the Hildebrandslied

more likely demonstrates that the second scribe was able to correct errors much more quickly and easily, and therefore was more experienced.

Besides corrections, the two scribes also show marked differences in style. For example, all digraphs in the manuscript appear to have solely been written by the first scribe, and all of them are <ae> or <et> digraphs. The forms of the <ae> digraphs are mostly regular, but the <et> digraphs vary more in form (Figures 3.5., 3.6., and 3.7.). The first two are similar, though the round part of the <e> in the first is higher. However, a stain makes it difficult to see. One of these digraphs could be a correction, but these cases are still unclear. The form used by this scribe, shown in Figure 4.6., appears quite different from the first. The purpose of these digraphs is unknown. They may have appeared in the exemplar, which the first scribe seems to have attempted to emulate closely, or they may have been a matter of personal taste for the scribe. In contrast, ligatures were used by both scribes and showed little to no variation.

Figure 3.5: Manuscript Evidence

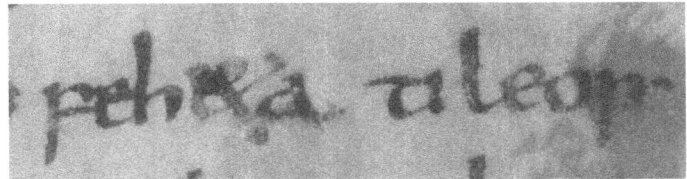

Figure 3.6: Manuscript Evidence

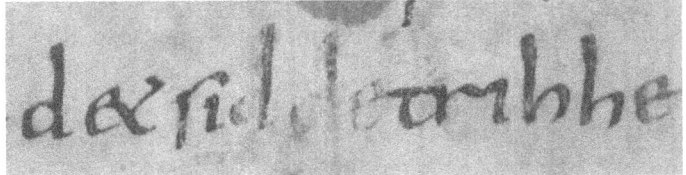

Figure 3.7: Manuscript Evidence

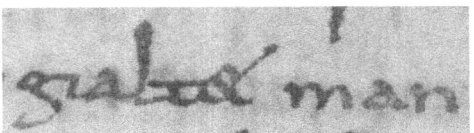

Even greater variation than that of digraphs and ligatures appears in the scribes' use of the letter <a>, but the reasoning for most of these variations is not entirely clear. The first scribe used two forms of the letter beside the "typical" Carolingian <a>, and these forms are pictured here:

Figure 3.8: Manuscript Evidence

Figure 3.9: Manuscript Evidence

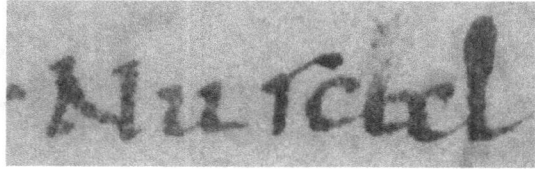

Figure 3.8. shows that cc-a is only a variation rather than a correction, a common feature for an early Carolingian manuscript.[30] The rest of the codex also uses double-c <a>, and a further study could help clarify why it appears in the *Hildebrandslied*: this letter form may have been typical for the scriptorium at Fulda at this time. Other atypical forms of <a> also appear in the manuscript, though under different circumstances. In Figure 3.9., the first scribe used an erasure and a double-horned <a> to correct a prematurely written <l>. This letter shape was, therefore, understandable as <a>, though the correction is rather obvious.

The <a> variations the second scribe wrote do not vary nearly as much (Figures 3.10. and 3.11.). These two letters that do not resemble the other forms of <a> by that scribe have a larger belly and a more upright back, perhaps to

---

[30] Karin Schneider, *Paläographie und Handschriftenkunde für Germanisten: Eine Einführung* 3rd. ed. *Sammlung kurzer Grammatiken germanischer Dialekte*, (Berlin: De Gruyter, 2014), 22.

save space. It is also possible that the scribe used these forms to relieve some of the monotony of writing. The scribe's motives, however, are impossible to know for certain.

Figure 3.10: Manuscript Evidence

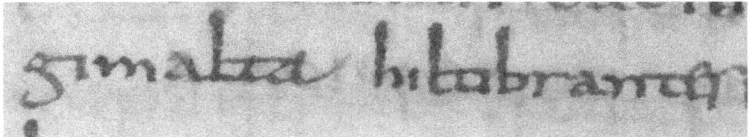

Figure 3.11: Manuscript Evidence

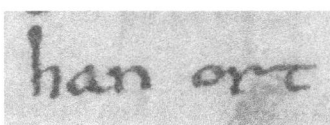

Even more unclear is the manuscript's one instance of double-footed <m> (Figure 3.12.). It could be a *calamo currente* correction: when a scribe writes a foot for <n> but intends to write <m>, they only need to make one further stroke. This variation could demonstrate that <m> was initially written as an <n>. It also occurred at the beginning of the text and was written by the first scribe, who tended to make more errors. It could also mean that the scribe wanted to vary the shape of the <m>. The text contains few hints as to which case occurred. Regardless, the variation is worth noting because it further demonstrates the variation of styles between the scribes and the ambiguity of counting errors and corrections in the text.

Figure 3.12: Manuscript Evidence

The text also contains only one instance of barred <b>, and this case is an abbreviation for part of the name element "-brant" in "heribrantes" (Figure

3.13.). Variations of the letter <e> in the text are also unclear because most of these could be less carefully written and may not be a full variation like shouldered <e>. The manuscript also contains one insular <f> (Figure 3.14.). It is unclear why the first scribe included this letter form; he demonstrates almost no other insular tendencies in the text. The exemplar may have been written in an insular script, which would explain the frequent occurrences of wynn in the text, but this is uncertain.

Figure 3.13: Manuscript Evidence

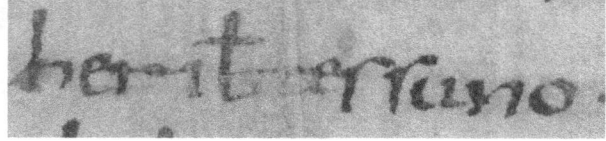

Figure 3.14: Manuscript Evidence

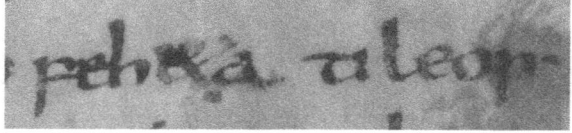

Tall <i> (shown in Figures 3.15. and 3.16.) appears ten times in the text and from both scribes. Nine of these examples are in the word <in>, and the tenth appears in the word <iro>. This pattern shows a propensity for this preposition to include tall <i>. Perhaps the letter is a recognition marker for such short words, though why is unclear. The height may be used to differentiate the beginning of a smaller word from words and letters of similar height around it, making it both easier to read and to copy. This choice, which could have been made for ease of reading, may hint that the text was intended to be read and not simply used to practice writing.

Figure 3.15: Manuscript Evidence

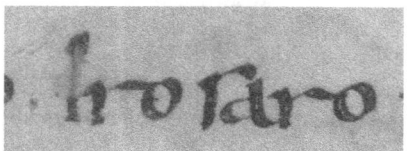

Figure 3.16: Manuscript Evidence

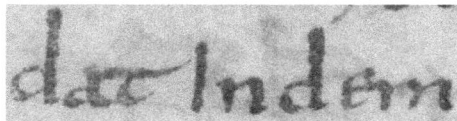

The scribes wrote three different forms of <d>: the standard Carolingian <d> (the unbarred, unrounded form), barred <d>, and rounded <d>, but each scribe has different patterns of using these forms. The first scribe uses all three forms, while the second writes only the standard and rounded forms. The environment that triggered these different forms is unclear, but a possible *calamo currente* correction demonstrates that the second scribe had at least some method for each form. In the second line of the 76th folio, the second scribe corrected a rounded <d> into a standard Carolingian <d> (Figure 3.17.). There are several reasons for this: the exemplar may have had a straight-backed <d> instead of a rounded <d>. Perhaps the scribe wrote a rounded <d> out of force of habit but felt that a more standard form was in order due to a personal paradigm for these letters. Either way, this hints at an intentional decision-making process on the part of the scribe.

Figure 3.17: Manuscript Evidence

For the most part, the miscellaneous cases are not unusual and include accents, nasal lines, dittography, and any letters that do not fit into other categories. Many of the special cases in this category are related. The letter <u>, for example, arises in an unusual form when written by the first scribe: in the word <ubar> (Figure 3.18.) and later near the end of the text in <dunu> (Figure 3.19).

Figure 3.18: Manuscript Evidence

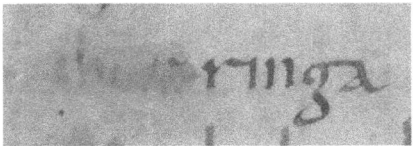

Figure 3.19: Manuscript Evidence

The case with the stain is not entirely clear, but the <u> appears to have a rounder first stroke. Danielowski saw this correction as a <u> formed from the stroke of an <i>, but that is not entirely clear in the manuscript.[31] The second <u> in <dunu> also shows this shape, but the reasoning behind it is hidden. The scribe could have possibly begun to write a rounded letter like <o>, but even if this is the case, it is not clear why.

Conclusions

The differences between the scribes and their writing techniques demonstrate much about the two scribes themselves, the exemplar, and scribal practices at the monastery at Fulda. The two scribes made the same number of *calamo currente* corrections, but the first scribe also used the penknife to erase many mistakes. These numbers could mean that the second scribe was more experienced and could quickly correct mistakes. The first scribe exhibited several copying mistakes, particularly those corrected with erasure. In contrast, the second scribe corrected most, if not all, errors *calamo currente*.

More than half of the *calamo currente* corrections are caused by the scribe looking to see what word or letters to copy next and accidentally copying the wrong letter. This wrong letter is often only one or two letters removed from the correct letter. This type of *calamo currente* correction also confirms letters and words that must have been in the exemplar: if a scribe corrected an error *to* a particular letter, that letter must have existed in the exemplar and have been intentional on the part of the scribe. Perhaps the most interesting example is "hiltibraht" (in Figure 3.3.). On the first page of the manuscript, in the second line, the second <h> in "hiltibraht" appears to be corrected from an <n>. Emma Danielowski also noted this correction.[32] This error shows that the second <h> in the name "Hiltibraht" was most likely in the exemplar – not a new addition from the scribe. Likewise, the corrected <d> in Figure 3.17. shows that one of

---

[31] Danielowski, 64.
[32] Ibid, 63-4.

these forms, likely the straight-backed form, existed in the exemplar, judging by its height. These changes suggest intentionality on the part of the scribes: this text needed to be correct and accurate to at least a certain degree (regardless of the level of success the scribes achieved). The *Hildebrandslied* was most likely intended to be used by later readers. For what reason, however, is unknown.

The scribes also differed widely in the uniformity of their letters. The second scribe (who wrote the first seven lines of the second folio of the manuscript) shows only a small breadth of variation in letters per line. The shortest line contains 41 characters, while the longest contains 45, creating a variation distance of only four characters. The scribe's letter sizes and shapes would appear to be mostly consistent by this measurement. In contrast, the longest line for the first scribe is 45 characters long, while the shortest contains 33 (one line has 27 characters, but is most likely an outlier due to being at the end of the text). By this metric, this scribe was much more inconsistent and likely had less experience than the second.

The second scribe, however, appears to have influenced the first scribe. The second section, written by the first scribe, shows a marked difference from the first section, written by the same scribe. For example, the number of letters per line for the first scribe becomes more regular toward the end of the text after the second scribe wrote a section. D'Alquen and Trevers write about this possibility and speculate that the second scribe may have been the teacher of the first.[33] While this is merely speculation, and the text does not seem to have been used for practice, it appears that the first scribe looked to the second scribe's writing for guidance.

The types of letters used by both scribes also reveal that they most likely had different training and approaches to writing. The forms of a <a> are, for example, completely different for each scribe when they choose to deviate from the typical Carolingian <a>: the first scribe used forms like horned <a> and double-c <a> (Figures 3.8. and 3.9.), while the second scribe wrote two with a longer back and a larger belly (Figures 3.10. and 3.11.). The first scribe also is the only one of the two to use digraphs. It is unclear why the second scribe chose not to use them.

The scribes may have spoken two different languages, though this is vague in their scribal practices. The first scribe copies the beginning of the text, written in incorrect Old Saxon, but the scribe also copies the end, written in Old High German. The first scribe also does not seem to recognize certain words and characters in the text, hinting they were unfamiliar with written Old High

---

[33] D'Alquen and Trevers, 21-22.

German. Examination of both scribes' practices compared to other manuscripts may help clarify what traditions the scribes adhered to.

An investigation of the physical manuscript would reveal even more information because the digital facsimile of the manuscript limited the parameters of this study. For example, the erasures were difficult to see in the digital version and proved a major disadvantage of this project. The second scribe may have used erasures that were not digitally observable. Investigating the physical manuscript would reveal even more about the handwriting and practices that created the manuscript.

The linguistic aspects of this manuscript also merit further investigation based on scribal tendencies. The *calamo currente* corrections, for example, confirm letters in the exemplar. By confirming whether certain words or word forms are older than this manuscript, these corrections could help with the dating of the text itself, or at least of this iteration. What we can confirm, however, is that the text was indeed copied from an exemplar and has a longer transmission history than what is readily seen. Future scholarship must consider this when investigating the lay.

Furthermore, almost no studies analyze the manuscript in the context of the rest of the codex. This text needs to be investigated alongside the codex paleographically because it is still unclear whether the script of the rest of the codex influenced the writing of the *Hildebrandslied*. The rest of the text may contain similar scribal features. For example, the codex contains the same variant forms of <a> that the first scribe used in the *Hildebrandslied*. The first scribe (and perhaps the second) could have easily been influenced by other texts in the codex and Latin writing. Because the text was written early in the process of the literalization of Old High German, these scribes may have only had Latin examples to draw on and were, therefore, less familiar with written forms of Old High German. Further investigation of the *Hildbrandslied* in the context of the entire codex may answer some of these paleographic questions, lending insight into both the *Hildebrandslied* and Old High German writing.

The paleography of the *Hildebrandslied* allows us to glimpse what the complicated text looked like at its inception. It hints at the diversity of scribes who copied the text and offers information on the tools, the exemplar, and the experience they had to make the manuscript. This knowledge could help us better understand, in tandem with linguistic studies, the transmission of the text and perhaps help us better guess why this unusual manuscript has survived. What is certain, though, is that the *Hildebrandslied*'s scribes were human. They display their faults, creativity, and experiences in their writing, In contrast, most scholarship tends to focus on the language and content of the lay, and while these topics are important, the scribes' writing is as well. It shows that several written aspects of the text had been passed on beforehand and offers insight into how scribes and readers reacted to the text. Although only the manuscript survives physically, the people who wrote it survive in a way, too, showing that modern writers and readers, even with technological advancements, are not that different from medieval ones.

Bibliography

Baesecke, Georg. *Das Hildebrandlied: Eine geschichtliche Einleitung für Laien, mit Lichtbildern der Handschrift, alt- und neuhochdeutschen Texten*. Halle: Max Niemeyer Verlag, 1945.

D'Alquen, R., and H. G. Trevers. "The Lay of Hildebrand: The Case for a Low-German Original." *Amsterdamer Beiträge zur älteren Germanistik* 22 (1984): 11-72.

Danielowski, Emma. *Das Hiltibrantlied: Beitrag zur Überlieferungsgeschichte auf paläographischer Grundlage*. Berlin: Mayer & Müller, 1919.

Enneccerus, Magda. *Die ältesten deutschen Sprach-Denkmäler in Lichtdrucken herausgegeben*. Frankfurt am Main: Verlag von F. Enneccerus, 1897.

Grimm, Wilhelm. *De Hildebrando: Antiquissimi Carminis Teutonici Fragmentum*. Gottingae Sumtibus Editoris, 1830.

Klingenberg, Heinz. "Braht Und Brand: Zum Althochdeutschen Hildebrandlied." In *Comparative-Historical Linguistics: Indo-European and Finno-Ugric: Papers in Honor of Oswald Szemerényi, III*, edited by Bela Brogyanyi and Reiner Lipp, 407-467. Amsterdam: John Benjamins, 1993. Amsterdam Studies in the Theory and History of Linguistic Science IV: Current Issues in Linguistic Theory (CILT): 97.

Krogmann, Willy. *Das Hildebrandslied in der langobardischen Urfassung hergestellt*. Berlin: Erich Schmidt Verlag, 1959.

Lawson, Richard H. "Displacement of Stabreim in the Old High German Hildebrandslied." *Studies in Medieval Culture* 8-9 (1976) 9-14.

———. "The Hildebrandslied Originally Gothic? Some Morphological and Syntactical Considerations." *Neuphilologische Mitteilungen: Bulletin De La Société Neophilologique/Bulletin of the Modern Language Society* 74 (1973): 333-339.

Lühr, Rosemarie. "Zum Hildebrandslied." *Sprachwissenschaft* 38, no. 2 (2013) 147-170.

Molinari, Maria Vittoria. "Appunti Sulla Lingua Del Hildebrandslied." *Incontri Linguistici* 1 (1974): 91-102.

Muir, Bernard J. "Issues for Editors of Anglo-Saxon Poetry in Manuscript Form." *Inside Old English: Essays in Honour of Bruce Mitchell*, Edited by John Walmsley, 181-202. Hoboken: Blackwell Publishing, 2006.

Murdoch, Brian. "*Das Hildebrandslied*." In *German Writers and Works of the Early Middle Ages, 800-1170*, edited by Will Hasty and James N. Hardin. Dictionary of Literary Biography Vol. 148. Detroit, MI: Gale, 1995. *Gale Literature Resource Center* (accessed February 11, 2022). https://link.gale.com/apps/doc/H1220000434/LitRC?u=wisc_madison&sid=bookmark-LitRC&xid=1523f3ac.

Price, Timothy Blaine. *Luther's "Hêliand": Resurrection of the Old Saxon Epic in Leipzig.* Pieterlen: Peter Lang Inc., 2011. Berkeley Insights in Linguistics and Semiotics: 80.

Schneider, Karin. *Paläographie und Handschriftenkunde für Germanisten: Eine Einführung.* 3rd. ed. *Sammlung kurzer Grammatiken germanischer Dialekte.* Berlin: De Gruyter, 2014.

Universitätsbibliothek Kassel, Landesbibliothek und Murhardsche Bibliothek der Stadt Kassel, 2° Ms. theol. 54, 1 recto and 76 verso. *Hildebrandlied. Origenes, lat. Liber Sapientiae. Liber Iesu filii Sirach,* 2011, https://orka.bibliothek.uni-kassel.de/viewer/image/1296741113093/169/.

Van der Kolk, Helmich. *Das Hildebrandlied: Eine forschungsgeschichtliche Darstellung.* Amsterdam: Scheltma & Holkema N. V., 1967.

Chapter 4

gedencken der pender: A New Reading of Hugo von Montfort's "min dienst und gruzz me tausent stunt" (no. 6)

Alexander Sager
University of Georgia

Abstract: Concerning the merits of the late medieval Styrian poet Hugo von Montfort (1357-1423), scholarship long held a uniformly low opinion. F. P. Knapp's 2004 judgement that Hugo's oeuvre is "aethetically very unsatisfying on the whole" and that his verse "bumps and hops along in a pathetic manner" reflects the traditional view, which we can trace, in the relatively little that has been written on this poet, from J. Wackernell in the 1880s through M. Wehrli in the 1980s. More recent scholarship (W. Hofmeister's 2005 edition; K. Amann and E. De Felip-Jaud's edited collection *aller weishait anevang*, 2010) has come to appreciate Hugo's poetic merits much more than in the past and have uncovered the poet's surprisingly complex relationship with the "classical" German vernacular poetic tradition.

This essay focuses on one of Hugo's cansos, "min dienst und gruzz me tausent stunt" (no. 6 in the Cpg 329 codex). On the evidence of some genealogical terms based on the lexeme *Band* surviving in Allemanic and Bauivaric dailects into the 19th century, I proposes a new, quasi-autobiographical readingof the crux *gedencken der pender* ("an die Bänder/Bande denken"; "to contemplate the ribbons/bonds"), for which no satisfying interpretation has yet been found.

While arguing that this poem is a good example of what scholars have come to recognize as Montfort's subtle aesthetic "Spiel mit der Ich-Rolle" (W. Achnitz, 2010; Böcking-Politis, 2015), I also claim that this is the only medieval German love poem in the minnesang tradition where the poet makes reference to his children.

Keywords: Late MHG, ENHG, lexical analysis, poetry

***

Scholarship long held a generally low opinion of the literary merits of the late medieval Styrian poet Hugo von Montfort (1357-1423). Fritz Peter Knapp's 2004 judgement that Hugo's oeuvre is "ästhetisch großteils wenig befriedigend" and that his verses "jämmerlich daher[holpern]" ['aesthetically largely unsatisfying;' 'limp along pitifully'] reflects the traditional view,[1] which we can trace, in the relatively little that has been written on Hugo, from Joseph Wackernell in the 1880s through Max Wehrli in the 1980s.[2] While he has always had his defenders, they have tended to emphasize how the poet's work gives us interesting insight into questions of authorship or the history of mentalities rather than seeking to defend the poetic quality of his work. Albrecht Classen, for example, writes that while we would look in vain for "bisher nicht wahrgenommene poetische Perlen" ['hitherto unnoticed poetic pearls'], Hugo's work nonetheless represents a notable milestone in the development of late medieval poetry into a mode of literary self-reflection, one with a strong autobiographical component.[3] That view has always been there. Already Wackernell noted that the manner in which Hugo represents the "Seelenleben" ['soul-life' or 'mentality'] of his era must compel our interest.[4]

In the last twenty years or so, however, the quality and craftsmanship of Hugo's poetry has been recognized more than in the past. The term most frequently used is *raffiniert* ['subtly clever,' 'sophisticated']. In Hugo's poem "Mich straft ein wachter morgens fru" (no. 11), for example, Cordula Böcking discusses the subtly clever way in which the topos of the "slave of love" (characters like Samson, King David, or Aristotle who fall victim to feminine wiles) is turned on its head in the service of a critique of those who hold women in contempt.[5] Jan Mohr writes appreciatively of the way Hugo subverts the

---

[1] Fritz Peter Knapp, Die Literatur des Spätmittelalters in den Ländern Österreich, Steiermark, Kärnten, Salzburg und Tirol von 1273 bis 1439, vol. 2, Die Literatur zur Zeit der frühen habsburgischen Herzöge von Rudolf IV. bis Albrecht V. (1358-1439) (Graz: Akademische Druck- und Verlagsanstalt, 2004), 397, 399. All English translations in this essay are mine.

[2] For an overview of Hugo reception see Elisabeth De Felip-Jaud, "Hugo von Montfort in Anthologien," in Aller weishait anevang Ist ze brúfen an dem aussgang. Akten des Symposiums zum 650. Geburtstag Hugos von Montfort, ed. Klaus Amann and Elisabeth De Felip-Jaud (Innsbruck: Innsbruck University Press, 2010), 143-153.

[3] Albrecht Classen, "Literatur und dichterische Selbstreflexion im Werk Hughos von Montfort. Ein Zeuge aus einer kulturhistorischen Spät- oder Frühzeit," in Aller weishait anevang, 167-189, here 167, 184.

[4] Joseph E. Wackernell, Hugo von Montfort. Mit Abhandlungen zur Geschichte der deutschen Literatur, Sprache, und Metrik im XIV und XV Jahrhundert (Innsbruck: Verlag der Wagner'schen Universitätsbuchhandlung, 1881), 7.

[5] Cordula Böcking-Politis, "ain iunkfrow rait der kúnsten perkh. Der Minnesklaventopos bei Hugo von Montfort," in Aller weishait anevang, 109-126.

medieval dawnsong. Normally the watchman, often a figure for the human conscience in later minnesang, wakes up the sleeper and exhorts him to arise from his sinful sloth. In Hugo's poem "Ich fragt ein wachter, ob es were tag" (no. 10), however, it is the watchman-conscience that is caught napping, an original poetic figure for the disordered life.[6] Perhaps the strongest case for Hugo's aesthetic is made by Wolfgang Achnitz, who argues that the poet's entire oeuvre is a "raffiniertes Spiel mit der Ich-Rolle," a sophisticated game with the first-person narrator, characterized by the methodical setting up and intentional disappointment of audience expectations for a whole range of traditional literary genres. In fact, the disappointment felt by modern-day scholars over the quality of Hugo's work may be testimony to how successful he was in this new aesthetic approach, which Achnitz calls "avantgardistisch" ('avant-garde').[7]

It is against this revaluation of the sophistication of Hugo's poetry that I would like to examine what I consider—with deference to Albrecht Classen—a hitherto underappreciated pearl in Hugo's work: poem no. 6, the canso "min dienst und gruzz me tausent stunt." Before turning to the poem, however, a brief synopsis of the author's life and work is in order, since he remains unfamiliar even to many medieval Germanists today.

Hugo Montfort's Life

As a member of the high nobility, Hugo led a well-documented life.[8] He was born in 1357 to Wilhelm III von Montfort, Count (*Graf*) of Bregenz, and was the twelfth Hugo to bear that name since the founding of the comital house in Bregenz by Hugo I in the early thirteenth century. In addition to the Swabian territories in and around Bregenz, the nobleman-poet possessed extensive lands in Vorarlberg and Styria, the latter through his first marriage to the wealthy Styrian noblewoman Margaretha von Pfannberg. His lifelong loyalty to the Habsburgs, including active participation in their military campaigns, brought him further honors and titles throughout his life and kept him in constant motion—his travels are a frequent theme in his poetry—over the more

---

[6] Jan Mohr, "Textreihe und Gattungsstrukturen. Zur Tageliedrezeption in Hugos von Montfort cpg 329," Beiträge zur Geschichte der deutschen Sprache und Literatur 138, no. 1 (April 2016): 76-106, here 87.

[7] Wolfgang Achnitz, "Man mocht es griffen mit der Hand. Das Durchbrechen von Erwartungshorizonten als Merkmal der Dichtungen Hugos von Montfort," in Aller weisheit anevang, 127-142, here 132, 139.

[8] Further biographical information can be found at Hugo von Montfort, Das poetische Werk, ed. Wernher Hofmeister (Berlin: Walter de Gruyter, 2005), xv-xvii, and Gernot Peter Obersteiner, "Hugo von Montfort und die Steiermark," in Aller weisheit anevang, 33-52, from which my account borrows.

than 500 kilometers between his Swabian and his eastern lands and interests. After Margaretha's death in 1388 or 1389, Hugo twice remarried: in 1395 or 1396 to Clementia von Toggenburg, who died young in 1399; and finally in 1402 to the widow Anna von Neuhaus, another Styrian noblewoman. The number of his progeny is uncertain. His funereal fresco in Pfannberg depicts his body in the company of six children, three boys and three girls. Of these, we know the name of only one, his eldest son Ulrich, by Margaretha von Pfannberg. Since the likelihood of natural as well as stepchildren in Hugo's household will be significant for our analysis below, I note that Margaretha (herself the stepdaughter of Hugo's father) was widowed before marrying the poet and may well have had children by her previous marriage, as well as further children by Hugo who remain unattested. Of Hugo's later wives, we know that at least Anna von Neuhaus had two daughters from her previous marriage,[9] and Clementia may have as well. Hugo withdrew from political life in 1416, devoted himself to religion, and died in 1423. He was buried in the Styrian town of Bruck.

Hugo's poetic corpus consists of some forty songs various in form, type, and length, ranging from traditional cansos and dawnsongs to extended didactic meditations on God and the world. On two occasions the poet himself provided overviews of his work, listing in one poem of 17 *reden* ['discourses'], 10 *lieder* ['songs' or 'cansos'], and an unnamed number of *frey brief* ['blithe letters']. In another poem, he divides his oeuvre into *brief, tagweis und red* ['letters, ', and discourses'].[10] He took pains to have his work collected, organized, and passed down, commissioning a beautiful codex that survived the centuries and is now in the Heidelberg University Library (Col. pal. germ. 329). Despite this effort, Hugo seems not to have taken his status as a poet terribly seriously, or at least he represented himself in this manner. In one poem, he notes that his rhymes may need improvement by an external party, and later in the same text he casually mentions that he outsources the melody-writing to a certain Mangolt.[11] Although surviving fragments in other and later manuscripts speak to considerable interest in Hugo's poetry in the decades after his death,[12]

---

[9] See Obersteiner, "Hugo von Montfort," 45.
[10] Hugo von Montfort, Das poetische Werk, ed. Hofmeister, poem no. 31, stanzas XLII-XLIV, and no. 38, stanza XXVI. "Blithe letters" is based on Hofmeister's conjecture, "unbekümmerte/freimütige Briefe" ["carefree/freely-spoken letters'], 149, note 2.
[11] Ibid., no. 31, stanza XXXVI: han ich mit meinem tichten / in den reimen iendert vergessen, / das tuo ein ander schlichten - / ich kan es nicht als messen. ("If in my poetry / I have neglected anything in the rhymes, / let someone else straighten it out; / I cannot measure it all"); stanza XLVI: die weysen hat gemachen Burk Mangolt / unser getrewer knecht. ("The melodies were made by Burk Mangolt, / our faithful servant").
[12] See Ibid., xix-xx (discission) and 195-208 (fragments).

gedencken der pender

modern scholarship, as exemplified in the quote from Fritz-Peter Knapp above, long considered him little more than a dilettante.

Classifications

If we follow Hugo's own classification of his work into *brief, tageweis und red* ['letters, dawnsongs, and discourses'], the refrain suggests that "min dienst und gruzz me tausent stunt" (no. 6) is one of the songs, although it is not one of the eight for which the poet included written melodies. I develop my reading from a solution proposed for a difficult passage in the poem's second stanza, underlined below:

II. I. Min dienst und gruzz me tausent stunt,
denn gestupp ist in der sunnen!
aller zwifel ist mir unkunt,
unmut ist mir zerunnen.
hett ich din huld (ich furcht din zorn),
so wer mir wol ze mute.
lazz ab, du lieber engel vin —
es kumpt dir noch ze gute!
sich an mir rew, nim von mir puss,
durch got tu mir vergeben!
wenn ich verlur din wiplich zucht,
so laidet mir das leben.
[Rep.] mit willen fro des bin ich zwar,
wan ich sich an dir itel recht.
und solt ich leben tusent iar,
so bin ich doch din aigen knecht.

II. <u>das ich der pender ye gedacht</u>
<u>mitt grunen sunder wenkhen</u>,
daz hat mir oft ain ruw bracht
mit mengerlay gedenkhen.
"der vatter zurnet dik dem kind":
das kunt von trewen stet.
das er aim andern nit entut,
der in es fleisslich bet.
was mir ist lieb, da ist mir lait:
was im kumpt nicht ze gut
an leib, an er, an wirdikait,
das bekrenkt mir den mut.
[Rep.] mit willen fro des bin ich zwar,

wan ich sich an dir itel recht.
und solt ich leben tusent iar,
so bin ich doch din aigen knecht.

III. ich bin dir doch mit trewen by
und stan des ane logen.
ich waiss ir yetz nit lebend fry,
die bass gevall min ogen.
din wiplich zucht und och din scham,
du hast die mazz gemessen.
und hett ich aller welt frod,
ich kann din nit vergessen:
"die fromdi schadt den steten icht"—
wie man tut selten sehen
so "vervacht gehaim gen wankel nicht,"
das ist och dik beschehen.
[Rep.] mit willen fro des bin ich zwar,
wan ich sich an dir itel recht.
und solt ich leben tusent iar,
so bin ich doch din aigen knecht.[13]

[I. To you my service and my greeting, a thousand times more / than the dust particles in a sunbeam! / I know no doubts, / and ill moods have passed away. / If only I had your favor (for I fear your anger), / I would be in a good mood. / Oh dear fine angel, desist! / It will be to your gain. / Behold my contrition, receive my penance, / forgive me for God's sake! / If I were to forfeit your womanly greeting, / my life would be ruined. *Truly, I am of a mind to be joyful, / for I see in you all that is fitting. / And were I to live a thousand years, / I am but your servant boy.*

II. <u>I have always thought about the relationships between parents and children, / with their ceaseless strife</u>. / Upon reflection, this has often / been a source of comfort to me. / "The father is often angry with the child": / that comes from deep loyalty. / He wouldn't do that with a child not his own, / even if that child were to beg him persistently! / What is dear to me causes me pain. / Whatever harms the dear one / in body, in honor, or in reputation, / hurts me in spirit. *Truly, I am of a mind to be*

---

[13] Quoted from Hugo von Montfort, Das poetische Werk, ed. Hofmeister, 33-34.

joyful, / for I see in you all that is fitting. / And were I to live a thousand years, / I am but your servant boy.

III. To you I am bound in loyalty, / and will never deny it. / Among the living and the free / I know of none who pleases my eye more. / In feminine breeding and modesty / you set the very standard. / And if I could enjoy the whole world, / I could not forget you. / "Separation always does damage to those who are constant" — / as one sees one another very rarely. Thus "secrecy has no power over fickleness;" / that has also happened often. / *Truly, I am of a mind to be joyful, / for I see in you all that is fitting. / And were I to live a thousand years, / I am but your servant boy.*]

The most traditional language is that of the first two quatrains of the third stanza (lines III.1-7), devoted to praise of the lady in terms conventional since the early thirteenth century. The poem also begins with what looks like a routine assurance of courtly service. However, the speaker's claim that he knows no doubts and ill moods have passed away is quickly shown to be false, for in the second stanza, we are suddenly in the middle of a relationship conflict, in which the favor of the lady is at stake, and her wrath looms. We do not learn what the problem was, only that the speaker caused it and how he intends to solve it: "sich an min rew, nim von mir puss, durch gott tu mir vergeben" ['Behold my contrition, receive my penance, / forgive me for God's sake!']. The sacramental analogy elevates the lady to a quasi-divine position. It also, perhaps, subtly pressures her to confer absolution as a matter of routine. At its first sounding (lines I.13-16), the refrain picks up on this motif: behind "itel recht" ['all that is fitting/right'], we detect a resonance of God's perfect righteousness in the lady, and the idea of contentedly being her : "eigen Knecht" ['feudal underling'] for a thousand years suggests a paradisiacal or millenarian state. None of this is new; from its beginnings in the early 12th century, courtly love poetry talked about the lady in sacral terms.[14]

The second stanza is more original. The basic move is to establish another analogy to the amorous conflict at hand, this time the conflict between parent and child. This scenario is clear from the fifth line (II.5), "der vatter zürnet dick dem kind" ['The father is often angry with the child']. Since it is perfectly natural for fathers to be angry at their children, and testimony to their deep affection (II.6: *daz kunt von triwen stet*), this analogy, too, like the sacramental one, normalizes the amorous conflict and the prospect of its resolution.

---

[14] On the divinity of the courtly lady see Peter Dronke, Medieval Latin and the Rise of European Love-lyric, vol. 1 (Oxford: Clarendon Press, 1968), 4-5.

However, the refrain acquires an additional resonance, based on an alternative common meaning of the word *knecht*. The speaker is now the "son" of the lady as a loving but wrathful parent, and as such, like the sinner can expect of God, he can expect her anger to end.

But there are complications. First, the stanza's opening four lines are very obscure and seem to bear no clear relationship to the parental analogy that follows. Secondly, after the proverbial expression about the father and the son in line II.5, the speaker goes off on an extended reflection on his own fatherhood, which seems to hijack the poem. In his recent edition of Hugo's complete work, Wernfried Hofmeister calls this a "dunkle Stelle," an obscure passage, a crux.[15]

The main problem is the first two lines (*das ich der pender ye gedacht / mitt grunen sunder wenkhen*), most notably the word *pender*. This is an upper German variant of *bender*,[16] singular *bant*, which means all the things that English "band" and "bond" do—with the possible exception of "rock group." There are two uncertainties. First, what exactly *bant* means in this context, and secondly, how we should interpret the definite article *der* (genitive plural, the case taken by the verb *gedencken*), which implies that the *bender* have either already been referred to or are somehow understood between the speaker and the lady.

As Hofmeister notes in his short discussion, two interpretations have been offered for these lines in the scholarly literature. The first is by Joseph Wackernell, who considers *bender* to be "bands" in the sense of "ribbons," here love tokens. He translates II, 1-2: *dass ich fortwährend der (versprochenen) Bänder gedacht mit unaufhörlichem Zanken* ['that I continually thought about the promised ribbons with non-stop bickering'].[17] Since ribbons have not been referred to in the poem, Wackernell concludes that they are considered understood between the speaker and the lady. Hence "the promised" ribbons, in this case, promised by the lady but never delivered. (Wackernell sees the non-delivery of love ribbons as the cause of the quarrel). The other difficult word, *grunen*, is in this reading a dialect version of standard MHG *grînen*, ['to weep, bawl, bicker, yammer'] modern German *greinen*. Already in MHG the word is used to characterize children.

---

[15] Hugo von Montfort, Das poetische Werk, ed. Hofmeister, 33, note 5.
[16] In the so-called Medienverschiebung, the West Germanic voiced stops (Medien) /b,d,g/ shifted in upper German dialects (Bavarian and Alemmanic) to /p, t, k/. See Hermann Paul, Mittelhochdeutsche Grammatik. 24. Auflage überarbeitet von Peter Wiehl und Siegfried Grosse (Tübingen: Niemeyer, 1998), 114.
[17] Wackernell, Hugo von Montfort, 219.

Wackernell himself does not address the rest of the stanza, but a reading in his sense would be something akin to the following: "That I continually thought about the ribbons you promised, with constant bickering, has often given me peace, the more I think about it. The father is often angry at the child." The speaker finds his own behavior concerning the ribbons to be childish, but then he realizes that this is in order because fathers are often angry with their children, since they love them. Provided we accept the ribbons as an absent referent (a big assumption), this interpretation seems plausible, although it is rather strange in several ways. How can the speaker be both yammering *continually* about the ribbons and *often* find peace because of this very behavior? The expression *gedenken mit grunen*, ['thinking in a bickering or yammering way'], also seems awkward and oxymoronic, rather than some more direct expression like "I was always yammering on about the ribbons." However, this is poetry, and Hugo's style is, as has been much remarked upon, a highly mannered one.[18]

The second interpretation of the passage is that of Franz Spechtler in his 1977 translation: *Das ich dieser Bänder immer / frisch und ohne Wanken gedachte*['That I always thought about these bands/bonds with verve and constancy'].[19] Here, *die bender* are construed as the figurative bonds uniting the lovers, and the problem of referentiality is easily solved, via the demonstrative article *dieser*, if we think of the whole first stanza as exemplifying "these bonds." The word *grunen* also admits of an alternative definition, here *grünen*, to become green, i.e. fresh. Although the phrase *gedenken mit grünen*, "thinking with greenness," seems even more awkward than Wackernell's suggestion, if we accept it, this reading makes more sense in terms of an expected psychological profile: Fresh and unwavering thoughts of the beloved can bring the speaker peace. The problem with this reading is that the shift to the father-child theme, which dominates the rest of the stanza, makes no sense.

In his recent edition of Hugo's works, Wernfried Hofmeister writes that he does not wish to add a third suggestion for how to read this obscure passage.

---

[18] Achnitz discusses the influence of Albrecht's Jüngerer Titurel ("Man mocht es griffen mit der Hand," 133-135). I note that Albrecht too favors such gerund constructions with mit + verb infinitive: mit lieben so mit leiden her im vor Parille / gerumet von den heiden (st. 119, 1-2); mit timpen tampen dar und widere (st. 200, 3); und lob der magt mit lesen und mit singen (439,3); ir rihtaer, sit so lebende, / daz ir den temel riche mit bowen tegeliche sit got gebende! (st. 439, 3-4).
[19] Franz Viktor Spechtler, Hugo von Montfort. Einführung zum Faksimile des Codex Palatinus Germanicus 329 der Universitätsbibliothek Heidelberg. Mit Beiträgen von Franz Viktor Spechter, Ewald M. Vetter, Vera Trost, Lorenz Welker und Wilfried Werner. Die Texte der Handschrift in vollständiger Übersetzung von Franz Viktor Spechtler (Wiesbaden: Reichert, 1988), 96.

However, another interpretation is possible. Among the figurative meanings of the word *band*, there is an old one in southern German dialects, both Bavarian and Alemannic, that I believe is being used here. *Band*, in this sense, denotes the specific relationship between the child and either the biological father or the biological mother.[20] A child in the keeping of one biological parent was an *einbändiges Kind* or a child *aus einem Band*. A child in the keeping of both biological parents was *zweibändig* or *aus beiden Banden*. In old Europe, prior to the dominance of bourgeois social relations, the distinction between *zweibändig* and *einbändig* children was more salient than it came to be later. Here, for example, is an excerpt from a late eighteenth century *Trauerordnung*, i.e., statutes governing how people are to be publicly mourned in a community:[21]

> "[Trauerordnung vom Jahr 1775] Nachdem Se. Churfürstl. Durchlaucht gnädigst einzusehen geruhet haben, daß bis anher bey den sich ergebenden Trauerfällen niemals eine sichere Gleichförmigkeit der Trauerzeit beobachtet worden, auch in Betreff des Trauerkleideranzuges so vieler Unfug sich eingeschlichen und bezeigt habe, daß hierin nicht allein der gebührend standesmäßige Unterschied gänzlich ausser Acht gesetzt, sondern auch ein in viel Wege eitel und unnützer Aufwand leererdings verschwendet worden: als haben höchstgedacht Se. Churfürstl. Durchlaucht, damit sowohl in Betreff der Trauerzeit eine gewiese Richtschnur beybehalten werde, als auch jeder des sich ihm gebührenden Kleideranzuges versichern könne, nachstehendes Trauer-Regulativ zu verfassen, und der genauen Darobhaltungswillen in offenen Druck legen zu lassen, gnädigst anbefohlen. München den 2. Jänner 1775.
>
> [...] Zwote Classe: Auf 3 Monat, mit 4 Änderungen, für die Stiefeltern, für die zweybändig leiblichen Geschwistere, für der Ältern und Großältern leibliche Geschwistere, die *Liberi adoptivi* für ihre *Parentes adoptivos*.

---

[20] Bayerisches Wörterbuch, ed. J. A. Schmeller, 2nd edition, ed. G. Karl Frommann (Munich: Rudolf Oldebourg, 1872), vol. 1, 246, https://books.google.com/books?id=OvzhAA AAMAAJ&dq=editions%3AAcVNm6v78EsC&pg=PP7#v=onepage&q&f=false; Schwäbisches Wörterbuch, ed. H. Fischer et al. (Tübingen: Verlag der Laupp'schen Buchhandlung, 1904), 601, https://books.google.com/books?id=h0Y_AAAAMAAJ&dq=schw%C3%A4bis ches%20w%C3%B6rterbuch&pg=PP1#v=onepage&q&f=false.

[21] Sammlung der Kurpfalz-Baierischen allgemeinen und besonderen Landesverordnungen, vol. 4, ed.J. K. Mayr (Munich: Anton Franz, 1788), 634-636, https://books.google.com/books?id=cYdkAAAAcAAJ&dq=%22einb%C3%A4ndig%22&pg=PA533#v=onepage&q&f=f alse. I have slightly normalized the spelling with regard to the umlauts.

gedencken der pender 85

Dritte Classe: Auf 6 Wochen mit 3 Änderungen, für leibliche Kinder und Enkeln, für einbändig leibliche Geschwistere, für leibliche zweybändiger Geschwistere Kinder gegeneinander, für Schwiegersöhne und Töchter [*sic*], für Schwäger und Schwägerinnen.

Vierte Classe: Auf 4 Wochen mit 2 Änderungen, für Stiefkinder, und die Liberos adoptivos, für der leiblichen Geschwistere ihre Kinder, für der Eltern und Großeltern einbändig leibliche Geschwistere, und leibliche Geschwisterekinder."

['(Regulations for mourning, 1775) After Your Electoral Majesty graciously deigned to note that, in the cases of mourning that have hitherto taken place, a certain uniformity of the mourning period has never been observed; (and) that, with regard to the habiliments of mourning, a great deal of mischief has insinuated itself and revealed that the proper differentiation of social estate has not only been entirely neglected, but also much vain and unnecessary resources have been wasted; thereupon did Your High Electoral Majesty graciously ordain that a definite guideline be maintained with regard to the period of mourning. Munich 2nd of January, 1775.

[...] Second class: For 3 months, with 4 changes, for the step-parents, for the *zweybändig* natural siblings, for the natural siblings of the parents and grandparents, for the adoptive parents of adopted children.

Third class: For 6 weeks, with 3 changes, for natural children and grandchildren, for *einbändig* natural children, for the children of natural *zweybändig* siblings with regard to each other, for sons-in-law and daughters[-in-law], for brothers-in-law and sisters-in-law.

Fourth class: For 4 weeks, with 2 changes, for step children, and for adopted children, for the children of natural siblings, for the *einbändig* natural siblings of the parents and grandparents, and natural children of siblings.']

The passage shown concerns who is to wear what kinds of mourning garb and for how long. *Zweibändig* and *einbändig* siblings belonged to different social classifications and were subject to different sartorial rules, making their different familial status socially visible. The purpose of this *Trauerordnung*, commissioned by the princely ruler of the Rhenish Palatinate, was to preserve the "proper distinctions of social estate" (*der gebührende standesmäßige Unterschied*) in the face of a lot of recent "mischief" (*Unfug*) that had crept into mourning customs. Although the differences in genealogical degree denoted by *einbändig* and *zweibändig* did not themselves signal hierarchical differences in social estate (that is not what *Classe* means here), they were nonetheless part and parcel of the old European order, dominated by the nobility, which thought of society primarily in terms of the bonds of blood; which made very precise distinctions among blood relations; and in which remarriages for "dynastic" reasons, as well as households with large numbers of children from different unions, were very common. In this general sense, though a comparatively late witness, the *Trauerordnung* reflects social conditions little changed in Germany since the Middle Ages.

As reflected in the above usage, the *bender* to which Hugo refers are, I believe, those between an individual parent and his/her natural children. Therefore, I suggest the following translation of the problematic lines: "I have always thought about the relationships between parents and children, / with their ceaseless strife." Everything falls nicely into place in this interpretation. The fact that *Band* was a specific social classification explains the use of the definite article: *der Bender gedenken* is grammatically the same sort of construction as *der Gefallenen gedenken* or *der Verstorbenen gedenken* ['to remember/ commemorate the fallen,' 'to remember the dead']. The motif of constant bickering or strife—*greinen* and not *grünen*—is retained, but it more logically characterizes the parent-child relationship than the speaker himself, in either of the senses discussed earlier. It is also the precisely genealogical term to use when one wishes to underscore the relationship a father has with his own biological child, as opposed to one not his own, which is very clearly the meaning intended in lines II.7-8: *das er aim andern nit entut, der in es fleisslich bet* ['He wouldn't do that with a child not his own, even if that child were to beg him persistently!']. Finally, this is the very relationship the poet humorously plays upon in the final words of the stanza. The speaker is not merely the "son" of the lady, as we saw, playing with the alternative sense of *knecht*, but *din eigen knecht*, "your own son," playing with the alternative meaning of *eigen*.

Two things are highly original about this stanza. On the one hand, is the sophistication of the paternal reflection. In a very short space, the speaker manages eloquently to characterize a very emotionally complex and rich parent-child relationship. The social wisdom contained in the proverb *der vater zürnet dick dem kind* ['The father is often angry at the child'] is given a psychological grounding, and this is exemplified via the speaker's personal experience with his own child. Notice the particular way the the *lieb/leid* topos—the courtly love truism that love causes both delight and suffering—is transposed into a filial context: *was mir ist lieb, da ist mir lait: / was im kumpt nicht ze gut / an leib, an er, an wirdikait, / das bekrenkt mir den mut* ['What is dear to me causes me pain. / Whatever harms the dear one / in body, in honor, or in reputation, / hurts me in spirit']. The depth of empathetic identification expressed here with the person and the interests of the beloved—the beloved child in this case—is both far simpler and far less superficial than the elevated solipsism of courtly love.

On the other hand, all this ultimately serves a courtly love agenda in a sophisticated and original way. Above I mentioned that the speaker's reflection on his own fatherhood seems to hijack the poem. This move is a poetic feature, not a bug. The speaker showcases his emotions and experiences as "real" parent of a child in difficulty so as to better model to the angry lady how she should behave as the metaphorical "parent" to him as her wayward *eigen knecht*. Just as the loving parent forgives the wayward child after a spell of anger, so the lady should forgive the wayward speaker. But the parental metaphor occasions a moral jolt at the end. Moved by the speaker's insights as parent and by his love for his child, we are shocked by the twist this takes in the last two words of the refrain: he is his lady's lover, her feudal underling—and now her own son! I know of no other courtly love poem so brazenly Oedipal in its suggestiveness.

Now that the speaker has professed his contrition and asked for forgiveness (first stanza) as well as elaborated a common familial scenario in which transgression and forgiveness occur as a matter of course (second stanza), it would now seem that he can be assured that the lady's *huld* ['favor'] will indeed be restored. Accordingly, the fact, noted above, that the third stanza contains rather conventional language in praise of a lady and the reassurance of the speaker's devotion makes sense within the economy of the poem. Nevertheless, in the final quatrain, the poet seems to pull the rug of courtly convention out from underneath the reader—and the lady. If we follow Hofmeister, the speaker is quoting and commenting on two further common proverbs. Both of them have as their subject how constancy in love is endangered, on the one hand by physical distance, *fromdi* ['foreign parts' or 'abroad'], and on the other—well, one is not exactly sure how "secrecy is of no help against fickleness," but apparently this is found to happen often as well. What the speaker's position vis-à-vis this received wisdom is, is also unclear. He has just assured the lady of his loyalty—*ich bin dir doch mit triuwen bi* [III, 1: 'To you I am bound in loyalty']. Is he calling that into question here, near the end? That is, is he trying to say that while constancy is his firm resolve, to judge by what actually happens in the world, it may be more difficult? I.e., "Hate the game, not the player"? If that is true, it is important to note that the refrain does formally rescue the loyalty of the speaker at the end—*so bin ich doch din eigen knecht*— but perhaps, a third iteration, now with a kind of verbal automatism that— rather devilishly—belies the sincerity of the sentiment.

The canso "min dienst und gruzz me tausent stunt," far from "bumping and hopping along in a pathetic manner" (Knapp), is the work of a highly skilled poet. It represents a particular bravura example of what Wolfgang Achnitz calls the "raffiniertes Spiel mit der Ich-Rolle" ['sophisticated play with the lyrical I'] of traditional courtly poetry and confirms the appreciative re-evaluation of Hugo's work found in more recent scholarship. Of particular interest here is the original way the rhetoric of fatherhood is made to serve an amorous agenda. This stanza is the underappreciated pearl, both with regard to the poem and, in isolation, as a medieval reflection on parenthood.

This brings up the question of the autobiographical character of Hugo's poetry. The traditional view of the scholarship is that Hugo's oeuvre reflects his lived experience to some extent.[22] Achnitz strongly disagrees, noting that while it is true that Hugo allocates elements ("Versatzstücke") of his own biography to his lyrical I and to what is narrated, "[d]ennoch handelt es sich nicht um autobiographische oder gar 'private' Texte. Sie sind Bestandteil einer repräsentativen Selbstdarstellung des einflussreichen und hochadligen Landespolitikers und das raffinierte Spiel mit der Ich-Rolle weist lediglich die literarische Kompetenz des Verfassers aus" [‚However, we are not dealing with autobiographical texts, much less 'private' ones. They are part and parcel of a program of self-representation on the part of this influential politician from the high nobility, and the sophisticated play with the lyrical I simply demonstrates the literary competence of the author'].[23]

This statement is too dogmatic, especially for late medieval poets about whose lives we know a decent amount. To cite a well-known example, the courtly love imprisonment drama Oswald von Wolkenstein orchestrates around the figure of the *Hausmännin* may very well have been something more

---

[22] See for example Gustav Moczygemba, Hugo von Montfort (Self-published: Fürstenfeld, 1967), 6: "Außer in [Gedicht] III ist es immer die kleine traute Welt der ehelichen Liebe, die Beziehungen zu den drei Ehefrauen, die seine Minnedichtung erfüllen. Der in der Blütezeit konventionelle Minnedienst als Verehrung einer fremden Herrin wird in den der eigenen Gattin umgewandelt, der Realismus des neuen bürgerlichen Zeitalters setzt sich hier bereits durch." ("With the exception of poem no.3, it is always the familiar little world of conjugal love, [Hugo's] relationships with his three wives, that fill his love poetry. The conventional love service, which in the Classical period took the form of devotion to an external lady, is now changed to service dedicated to the poet's own spouse. The realism of the new bourgeois era asserts itself already here"). See also Classen, "Literatur und dichterische Selbstreflexion," passim and Achnitz, "Man mocht es griffen mit der Hand," 130 on the autobiographical question as well as the literature referenced there. I note also that Wernfried Hofmeister, the most recent editor of Hugo's oeuvre, espouses the traditional position that some of Hugo's poetry seems to have been addressed to his wives (xix).

[23] Achnitz, "Man mocht es griffen mit der Hand," 132.

than the mere "allocation of autobiographical elements to the lyrical I," especially given that traces of the physical torture Oswald describes in his poems have been found on his skeleton. In the case of Hugo's poem discussed above, an autobiographical reading seems especially apt. We know Hugo was married three times. He had at least one son, Ulrich, from his first marriage, and we know that his third wife had her own children from an earlier husband, probably his second wife as well.[24] If Hugo's love poems are addressed to his wives, as many scholars think,[25] "min dienst und gruzz me tausent stund" seems specific to his situation in one of his latter two marriages (to Clementia von Toggenburg from 1395/96-1399 or to Anna von Neuhaus after 1402), when there were children from multiple unions around the castle. Hugo's reflection on parenthood, his *gedenken der bender* (we recall it means relationships between individual parents and their biological children), would have been conditioned by his experience of children in his family who were not his own.

Bibliography

Achnitz, Wolfgang. "Man mocht es griffen mit der Hand. Das Durchbrechen von Erwartungshorizonten als Merkmal der Dichtungen Hugos von Montfort." In Aller weishait anevang Ist ze brúfen an dem aussgang. *Akten des Symposiums zum 650. Geburtstag Hugos von Montfort*, edited by Klaus Amann and Elisabeth De Felip-Jaud, 127-142. Innsbruck: Innsbruck University Press, 2010.

Amann, Klaus, and Elisabeth De Felip-Jaud, eds. Aller weishait anevang Ist ze brúfen an dem aussgang. *Akten des Symposiums zum 650. Geburtstag Hugos von Montfort*. Innsbruck: Innsbruck University Press, 2010.

Bayerisches Wörterbuch. Edited by J. A. Schmeller, 2nd edition, ed. G. Karl Frommann. Munich: Rudolf Oldebourg, 1872), vol. 1. https://books.google.com/books?id=OvzhAAAAMAAJ&dq=editions%3AAcVNm6v78EsC&pg=PP1#v=onepage&q&f=false

Böcking-Politis, Cordula. "ain iunkfrow rait der kúnsten perkh. Der Minneklaventopos bei Hugo von Montfort." In Aller weishait anevang Ist ze brúfen an dem aussgang. *Akten des Symposiums zum 650. Geburtstag Hugos von Montfort*, edited by Klaus Amann and Elisabeth De Felip-Jaud, 109-126. Innsbruck: Innsbruck University Press, 2010.

---

[24] See Wackernell, Hugo von Montfort, III-XXIX; Hugo von Montfort, Das poetische Werk, ed. Hofmeister, xv-xvii; and Obersteiner, "Hugo von Montfort und die Steiermark, " in Aller weishait anefang, 33-50. The deep feeling expressed by the father towards the son in poem no. 6 also suggest that Hugo's didactic poem "Ein vater seinem sun riet" (Hugo von Montfort, Das poetische Werk, no. 14) had an autobiographial dimension.

[25] In addition to the references under footnote 18, see Max Wehrli, Geschichte der deutschen Literatur vom frühen Mittelalter bis zum Ende des 16, Jahrhunderts. 2nd edition (Stuttgart: Reclam, 1984)("die meisten als Dienstlieder ausdrücklich an die Braut oder Ehefrau gerichtet" ["most of the songs, thematizing love-service, addressed to his bride or wife"], 746).

Classen, Albrecht. "Literatur und dichterische Selbstreflexion im Werk Hughos von Montfort. Ein Zeuge aus einer kluturhistorischen Spät- oder Frühzeit." In Aller weishait anevang Ist ze brúfen an dem aussgang. *Akten des Symposiums zum 650. Geburtstag Hugos von Montfort*, edited by Klaus Amann and Elisabeth De Felip-Jaud, 167-189. Innsbruck: Innsbruck University Press, 2010.

De Felip-Jaud, Elisabeth. "Hugo von Montfort in Anthologien." In Aller weishait anevang Ist ze brúfen an dem aussgang. *Akten des Symposiums zum 650. Geburtstag Hugos von Montfort*, edited by Klaus Amann and Elisabeth De Felip-Jaud, 143-153. Innsbruck: Innsbruck University Press, 2010.

Dronke, Peter. *Medieval Latin and the Rise of European Love-lyric*, vol. 1. Oxford: Clarendon Press, 1968.

Knapp, Fritz Peter. *Die Literatur des Spätmittelalters in den Ländern Österreich, Steiermark, Kärnten, Salzburg und Tirol von 1273 bis 1439*, vol. 2, *Die Literatur zur Zeit der frühen habsburgischen Herzöge von Rudolf IV. bis Albrecht V. (1358-1439)*. Graz: Akademische Druck- und Verlagsanstalt, 2004.

Moczygemba, Gustav. *Hugo von Montfort*. Self-published: Fürstenfeld, 1967.

Mohr, Jan. "Textreihe und Gattungsstrukturen. Zur Tageliedrezeption in Hugos von Montfort cpg 329." *Beiträge zur Geschichte der deutschen Sprache und Literatur* 138, no. 1 (April 2016): 76-106. https://www.degruyter.com/view/journals/bgsl/138/1/article-p76.xml

Montfort, Hugo von. *Das poetische Werk*, ed. Wernher Hofmeister. Berlin: Walter de Gruyter, 2005.

Obersteiner, Gernot Peter. "Hugo von Montfort und die Steiermark." In Aller weishait anevang Ist ze brúfen an dem aussgang. *Akten des Symposiums zum 650. Geburtstag Hugos von Montfort*, edited by Klaus Amann and Elisabeth De Felip-Jaud, 33-50. Innsbruck: Innsbruck University Press, 2010.

Paul, Hermann. *Mittelhochdeutsche Grammatik*. 24. Auflage überarbeitet von Peter Wiehl und Siegfried Grosse. Tübingen: Niemeyer, 1998.

Sammlung der Kurpfalz-Baierischen allgemeinen und besonderen Landesverordnungen, vol. 4. Edited by J. K. Mayr. Munich: Anton Franz, 1788. https://books.google.com/books?id=cYdkAAAAcAAJ&dq=%22einb%C3%A4ndig%22&pg=PA533#v=onepage&q&f=false

Schwäbisches Wörterbuch. Edited by H. Fischer et al. Tübingen: Verlag der Laupp'schen Buchhandlung, 1904. https://books.google.com/books?id=h0Y_AAAAMAAJ&dq=schw%C3%A4bisches%20w%C3%B6rterbuch&pg=PP1#v=onepage&q&f=false

Spechtler, Franz Viktor. *Hugo von Montfort. Einführung zum Faksimile des Codex Palatinus Germanicus 329 der Universitätsbibliothek Heidelberg. Mit Beiträgen von Franz Viktor Spechter, Ewald M. Vetter, Vera Trost, Lorenz Welker und Wilfried Werner. Die Texte der Handschrift in vollständiger Übersetzung von Franz Viktor Spechtler*. Wiesbaden: Reichert, 1988.

Wackernell, Joseph E. *Hugo von Montfort. Mit Abhandlungen zur Geschichte der deutschen Literatur, Sprache, und Metrik im XIV und XV Jahrhundert*. Innsbruck: Verlag der Wagner'schen Universitätsbuchhandlung, 1881.

Wehrli, Max. *Geschichte der deutschen Literatur vom frühen Mittelalter bis zum Ende des 16. Jahrhunderts*. 2nd edition. Stuttgart: Reclam, 1984.

Chapter 5

Yiddish, Power, and Compassion: Emotive Language in Wagenseil's Belehrung (1699)

Annegret Oehme
University of Washington

Abstract: Perhaps not the most famous of King Arthur's knights, but Wigalois, son of Gawein, has fascinated many audiences and inspired adaptations in German and Yiddish, in medieval manuscript and graphic novel. The *Wigalois* adaptations have crossed borders of supposedly "separate audiences" repeatedly: Composed originally for a Middle High German speaking Christian audience at a court (1215, Wirnt von Grafenberg: *Wigalois*), a 14th ct. adaptation made the text accessible to the Yiddish-speaking Jewish community of the Holy Roman Empire.

A Yiddish textbook (*Belehrung der Jüdisch-Teutschen Red- und Schreibart*, 1699) by the Protestant theologian and father of the Humanist Yiddishist movement, Johann Christoph Wagenseil ensured the continuity of the *Wigalois* transmission and created an interest for Yiddish among German speakers. Later adaptors would access the *Wigalois* narrative through Wagenseil's editions, including the famous German romantic poet Ludwig Uhland and his fragmentary poem *Ritter Wieduwilt* (1809/10). Wagenseil's seemingly minor contribution to the Arthurian tradition has crucial significance for the German-Yiddish tradition for two reasons: it ensured a German adaptation tradition built on the Yiddish—in itself a rare case—and shows how Wagenseil overcame common conceptions of separated lingual traditions.

In this paper, I explore how Wagenseil impacts the reception of this shared narrative by analyzing his portrayal of the relationship between Yiddish and German and his employment of the Antiqua and Fraktur typefaces. By emphasizing the English, German, and Jewish roots of the material in combination with the different languages and typefaces used in his edition of the Arthurian romance, Wagenseil enables the respective other group to access the language they were less familiar with.

Keywords: Yiddish; MHG; ENHG; sociolinguistics; typefaces

***

Mit keiner Sprach sind die Juden iemals / so / wie man zu reden pflegt / låsterlich / als mit unserer Teutschen umbgangen / dann sie haben solcher einen ganz frembden Thon und Laut gegeben / die guten teutschen Wörter <u>gestůmmelt /</u> <u>geradbrecht</u> / <u>verkehret</u> / neue uns unbekandte erdacht / wie auch / unzåhlich viel Hebreische Wörter und Red-Arten in das Teutsche gemischet / das solcher gestalt / wer die Teutsch reden höret / nit anders glaubt / als / sie reden pur lauter Hebreisch / indem fast kein einiges Wort verståndlich fůrkommet.
(*Belehrung*, B1r)

[The Jews have never treated any other language as, so to speak, blasphemously, as our German. They have imported an utterly foreign tone and sound, have mutilated, deformed, and perverted the good German words, invented new ones unfamiliar to us and also mixed innumerable Hebrew words and expressions into German, so that whoever hears them speak German can only believe them to be speaking pure Hebrew, since scarcely a single word seems comprehensible.]

With these polemical words, Johann Christoph Wagenseil (1633-1705) aims at capturing the development of Yiddish as a defiled and base hybridity. Although his resentments seem to reflect common anti-Yiddish and anti-Jewish resentment of the seventeenth century, they are surprising for two reasons. Firstly, Wagenseil was not just an early philologist but a prominent Protestant Hebraist[1] and is often considered the father of the Christian Yiddishist movement, which promoted the study of Yiddish among Christian—almost exclusively Protestant—German speakers.[2] Secondly, Wagenseil offers these

---

[1] Christian Hebraists were part of the Humanist *ad fontes* [back to the sources] endeavor, which embodies the increased interest in studying languages (especially those considered of ancient origin) since the late Middle Ages. The goal of the Christian Hebraists was an accurate understanding of Hebrew scripture, particularly the Hebrew bible.

[2] Wagenseil took the Christian Hebraist movement further by emphasizing the study of Yiddish, making him a catalyst of a new movement: the Christian Yiddishists. With reference to their origin and indebtedness to these ideas of Renaissance Humanism, Jerold Frakes refers to the participants in this movement as "Humanist Yiddishists" in his comprehensive edition of influential early modern writings on Yiddish (Jerold Frakes, *The Cultural Study of Yiddish in Early Modern Europe* [New York: Palgrave Macmillan, 2007], p.ix. See further Aya Elyada, *A Goy Who Speaks Yiddish: Christians and the Jewish*

observations in the least expected place: his Yiddish textbook, *Belehrung der Jüdisch-Teutschen Red- und Schreibart* [Introduction to Written and Spoken Jewish-German] written in Königsberg in 1699.[3] Wagenseil's assessment is no slip of the pen, however, but a fair representation of Wagenseil's attitude towards the Ashkenazi (Central and Eastern European) Jews' vernacular. Throughout *Belehrung*, Wagenseil makes no pretense of his opinion but rather intensifies his attacks on Yiddish, which, in his eyes, does not even attain the status of a language but is instead a hybrid socio-/dialect. This article explores the apparent conflict inherent in Wagenseil's deprecating attitude towards Yiddish alongside his goal of teaching Yiddish, focusing on the strategies and mechanisms he employs, especially regarding the underlying power relations, to market his book and urge his audience to learn Yiddish.[4] Wagenseil emphasizes the German-speaking Protestants' majority status in the face of a minority population that, according to Wagenseil and kindred spirits, needs saving from itself, its culture, its religion, and its language, with the ultimate goal of converting the Jews to Christianity. He identifies language as the core of a successful missionizing strategy.

At the center of Wagenseil's approach to turning his German-speaking audience into Yiddish speakers lies emotive writing, with the goal of triggering his primary (Protestant) audience's compassion.[5] Wagenseil aims to move his audience by including the story of Löbl Kurtzhandl, a Jew who was tortured and executed in Prague in 1694 for the alleged murder of a Jewish boy. According to Wagenseil, the juridical proceedings leading up to Löbl's conviction and execution were flawed because the Christian officiaries did not speak Yiddish, and Jewish core witnesses were fluent in neither Hebrew nor German. A tale of miscommunication unfolds. To elicit his audience's compassion for a suspected

---

Language in Early Modern Germany [Stanford: Stanford University Press, 2012], pp.6–7, Jeffrey A. Grossman, *The Discourse on Yiddish in Germany from the Enlightenment to the Second Empire* [Columbia, S.C.: Camden House, 2000], pp.120–127).
[3] Johann Christoph, *Belehrung der jüdisch-teutschen Red- und Schreibart* (Königsberg, 1699). The text will be shortened to *Belehrung* and all page numbers will be given in text.
[4] Wagenseil identifies the Yiddish-speaking Jews as a secondary audience and suggests that *Belehrung* could be of use for them too, albeit in an inverted way: "Diese nun / koennen auf eine umgekehrte Weise / indem sie unser Teutsch gegen das ihrige halten / gleich wie wir das ihrige mit dem unsern vergleichen / gegenwaertiges Buch brauchen / das rechte Teutsch mit der Zeit nach und nach dadurch lesen zu lernen / dessen sie allermeisten unwissend." [They can in turn use this very book in reverse to learn gradually to read correct German, which they mostly do not know, by setting our German against theirs just as we compare theirs with ours.] (*Belehrung*, Hiiv).
[5] As we will later see, Wagenseil repeatedly includes general anti-Catholic remarks and criticism of Catholic officials' language skills and philosophy.

murderer whose suffering could have been alleviated by the employment of Yiddish, Wagenseil offers a thorough description of the case, omitting no salacious detail (including the breaking wheel and a multiple-stage beheading). It is in the hand of *Belehrung*'s reader to prevent future similar travesties of justice by learning Yiddish. Ultimately, this analysis shows that Wagenseil's call for compassion can easily be misread. Wagenseil is no proponent of a German-Jewish dialogue characterized by mutual tolerance; instead, he argues from within a power matrix in which Yiddish-speaking Jews remain inferior. Their only salvation lies in learning German and, ultimately, converting to Christianity.

Why Yiddish?

Despite its disdaining view of Yiddish, Wagenseil's *Belehrung* was the most influential pre-modern Yiddish textbook and subsequently inspired the linguistic-theoretical study of Yiddish as well as an increased interest in the practical learning of Yiddish. It proved so successful after its publication in 1699 that a second edition was published 16 years later.[6] Its success can be attributed to multiple factors. Firstly, Wagenseil persuasively identifies the value of learning Yiddish for a broad audience ranging from "common" people to high officials.[7] Secondly, Wagenseil boldly argues for the benefits of reading Yiddish religious and non-religious literature. And, finally, his book offers an easily accessible structure that aims to create actual pedagogical value for the language learner without requiring additional resources.

Printed in Königsberg, Wagenseil's book offers a linguistic introduction to Yiddish grammar and language supplemented by longer texts as exercises. These practice texts include a memorial account concerning the so-called Fettmilch uprising (violent anti-Jewish riots in Frankfurt am Main in 1614), several Passover songs,[8] and the Yiddish Arthurian romance *Viduvilt,* by far the longest exercise, consisting of 152 pages of storytelling plus a 7-page

---

[6] This time printed in Frankfurt in 1715 by Peter Conrad Monath.

[7] Wagenseil commends *Belehrung* especially to an educated elite but also remarks that anyone willing to commit to the learning would benefit from his book: "In einem weitlåufigen Fůrtrag wird klårlich erwiesen / Daß solche Erfahrenheit / Denen hohen und niedern Obrigkeiten / wie auch deren Rathgeben / und anderen Rechtsgelehrten / denen Theologis, Medicis, Handels-Leuten / und insgemein Jedermann / nutzlich / auch fast nothwendig sey." [In a comprehensive discourse, it will be illustrated that counselors, jurists, theologians, doctors, merchants, and everyone else will profit from, even almost need, such knowledge.] (*Belehrung,* title page).

[8] For a discussion of the Passover songs, see Hartmut Dinse, *Die Entwicklung des jiddischen Schrifttums im deutschen Sprachgebiet* (Stuttgart: Metzler, 1974), pp.41–46.

introduction to the Arthurian material.[9] Most of the exercises are presented as facing-page translations with one version of the text in Hebrew letters and the corresponding German translation in the Latin alphabet on the opposite page. Yiddish is printed in the so-called *Vayber-taytsh*, a semi-cursive version of the Hebrew alphabet (Wagenseil: "current," Xiiir) commonly used for early Yiddish publications, in contrast to the more common square script used for the Hebrew Bible and other Hebrew literature.[10]

Even though we speak of Wagenseil's *Belehrung* as a Yiddish textbook, he does not use the word "Yiddish" (a term not used before the 18th century) but uses two different terms to describe what he considers to be a dialect that originated from the Jews' engagement with German: "Juedisch-Teutsche" [Jewish-German] for the spoken usage and "Hebraeisch-Teutsche" [Hebrew-German] for the written, due to the use of the Hebrew alphabet.[11] While we cannot expect Wagenseil to use a term that did not yet exist, the fact that he characterizes Yiddish as "Red- und Schreibart" [Speaking and Writing Style] emphasizes that he does not consider it a language in its own right but a distorted version of German (*Belehrung*, Fiir-v).

Clearly, Wagenseil's book contains myriad contradictions. Dismissing the status of Yiddish itself on one hand, Wagenseil promotes it extensively for

---

[9] The Yiddish text is a reprint of Yosl von Witzenhausen's *Kinig Artis Hof* [Court of King Arthur] (1671, Amsterdam) itself an adaptation of an earlier Yiddish source. These Yiddish texts are adaptions of Wirnt of Grafenberg's Middle High German *Wigalois* (1210/20).

[10] Sometimes used synonymously with máshkit (Dovid Katz, *Yiddish and Power* [New York, NY: Palgrave Macmillan, 2015], p.59). The term *Vayber-taytsh* name is derived from the – now mostly refuted – idea that women (Old Yiddish: ווייבער [vayber]) presented the major audience for the Yiddish literature because of their insufficient Hebrew skills. The term further implies a polite fiction that most men had sufficient Hebrew skills that they didn't need a vernacular literature. The reason this idea has been refuted is because more men read Yiddish than acknowledged, albeit not more women necessarily read Hebrew. Already Wagenseil foregoes this conclusion, using examples that show that the Hebrew-proficiency among Jewish man is overrated by non-Jews, which leads him to the conclusion that Yiddish is the key to successful interactions with both Jewish men and women (although his focus was Jewish men). Pointing out that Jewish men generally were not truly fluent in Hebrew is one of Wagenseil's key selling points of *Belehrung*. About this paradigm, see the conclusive essay by Chava Weissler, "For Women and for Men Who Are Like Women. The Construction of Gender in Yiddish Devotional Literature." *Journal of Feminist Studies in Religion* 5 (1989): pp.7–24, and Diane Wolfthal, *Picturing Yiddish: Gender, Identity, and Memory in the Illustrated Yiddish Books of Renaissance Italy* (Leiden: Brill, 2004), pp.81–82. Dovid Katz 'translates' the paradigm: "Buy this book, it is for regular people like you and me who like a good fun read, not for those great rabbis busy with their legal works in those inscrutable languages." (Katz, *Yiddish and Power*, p.45).

[11] In general, he differentiates between these two, but not always consistently.

theoretical as well as practical reasons on the other. Concerning the German-speaking Protestant audience, Wagenseil lists several reasons, both common and unusual, for learning Yiddish. The first, more conventional, reason illustrates his own background in the Christian Hebraist movement. Yiddish was considered a first step towards learning Hebrew for German speakers. As a Germanic language with Hebrew elements and written in a Hebrew alphabet, a familiarity with written Yiddish made the subsequent study of Hebrew—with the ultimate goal of reading the Hebrew Bible—more straightforward. But Wagenseil goes further. Even if learning Hebrew was not a reader's ultimate goal, Wagenseil argues, theologians and other interested parties would benefit tremendously from knowing Yiddish because they would learn a lot from Yiddish translations of the Talmud and other commentaries to the Hebrew Bible (*Belehrung*, Eiiiir-v, Kiiiv).[12] In particular, Wagenseil recommends a Yiddish bestseller, the *Tsene-rene* (so-called "Women's Bible;" *Belehrung*, Eiiiir-v), a Yiddish prose adaptation (not translation) of the Hebrew Bible that draws extensively on rabbinic interpretations and is structured according to the weekly Torah readings (*Parashot*).[13] While Christian Hebraists regularly consumed Hebrew literature and even engaged closely with Kabbalistic writings, Wagenseil's recommendation of Yiddish literature is relatively new and unconventional.[14] The general disregard for Yiddish prevented an erudite audience from learning Yiddish and reading this material. Wagenseil's positive approach to Yiddish religious literature led to his being considered the father of the Christian Yiddishist movement.

However, he moves even beyond this explicitly religious rationale for Yiddish study. In a bold move against the conventions of his contemporary Christian Hebraists, he recommends not just religious literature but also non-religious literature. Non-religious Yiddish literature, Wagenseil suggests, offers excellent works of fiction and non-fiction particularly well suited for entertainment (*Belehrung*, Hiv). Consequently, Wagenseil's *Belehrung* explicitly adheres to the Latin concept of *prodesse et delectare*, education and entertainment ("zum Nutzen als auch zur Belustigung dienen," *Belehrung*, Liv) and contains

---

[12] See also Elyada, *A Goy Who Speaks Yiddish*, pp. 65–75.

[13] The earliest preserved edition (the fourth) dates from 1622, by which time the *Tsene-rene* was already widely read in Ashkenazi communities. This popular book was distributed throughout Europe and was even translated into Eastern (or modern) Yiddish in the 18th ct. (Shlomo Berger, "A Bestseller in Context. Referring to the 'Tsene Rene' in Early Modern Yiddish Books." *Studies in the History of Culture and Science. A Tribute to Gad Freudenthal*, edited by Resianne Fontaine, Ruth Glasner, Reimund Leicht, and Giuseppe Veltri, 2011, p. 421).

[14] Most famously Johannes Reuchlin 1455–1522) and Marsilio Ficino (1433-1499).

exercises with an explicit focus on Jewish religion, culture, or history but also material meant overtly to entertain, such as the Arthurian romance *Viduvilt*.

Beyond all the benefits of knowing Yiddish for his German-speaking audience, the ultimate goal of *Belehrung* is the mission to the Jew. While learning a language with the goal of missionizing is a conventional Christian practice even today, Wagenseil's focus on Yiddish presents a radical departure from the convention. Previous attempts employed Hebrew based on the false assumption that most Jews spoke the language well (*Belehrung*, Fiir).[15] At the same time, German promised no advantage in missionary attempts either, as contemporaneous Jews were rarely fluent in German. Thus, Wagenseil argues, Yiddish presents the key—for better or worse—to reach the Jews: "Bleibt demnach nichts uebrig / als / woferne es uns ein rechter Ernst ist / denen Juden die mitleidige und huelffliche Hand zu bieten / damit sie aus der Tieffe des Unglaubens darinnen sie stecken / moegen gezogen werden / daß man / damit sie gewonnen werden / sich ihnen gleichfoermig mache / und nach ihrem Dialecto schreibe / auch das verabfassete mit ihren Buchstaben drucken lasse." [If we are serious about offering the Jews a sympathetic and helping hand to pull them from the depths of unbelief in which they founder, then there is no option but to become like them and write in their dialect and to print what is written in their alphabet.] (*Belehrung*, Fiir-v).

Wagenseil's recommendation of Yiddish for educational and missionary purposes anchors in Protestant language philosophy. Most famously, Luther's Bible translation project embodied the idea of enabling Christians to access God in their vernacular and significantly impacted the standardization of the German language.[16] Luther's project itself was inherently Humanist and motivated by the *ad-fontes* impetus. Therefore, Protestant religious education and missionary endeavors were grounded in the belief that a higher chance of success existed if such efforts were grounded in the use of the respective locally relevant vernacular.[17] Based on his own assessment of previous failed attempts due to the use of inapplicable languages, Wagenseil concludes that the actual vernacular of the Ashkenazi Jews holds the key to success.

---

[15] Wagenseil further points out that even in cases of Jews who speak fluent Hebrew, Christian-Jewish oral conversations are doomed to failure because the pronunciation differs (*Belehrung*, Fiir). These differences refer to the specific regional Jews' pronunciation of Hebrew in Central and Eastern Europe (Ashkenaz).

[16] Klaus J. Mattheier, "German," in *Germanic Standardizations. Past to Present*, ed. Ana Deumert and Wim Vandenbussche, Impact, Studies in Language and Society 18 (Amsterdam; Philadelphia: J. Benjamins, 2003), p. 217.

[17] Daniel Tröhler, *Languages of Education Protestant Legacies, National Identities, and Global Aspirations*, Studies in Curriculum Theory (New York: Routledge, 2011), pp. 21–36.

But one more feature of Wagenseil's approach sets him apart. Even speaking the everyday language of the to-be-converted target group does not suffice; the tone of the missionizing attempts is of utmost importance. Wagenseil identifies compassion as the guiding principle that should motivate his audience to study Yiddish and interact with Jews, tying this argument back to the (not uncomplicated) Protestant reformer Martin Luther's temporary belief that, if instructed in the proper manner and spirit, Jews will finally discern the Christian belief and convert.[18] Wagenseil supports his argument with a direct quote from Luther's *Das Jhesus Christus ain geborner Jude sey* [That Jesus Christ is born a Jew] (Augsburg, 1523): "Ich hoffe wann man mit den Juden freudlich handelte / und aus der heiligen Schrifft sie saeuberlich unterweisete / es sollte ihr viel rechte Christen werden [...]" [I hope that if we treated the Jews kindly, and instructed them properly in the Holy Writ many would become good Christians [...].] (*Belehrung*, Fiiv; *Das Jhesus*, Aiiv).

Wagenseil paints the seventeenth-century situation he observes in stark contrast to Christianization efforts driven by compassion. He condemns Christian anti-Jewish resentments and pogroms as obstructing the overall mission to the Jews (*Belehrung*, Giiir) and refers to the participants of such violent outbursts as lowlife ("zusamm gelauffenen Gesinde," *Belehrung*, Bbiiiiv). In order to illustrate the horror and excesses of anti-Jewish violence, one of the exercises in *Belehrung* is a reprint of a Jewish account of the aforementioned so-called Fettmilch riots in 1614 in Frankfurt am Main.[19] Christians need to stop using violence against Jews and fundamentally change how they treat their Jewish neighbors in order to reach them (*Belehrung*, Bbiiiiv).

The Case of Löbl Kutzhandel

Wagenseil's emphasis on compassion alters the established mode of argumentation on this topic. After his dialectic explorations of reasons why

---

[18] (Martin Luther, *Das Jhesus Christus eyn geborner Jude sey*. Wittenberg, 1523). Luther's case is, admittedly, complicated. While he professed his hopes for a potential Christianization of the Jews in this treatise, his anti-Jewish resentments led him to harshly condemn Jews and even suggest the burning of synagogues in other places (most prominently in Martin Luther, *Von den Jůden und iren Lůgen*. Wittenberg, 1543).

[19] When his petition against the Jews of Frankfurt, presented to the emperor, was ignored, the Frankfurt guild leader Vincent Fettmilch led a group of followers to attack the local Jewish community. He and his followers were hanged in 1616, and his ultimate persecution was commemorated in the Jewish community as Purim of Vincent and captured in Yiddish and Hebrew literature. See for further reference: Elhanan Helen, *Turmoil, Trauma, and Triumph: The Fettmilch Uprising in Frankfurt Am Main (1612-1616) According to Megillas Vintz: A Critical Edition of the Yiddish and Hebrew Text Including an English Translation. Judentum und Umwelt;* Bd. 72 (New York: Peter Lang, 2001)

Yiddish is "terrible" and why it should be learned regardless, the transition to an emotive level of argumentation builds to Wagenseil's ultimate point. All weighing of pros and cons is abandoned as compassion, with its purely emotional component, renders all other argumentation futile. If suffering can be reduced, there is no alternative.

Wagenseil's call for compassion is tied to a strong criticism of current practices of Christian authorities engaging with Jews through Hebrew or German. Wagenseil explicates the urgency of this problem through the example of the common so-called "Jewish oath" (*More Iudaico*), usually taken in German. Jews had to take this oath in the context of legal disputes that involved Christian and Jewish parties. Wagenseil argues that Jews did not understand the oath (*Belehrung*, Eiiiir) and often mispronounced it, and, as a result, did not take it seriously (*Belehrung*, Biiiv). To illustrate the terrible consequences of this oath-taking for Jews, Wagenseil focuses on the recent ("ohnlångst," *Belehrung*, Biiiir) suspected homicide in Prague of Simon Abeles, with Löbl Kurtzhandl as one of his suspected murderers (*Belehrung*, Biiiir-Eiiv).

This case shattered the Jewish community of Prague in 1694. Simon Abeles, a Jewish boy of about 11 or 12 years, had supposedly been killed by his father Lazar Abeles, with Kurtzhandl's help, because Simon attempted to convert to Christianity under the guidance of local Jesuits.[20] Shortly after the events, word of Simon's death reached the authorities, who ordered the exhumation of Simon's body and initiated investigations. Although at first only Lazar Abeles was accused of murder, eventually, Löbl Kurtzhandl was tried and executed as a second suspect after the authorities heard from several more witnesses, including Lazar's wife Leah.[21] While Lazar died in custody without having undergone the full trial, Kurtzhandl was gruesomely tortured and ultimately executed.[22] Simon's body received an excessive second public funeral, and the boy was venerated as a martyr within the Prague Christian community.[23]

Wagenseil had easy access to details of the case. Documents concerning the case and, in particular, Lazar Abeles' trial were printed and circulated shortly

---

[20] To this day, it remains unclear whether Simon was murdered or died of natural causes. Elisheva Carlebach, "The Death of Simon Abeles: Jewish Christian Tension in Seventeenth Century Prague," in *Third Annual Herbert Berman Memorial Lecture* (New York: Queens College, 2003), p.10. See also Marie Vachenauer's critical source material study on the Kurtzhandl (Marie Vachenauer, *Der Fall Simon Abeles: Eine kritische Anfrage an die zugänglichen Quellen* [Berlin: Frank & Timme, 2011]).

[21] Rachel L. Greenblatt, "Saint and Countersaint: Catholic Triumphalism and Jewish Resistance in Baroque Prague's Abeles Affair." *Jewish History*, vol. 30, 2016, p.67.

[22] Ibid.; Carlebach, "The Death of Simon Abeles," p.7.

[23] Ibid., pp.61, 63, 67; Carlebach, "The Death of Simon Abeles," p.7.

after the events.[24] Two key sources describe the events surrounding Simon's death and the subsequent investigations.[25] The Old Yiddish "Ayn nay kloglid" ("A New Song of Lament"), preserved only in the second edition, tells the events from a Jewish viewpoint.[26] Almost half the text is concerned with the trials of Löbl Kurtzhandl and describes with horror the tortures he underwent. Kurtzhandl, in this account, becomes a kind of counter-saint, remaining steadfast in his religious belief until his death.[27] The (primarily German) *Processus Inquisitorius* (Prague, 1696), on the other hand, a text enhanced by anti-Jewish remarks and stereotypes,[28] is the most prominent source, a "stitched-together account of the Abeles affair"[29] containing nearly a hundred pages of legal proceedings, including interrogations and a commentary, presenting the Jesuit perspective. It concludes with Kurtzhandl's alleged forced conversion and baptism by torture during the trial.[30]

Wagenseil, at first, carefully summarizes the events based on the *Processus* but subsequently offers a long commentary establishing his anti-Catholic stance[31] and fashioning himself as a true expert in the matter of Jewish language, rites, and religion. In particular, he criticizes the authorities' and the author's lack of knowledge regarding the Hebrew language and Jewish customs. Wagenseil argues that the case of Simon Abeles is known among Catholics because of their "obsession" with Saints but not among Protestants. Wagenseil includes a lengthy summary of the case based on the *Processus* because he assumes that Protestants don't know about this case from Catholic Prague (*Belehrung*, B4r; also C2r-C4v) and, further, it enables him to deconstruct the Catholic authorities' engagement with the Jewish community. As Elisheva Carlebach has pointed out, Wagenseil's treatment of the *Processus* should be perceived in the context of his anti-Catholic program and the self-fashioning of his expertise of Yiddish and Hebrew as well as Jewish religion, much in contrast to the Jesuits' knowledge of Jewish language, culture, and religion.[32] I argue, however, that while inherently anti-Catholic, Wagenseil's core motivation for including this text lies in justifying the study of Yiddish and offering an ultimate reason that moves his argument from the level of logic to that of emotions by

---

[24] Carlebach, "The Death of Simon Abeles," p.10.
[25] Greenblatt, "Saint and Countersaint," p.61.
[26] Amsterdam, 1695; preserved in Bodleian Library, Oxford, Ms. Opp. 8° 460, no. 11.
[27] Greenblatt, p.72.
[28] Carlebach, "The Death of Simon Abeles," p.11.
[29] Greenblatt, "Saint and Countersaint," p.75. Carlebach, "The Death of Simon Abeles," p.10.
[30] Ibid., pp.75, 76.
[31] Carlebach, "The Death of Simon Abeles," p.34.
[32] Ibid., pp.33–34.

appealing to his audiences' compassion. Kurtzhandl's case is the conclusive argument Wagenseil makes for learning Yiddish by enabling him to use emotive rhetoric appealing to the reader. It is more than a supplement to his scholarly-logical preceding arguments; it presents a radical change of Wagenseil's rhetoric from the logical level to the emotional.

Rhetoric's goal is persuasion, to move the audience not only to feel something internally but to do something externally, to make a decision or act in a certain way.[33] The appeal to emotions transfers the argument to another level: "While mentioning abstract concepts such as pain, sorrow, injustice, and violence cannot awake the interlocutor's emotions, the use of words to depict painful, cruel, or unjust scenarios can actually evoke in the hearer anger, compassion, or contempt."[34] Wagenseil's appeal to emotions invokes Aristotle's theory, which is based on the persuasion of judges who—ideally—would make their determinations solely on the basis of law but who, as humans, are influenced by a multitude of information and circumstances and who often lack sufficient time and the necessary information to make a fully unbiased judgment.[35]

Wagenseil's first step in appealing to his audience's compassion is based on the extensive critique of the lingual and contextual misunderstandings of Jewish culture and religion within *Processus*, such as inconsistencies and issues with Yiddish names (*Belehrung*, D4v) and the misconception of tefillin[36] (*Belehrung*, E1r). The misunderstanding is particularly prevalent in the context of the oaths which witnesses—Lazar's wife, Rabbi Lipman, and the cook—had to swear (*Belehrung*, E1r). Wagenseil illustrates that because they misused the language, their oaths are rendered useless, and the witnesses' testimony is, therefore, implicitly unreliable (*Belehrung*, E3r). Further, Wagenseil points out that the *Processus* claims Kurtzhandl invokes Abraham, Isaac, and Jacob during his prolonged torture. This claim of invoking all-powerful saint-like forefathers, Wagenseil argues, does not align with Jewish religion but instead uncovers the inherent Catholic thought that permeates the *Processus* and the proceedings

---

[33] Rüdiger Campe, *Affekt und Ausdruck. Zur Umwandlung der literarischen Rede im 17. und 18. Jahrhundert* (Tübingen: Max Niemeyer, 1990), p. ix.

[34] Fabrizio Macagno, Douglas Walton, *Emotive Language in Argumentation* (Cambridge: Cambridge University Press, 2014), p.67.

[35] Rüdiger Campe, "Presenting the Affect. The Scene of *Pathos* in Aristotle's *Rhetoric* and Its Revision in Descartes's *Passions of the Soul*." *Rethinking Emotion. Interiority and Exteriority in Premodern, Modern, and Contemporary Thought*, edited by Rüdiger Campe and Julia Weber (Berlin, Boston: De Gruyter, 2014), p.44; Fabrizio Macagno: "Manipulating Emotions. Value-based Reasoning and Emotive Language." *Argumentation and Advocacy*, vol. 51, 2014, pp.119-120.

[36] Tefillin are small black boxes containing text from the Torah, attachable to head and arms as part of the morning prayer.

(*Belehrung*, E2r). All these misinterpretations and misunderstandings ultimately result, in Wagenseil's argument, from the Christian community's lack of Yiddish knowledge. Wagenseil supports his criticism with both Hebrew and Latin quotes and references to the Talmud and Maimonides' 13 Principles of Faith, therewith establishing him as a credible authority who possesses the required extensive knowledge of Jewish religion and language. Wagenseil does not point his finger at the Jewish witnesses or the accused. In his telling, the fault lies entirely with the Catholic authorities in the context of the trial and those who have created the oath and placed it centrally within juridical proceedings that included Jews.

The case of Simon Abeles, in Wagenseil's version, highlights a top-down process led by authorities completely out of touch with the realities of the people on trial and which was consequently unable to uncover any truth but instead caused significant suffering because it was essentially flawed. While Wagenseil is not critical of Kurtzhandl's forced conversion itself, he questions the events that led to the suspect's extended torture and final execution. Wagenseil indicates that this outcome is based entirely on a misunderstanding resulting from different parties not communicating in the same language (German or Yiddish) and assuming that Jews speak Hebrew well when they were actually fluent in Yiddish. Christian compassion, Wagenseil concludes, should prevent such pointless suffering by enabling the Jews to comprehend court procedures and the oath they take fully. To emphasize this point, Wagenseil identifies councilmen, magistrates, and high- and low-level members of the local authorities as core audiences on the title page of his book.[37]

By deconstructing the authorities' knowledge and practices, Wagenseil operates on an argumentative-logical level. Based on Wagenseil's examples, an audience potentially concludes that the judicial process was flawed. But Wagenseil's extended repetition and detailed account of Kurtzhandl's suffering (based on the *Processus*) achieves more than that. The graphic depiction of the suffering creates images in the audiences' imagination intended to trigger their

---

[37] Considering his audience's demands on their time, *Belehrung* is intended as an easily accessible and comprehensible text ("that anyone may grasp it easily without oral guidance." "daß sie jedermann leicht ohne einen muendlichen Belehrer begreiffen kan." *Belehrung*, Xiir) that promises nothing less than immediate success for the language learner within a few hours of independent study. ("Introduction to spoken and written Jewish-German by means of which anyone able to read true German can acquire these skills within a few hours." *Belehrung Der Jüdisch-Teutschen disch-Teutschen Red- und Schreibart. Durch welche / Alle so des wahren Teutschen Lesens kundig / für sich selbsten / innerhalb wenig Stunden / zu sothaner Wissenschaft gelangen können.* [*Belehrung*, title page]).

compassion, a compassion that should lead to action.[38] Wagenseil achieves this vividness through a detailed account of the torture Kurtzhandl underwent. This means, in consequence, that the events present not just a flawed court case but the ways in which miscommunication and lack of cultural understanding caused Kurtzhandl's significantly prolonged suffering, which could have been cut short. Christian brotherly love, Wagenseil concludes, should prevent such pointless suffering. Appealing to his primary audience of Christian readers, he offers the key to preventing similar instances in the future: the knowledge of Yiddish.

Wagenseil does not just point to the fact that Kurtzhandl's torture was extensive but re-narrates it over several pages using the *Processus* material. In reading, the audience re-lives the moments as spectators of Kurtzhandl's suffering. By depicting the scenes that the audience can envision, Wagenseil ventures beyond logical arguments for learning Yiddish and focuses on the core power of emotive language. Fabrizio Macagno highlights this fictional-theatrical aspect of emotive language: "A speaker can depict initials, groups, or issues from an emotional perspective, representing people as actors in emotional events."[39] Wagenseil uses this strategy of the performative element, recounting the torture of Kurtzhandl in detail, with the hope that, in the sight of such suffering, his audience understands his plea for compassion and makes effective use of the actual language learning sections that follow in *Belehrung*.

Compassion and Power

The core requirements for receiving compassion are already established by Aristotle in his reflection on the tragedy. Aristotle argues—as is generally accepted—that we as spectators of suffering feel compassion when 1) the suffering is immense and not just trivial (e.g., death vs. a brief illness of little consequence, job loss vs. not getting a promotion) and 2) the sufferer is not responsible for his situation, but it is caused by another power (humans, nature, etc.[40] As we have already seen, Wagenseil repeatedly stresses Kurtzhandl's underserved, unmerited suffering. He achieves this by marking

---

[38] Traditionally, scholars strictly differentiate among the emotions between empathy and compassion: "Empathy is not sufficient for compassion, for a sadist may have considerable empathy with the situation of another person, and use it to harm that person." (Martha C. Nussbaum, *Political Emotions. Why Love Matters for Justice* [Cambridge MA: Harvard University Press, 2013], p.146). The generally accepted understanding is that empathy remains in the sphere of affect, while true compassion leads to action.
[39] Macagno, "Manipulating Emotions," p.115.
[40] Aristotle, *Poetics and Rhetoric*, edited by George Stade, translated by S. H. Butcher (New York: Barnes & Noble Books, 2005), 1386b26-29.

the lawmakers, the persecutors, and even the author of the *Processus* as deficient, lacking the knowledge and skills to understand the witnesses' and suspects' language, religion, customs, and life circumstances. The unmerited suffering is core to Wagenseil's strategy. For Wagenseil, his privileged Christian German-speaking audience has the power to prevent such suffering by learning Yiddish.

According to Aristotle, the third requirement is the "average character" of the sufferer, who should be neither saint nor villain for others to feel compassion. In line with the interpreters of the Aristotelian school of thought and studies of emotion, Martha Nussbaum adds a fourth requirement: not only should the person be average in character, but his social status should not differ widely from the person to be affected by compassion.[41] In other words, the suffering person and the person in whom compassion will be evoked should be similar, and their possibilities in life should be much the same. While Wagenseil clearly stresses the first two requirements, he reinterprets the third and fourth features very differently and in ways that uncover the hidden power matrix within Wagenseil's worldview and that of his readers. For Wagenseil and his readers, the Yiddish speakers' possibilities are decidedly different; the suffering person seems almost the same, capable of converting to Christianity and learning "proper" German but not there yet. And it is this essential "almost" that enables compassion within a matrix of power.

Wagenseil leaves no doubt, even within his compassion, that the Yiddish-speaking Jews in their "current" state are inferior to him and his German-speaking audience. In *Belehrung*, Wagenseil refers to the Jews as "obdurate Jews" ("verstockte Juden," Jir) whose only way to salvation as well as social advancement is by speaking "proper" German. By extension, this implies that Wagenseil's readers are supposed to learn Yiddish to teach "proper German" to Jews and to support their conversion to Christianity. Wagenseil's beliefs are grounded in the theology attributed to the apostle Paul, who accuses the Jews of murdering Jesus (1 Thessalonians 2:14-16). All of these ideas are well captured in a short prayer that concludes the introduction wherein Wagenseil prays for God's blessing on all those partaking in the mission of the Jews and for the eventual redemption of Israel.[42] The prayer ends with a quote from the

---

[41] Martha C. Nussbaum, *Upheavals of Thought. The Intelligence of Emotions* (Cambridge: Cambridge University Press, 2001), p.313.
[42] "May the Lord our God foster the work of those who attempt to convert the Jews, and may He be their shield and their great reward, and through his grace and salvation finally redeem Israel from all its sins, according to the prayer that his only son made for them upon the tree of the holy cross: Father forgive them for they know not what they do. Amen. Sela." ("Nun/ der HErr unser GOtt fördere noch ferner das Werck der Hånde derer / so sich um die Bekehrung der Juden annehmen / und sey ihr Schild und ihr grosser

passion of Christ as narrated in the Gospel of Luke that similarly links the Jews to murdering Jesus: "Father, forgive them, for they know not what they do" (Lk 23,34). Even in this quote, with its undertone of condescension, the focus is compassion. Similarly, Wagenseil takes a stand against forced conversions and physical violence. Yet, under the veil of Wagenseil's emotive strategy, using compassion as motivation to learn Yiddish, Wagenseil obscures profoundly anti-Jewish resentments. Learning Yiddish is only a temporary step for Christians, who must learn this inferior system to eliminate it.

Wagenseil believes that compassion for the Jews leads to Christians learning Yiddish as an act of Christian mercy, this mercy, however, still focuses on the "guilt" of being Jewish. Nussbaum, similarly, points out that mercy acknowledges the fault of an individual or group accused of wrongdoing by offering a reaction or penalty that is milder than the one appointed by law for the act.[43] Wagenseil's concept of compassion is based on the perception that the Jewish religion and language are inferior and deficient (compared to the Christian religion and German language). Jews are being found guilty of being Jewish; the Christians in power are in a position of acting mercifully. But it is their mercy that ultimately devaluates and condemns both Judaism and Yiddish. As Wagenseil's text lacks positive examples of such a double linguistic-religious conversion, whether the newly converted would be fully integrated or considered sort-off second-class Christians remains open.

The goal of the proposed mercy leads to the acculturation and assimilation of Jews into the majority culture of German-speaking Christians (ideally Protestants), placing the responsibility to reach out and enable Jews to overcome their limitations on the Christian German-speakers. Wagenseil emphasizes this Christian-dominated power structure by appealing to his fellows' constructs of compassion, which inherently contain implications of superiority. Wagenseil considers doing good to less fortunate others a foundational Christian responsibility. The power structure within which Wagenseil's concept of compassion works explains the inherent paradox and paternalism of *Belehrung*: Yiddish is bad, but a good Protestant should learn Yiddish to help the Jews.

Kurtzhandl's life ends, according to the *Processus* and Wagenseil's summary, with his conversion to Christianity (*Belehrung*, D2r-v)—and, according to

---

Lohn / erlöse auch endlich durch die Gnade und viele Erlösung die bey ihn ist / Israel aus allen seinen Sünden nach der Fürbitte / so sein einziger Sohn / am Stamm des heiligen Creutzes für sie gethan: Vatter / vergib ihnen / denn sie wissen nicht / was sie thun. Amen. Sela" *Belehrung*, Iiiv).

[43] Nussbaum, *Upheavals of Thought*, pp.356–366.

Wagenseil, there is nothing wrong with the fact that this conversion takes place. While the prolonged torture is a problem, the ultimate outcome is satisfactory in Wagenseil's eyes. Thus, even though Kurtzhandl ultimately died through the sword of the henchmen, Wagenseil describes his very violent death using the phrasing of the *Processus* as "passing away peacefully in the Lord" (seelig in dem Herrn entschlaffen," *Belehrung*, D2v). Wagenseil's wording underscores that, in his view, Kurtzhandl's conversion turns the gruesome death into a peaceful passing, with the implication of an afterlife within a Christian framework. The focus lies on the perceived salvation and not the details of the earthly death, underscoring once more that conversion is the superior goal that must be achieved with whatever means necessary. *Belehrung* only offers an intervention regarding the course of action, not an alteration of the outcome.

Conclusion

With his appeal to his primary audiences' compassion, Wagenseil tries to move the reader to learn Yiddish despite his belief in its base linguistic status, which he constantly underscores. Wagenseil attemps to rehabilitate the Jews and their writings while simultaneously describing them as an obdurate religious group in desperate need of salvation, a salvation directly tied to Christians' ability to speak Yiddish and Jews' ability to speak German.[44] While emotive language in the context of early modern non-Jewish debates (e.g., blood libel accusations) usually aims to provoke anti-Jewish policies and actions, Wagenseil uses emotive language to achieve the opposite: compassion and outreach. Wagenseil tries to improve the Jews' reputation by arguing that defamations are only contained in a small part of their literature and vehemently rebuking anti-Jewish superstition and blood libel accusations.[45]

Especially because of *Belehrung*, the first influential Yiddish teaching book, Wagenseil has been hailed as a pioneer of Christian-Jewish coexistence

---

[44] See Martin Friedrich, *Zwischen Abwehr und Bekehrung: die Stellung der deutschen evangelischen Theologie zum Judentum im 17. Jahrhundert* (Tübingen: Mohr, 1988), p. 142–3.

[45] This term commonly refers to the false and superstitious belief in the existence of a Jewish custom of murdering Christian children to use their blood for ritual purposes (often connected to the context of the Jewish holiday of Passover).

(Dickmann, Blastenbrei)[46] and his work as indispensable service to the field of Yiddish (Garrin).[47] Yet his argument remains inherently anti-Jewish. Wagenseil wanted to improve Jews' lives on the premise that they ultimately cease to be Jewish in a cultural-religious or linguistic sense and convert to Christianity. Therefore, Wagenseil's book, written in his view out of pragmatic necessity, is not targeted at founding an extensive field of Yiddish studies but at ending its very existence. That the conversion of the Jews turns Wagenseil's efforts into a monologue rather than a dialogue, grounded in anti-Jewish polemics, has often been overlooked in scholarship stressing either Wagenseil's service to the field of Yiddish or the controversial so-called "German-Jewish dialogue." The end goal, as professed in *Belehrung*, is to offer the Yiddish-speaking Jews a way out of their repressed minority status by turning them into "proper" German-speaking Christians. Only when the Jews abandon their cultural, religious, and lingual elements—nothing short of ceasing to be Jewish—will Wagenseil and his audience stop considering them "almost the same" and begin seeing them as equals.

Wagenseil successfully established the field for generations to come. His *Belehrung and* subsequent related publications frequently saw multiple editions within a short time;[48] these well-received and widely referenced texts shaped the (negative) reception of Yiddish until the twentieth century. The case of one of Wagenseil's followers, Johann Heinrich Callenberg (1694-1769), shows that the model could even expand onto other minorities. In 1728, the pietist and professor of philosophy and Oriental languages gave Wagenseil' Christian Yiddishist movement an institutional framework by establishing the *Institutum Judaicum et Muhammedicum* (1728-91; Halle). The institute's intellectual scope fostered Christian missionary efforts among Jews and Muslims.[49]

---

[46] Blastenbrei writes: "Anders als viele der bekannteren Philosemiten des 17. Jahrhunderts hat Wagenseil..." (Peter Blastenbrei, *Johann Christoph Wagenseil und seine Stellung zum Judentum* [Erlangen: Harald Fischer Verlag, 2004], p.38). Friedrich Dickmann takes this further: "Sich selbst würde Wagenseil gewiß als Judenfreund bezeichnen [...]" [Surely, Wagenseil would call himself a philosemite.] Dickmann, "Das Judenmissionsprogramm Johann Christoph Wagenseils," *Neue Zeitschrift für Systematische Theologie und Religionsphilosophie*, volume 16, issue 1, 1974, p.92.
[47] "[...] Wagenseil transcended these prejudices [against Yiddish] to the extent that he probed further into the internal principles of the language and presented examples of its literature as worthy of serious study." Stephen H. Garrin, "Johann Christoff Wagenseil's *Belehrung der teutsch-hebräischen Red- und Schreibart*," *The South Central Bulletin*, volume 39, issue 3, 1979, p.43.
[48] Elyada, *A Goy Who Speaks Yiddish*, pp. 20.
[49] Ibid. 26. On the history of the *Institutum*, see Matthias Morgenstern / Reinhold Rieger (ed.): *Das Tübinger Institutum Judaicum. Beiträge zu seiner Geschichte und Vorgeschichte seit Adolf Schlatter*. Stuttgart: Steiner, 2015; and Christoph Rymatzki: *Hallischer Pietismus und Judenmission. Johann Heinrich Callenbergs Institutum Judaicum und dessen*

Callenberg's institute illustrates Wagenseil's complicated philosophy. While the idea was to foster proficiency in Yiddish, the project established no Christian-Jewish dialogue but represents a one-sided effort of Christianizing religious minorities. The such-desired knowledge of Yiddish, as grounded in Wagenseil's work, thus serves as a tool for exerting power, a way to control and alter a minority group, ideally causing its extinction.

Bibliography

Aristotle. *Poetics and Rhetoric*. Edited by George Stade, translated by S. H. Butcher (*Poetics*) and W. Rhys Roberts (*Rhetoric*). New York: Barnes & Noble Books, 2005.

Berger, Shlomo. "A Bestseller in Context. Referring to the 'Tsene Rene' in Early Modern Yiddish Books." *Studies in the History of Culture and Science. A Tribute to Gad Freudenthal*. Eds. Resianne Fontaine, Ruth Glasner, Reimund Leicht, and Giuseppe Veltri. Leiden: Brill, 2011, pp. 419-30.

Blastenbrei, Peter. *Johann Christoph Wagenseil und seine Stellung zum Judentum*. Erlangen: Harald Fischer, 2004.

Campe, Rüdiger. "Presenting the Affect. The Scene of *Pathos* in Aristotle's *Rhetoric* and Its Revision in Descartes's *Passions of the Soul*." *Rethinking Emotion. Interiority and Exteriority in Premodern, Modern, and Contemporary Thought*. Eds. Rüdiger Campe and Julia Weber. Berlin, Boston: De Gruyter, 2014, pp. 36-57.

———. *Affekt und Ausdruck. Zur Umwandlung der literarischen Rede im 17. und 18. Jahrhundert*. Tübingen: Max Niemeyer, 1990.

Carlebach, Elisheva. "The Death of Simon Abeles: Jewish Christian Tension in Seventeenth Century Prague." *Third Annual Herbert Berman Memorial Lecture*. New York: Queens College, 2003, pp. 1-44.

Dickmann, Friedrich, "Das Judenmissionsprogramm Johann Christoph Wagenseils." *Neue Zeitschrift für Systematische Theologie und Religionsphilosophie*, volume 16, issue 1, 1974: 75-92.

Dinse, Hartmut. *Die Entwicklung des jiddischen Schrifttums im deutschen Sprachgebiet*. Stuttgart: Metzler, 1974.

Elyada, Aya. *A Goy Who Speaks Yiddish: Christians and the Jewish Language in Early Modern Germany*. Stanford: Stanford University Press, 2012.

Frakes, Jerold. *The Cultural Study of Yiddish in Early Modern Europe*. New York: Palgrave Macmillan, 2007.

Friedrich, Martin. *Zwischen Abwehr und Bekehrung: die Stellung der deutschen evangelischen Theologie zum Judentum im 17. Jahrhundert*. Tübingen: Mohr, 1988.

Garrin, Stephen H. "Johann Christoff Wagenseil's *Belehrung der teutsch-hebräischen Red-und Schreibart*," *The South Central Bulletin*, volume 39, issue 3 (1979): 87-113.

Freundeskreis (1728–1736) (Tübingen: Verlag der Franckeschen Stiftungen Halle im Max Niemeyer Verlag, 2004).

Greenblatt, Rachel L. "Saint and Countersaint: Catholic Triumphalism and Jewish Resistance in Baroque Prague's Abeles Affair." *Jewish History*, vol. 30, 2016, pp. 61-80 (2016).

Grossman, Jeffrey A. *The Discourse on Yiddish in Germany from the Enlightenment to the Second Empire* Columbia, S.C.: Camden House, 2000.

Helen, Elhanan. *Turmoil, Trauma, and Triumph: The Fettmilch Uprising in Frankfurt Am Main (1612-1616) According to Megillas Vintz: A Critical Edition of the Yiddish and Hebrew Text Including an English Translation.* Judentum und Umwelt; Bd. 72. New York: Peter Lang, 2001.

Katz, Dovid. *Yiddish and Power.* New York, NY: Palgrave Macmillan, 2015.

Luther, Martin. *Von den Jůden und iren Lůgen.* Wittenberg, 1543

———. *Das Jhesus Christus eyn geborner Jude sey.* Wittenberg, 1523.

Macagno, Fabrizio; Douglas, Walton. *Emotive Language in Argumentation* Cambridge: Cambridge University Press, 2014.

———. "Manipulating Emotions. Value-based Reasoning and Emotive Language." *Argumentation and Advocacy*, vol. 51, 2014: 119-120.

Mattheier, Klaus J. "German." In *Germanic Standardizations. Past to Present*, edited by Ana Deumert and Wim Vandenbussche, 211-44. Impact, Studies in Language and Society 18. Amsterdam; Philadelphia: J.Benjamins, 2003.

Nussbaum, Martha C. *Political Emotions. Why Love Matters for Justice.* Cambridge MA: Harvard University Press, 2013.

———. *Upheavals of Thought. The Intelligence of Emotions.* Cambridge: Cambridge University Press, 2001.

Tröhler, Daniel. *Languages of Education Protestant Legacies, National Identities, and Global Aspirations.* Studies in Curriculum Theory. New York: Routledge, 2011.

Vachenauer, Marie. *Der Fall Simon Abeles: Eine kritische Anfrage an die zugänglichen Quellen.* Berlin: Frank & Timme, 2011.

Wagenseil, Johann Christoph. Belehrung der jüdisch-teutschen Red- und Schreibart ... Königsberg, 1699.

Weissler, Chava. "For Women and for Men Who Are Like Women. The Construction of Gender in Yiddish Devotional Literature." *Journal of Feminist Studies in Religion* 5 (1989): 7-24.

Wolfthal, Diane *Picturing Yiddish: Gender, Identity, and Memory in the Illustrated Yiddish Books of Renaissance Italy.* Leiden: Brill, 2004.

Chapter 6

Gendered Variation in Spoken German: Has Prescriptivism Affected the Vernacular?

James M. Stratton
The Pennsylvania State University

Abstract: Over the last five decades, several gender-fair innovations have entered the German language as a result of feminist advocacy work (Trömel-Plötz, 1978; Guentherodt et al. 1980; Schoenthal, 1989; Hellinger, 1990; Grabrucker, 1993). Consequently, gendered language now pervades written and formal spoken German (Bußmann & Hellinger, 2003; Lamb & Nereo, 2012; Moser & Hannover, 2014; Diewald & Steinhauser, 2020). However, the extent to which such ideological prescriptivism has affected vernacular speech is an empirical question only recently investigated (Stratton, 2018). Building on previous research, the present study uses variationist methods to examine gendered language in two geographically distinct speech communities, namely a North East Frisian speech community and a North West Swiss speech community.

Native speakers of *Standarddeutsch* 'Standard German' from Germany and Switzerland were asked to describe 26 images which were deliberately chosen to examine their use of gendered language in informal spoken German. For instance, asking native speakers to describe an image of a group of female-only pupils examined whether speakers would employ the generic masculine variant *Schüler*, the gender-fair variant *Schülerinnen*, the gender-neutral form *Lernenden*, or a biologically determined variant such as *Mädchen* or *Frauen*.

While this study found that gendered language was used infrequently in vernacular speech compared to written and formal spoken German, results found age, education, and morphological composition to significantly influence the likelihood that gender-inclusive language is used in unrehearsed spoken German. However, relative to the frequency of the generic masculine, gendered language was rarely used, which may suggest something about the nature and overall impact of ideological change in vernacular spoken language, namely, it has little effect. The present study contributes to the growing body of variationist sociolinguistic scholarship on varieties of German that shows various linguistic and social factors influence variation.

Keywords: Modern Standard German; North East Frisian/ North West Swiss; gendered language; prescriptivism; German language variation and change; variationist sociolinguistics

***

Sociolinguistics differs from traditional philological approaches to language in its methodological framework, analyses, and interpretation of data. One area that sets sociolinguistics apart is the emphasis on real-life, unrehearsed spoken language. The present study uses variationist sociolinguistic methods to examine the factors that influence the use of gender-inclusive language in unrehearsed spoken German. It analyzes the use of gender-fair, gender-neutral, and generic masculine constructions in two speech communities: a speech community in Germany (Westoverledingen, Northwest Germany) and a speech community in Switzerland (Basel, Northwest Switzerland). Both language-internal (morphological composition) and language-external factors (sex, age, geography, education) are considered in the analysis. Two research questions are addressed. First, what is the distribution of variants in the two speech communities? In other words, of the three macro variants (i.e. gender-neutral, gender-fair, and generic masculine), which is used most frequently, and do choices differ across the two speech communities? Second, is the use of gender-inclusive or gender-exclusive language sensitive to linguistic and social constraints? For instance, is there a correlation between the use of a particular variant and social factors? Does the morphological composition of a word interact with the realization of a given variant? Answering these questions provides insight into the factors which currently influence the use of gendered language constructions while adding to the developing scholarship on German variationist sociolinguistics.[1]

---

[1] Examples of recent variationist sociolinguistic work include: James Stratton, "Adjective Intensifiers in German," *Journal of Germanic Linguistics*, 32, no. 2, (2020): 183-215; James Stratton, "Tapping into German Adjective Variability: A Variationist Sociolinguistic Approach," *Journal of Germanic Linguistics*, 34, no. 1 (2022): 63-101; Karen Beaman, "Swabian Relatives: Variation in the Use of the wo-relativiser," in *Advancing Sociogrammatical Variation and Change*, eds. Beaman et al., 134-164. (New York: Routledge, 2020); Bülow et al., "Linguistic, social, and individual factors constraining variation in spoken Swiss Standard German," in *Intra-Variation in Language*, eds. Werth et al., (Berlin: De Gruyter Mouton), 127-173. James Stratton and Karen Beaman, "*Expanding Variationist Sociolinguistic Research in Varieties of German*" (London: Routledge, 2024).

Background

Like many languages of the world, German has a grammatical gender system. Both animate (e.g. *der Lehrer* 'teacher') and inanimate nouns (e.g. *das Licht* 'light') belong to one of three grammatical genders: masculine, feminine, or neuter. However, when referring to a mixed-sex group (e.g. a group of both male and female referents), speakers often make use of the generic masculine, that is, the linguistic convention whereby the morphological masculine form of a word is used to refer to speakers of all sexes and gender identities, as in (1). Whether used in the singular (1a) or plural (1b), the meaning can be ambiguous: the referents can be exclusively male, they can be male and female, or they can be non-binary, trans, or intersex. While female, non-binary, trans, and intersex referents are theoretically included in the generic masculine reading, they lack overt morphological marking.

(1)   (a) der Student ist im Klassenzimmer

           'the student.masc is in the classroom'

       (b) Studenten sind im Klassenzimmer

           students.masc are in the classroom'

Views on the use of the generic masculine fall into two schools of thought: the semantic view and the arbitrary view. According to the semantic view, there is a close relationship between grammatical gender and biological gender. The semantic view is in line with traditional scholarship on linguistic relativism, where language and cognition are thought to be closely intertwined.[2] According to this association, use of the generic masculine is thought to be androcentric.[3] Luise F. Pusch illustrated this gender bias with the example: *99 Staatsbürgerinnen und ein Staatsbürger sind auf Deutsch 100 Staatsbürger* '99 female citizens and one male citizen, in German, are 100 male citizens.'[4] Even though there are 99 female citizens, the presence of one male citizen "makes

---

[2] The notion that the language you speak influences the way you think is the basis of the Sapir-Whorf hypothesis. See Benjamin Whorf, *Language, thought, and reality: Selected writings*, ed., J.B. Carroll, (Cambridge, Mass: Technology Press of Massachusetts Institute of Technology, 1956).

[3] For information on this claim, see: Senta Trömel-Plötz, *Linguistik und Frauensprache* (Frankfurt am Main: Fischer Taschenbuch Verlag, 1978); Ingrid Guentherodt, Marlis Hellinger, Luise F. Pusch, Senta Trömel-Plötz, "Richtlinien zur Vermeidung sexistischen Sprachgebrauchs," *Linguistische Berichte*, 69, (1980): 15–21; Marianne Grabrucker, *Vater Staat hat keine Muttersprache* (Frankfurt: Fischer, 1993).

[4] Luise Pusch, *Die Frau ist nicht der Rede wert* (Frankfurt am Main: Suhrkamp, 1999), 10.

the whole NP morphologically masculine."[5] Indeed, studies have found that a lack of overt morphological visibility can have societal implications; specifically, psycholinguistic studies have shown that the generic masculine evokes more mental images of male referents.[6] A job advertisement that reads *Journalist gesucht* 'journalist sought' is referentially ambiguous because it is unclear whether female, non-binary, trans, intersex, or agender speakers are included as permissible candidates. For this reason, other than cisgender men, people may be less likely to apply for a position than if gender-inclusive language were used (e.g. *Journalist*in gesucht* 'journalist sought of any gender identity').[7] Although gender-inclusive language is thought to impede readability and is less aesthetically-pleasing, Friedrich Marcus and Elke Heise found that comprehensibility ratings were not affected by the use or absence of gendered language.[8] Gender-inclusive language, in its more antiquated use, refers to language that includes both male and female referents (e.g. *Lehrer und Lehrerinnen* 'male and female teachers') in contrast to gender-exclusive language which does not (e.g. *Lehrer* 'teachers.masc'). However, more recently, efforts toward creating and using gender-inclusive language have moved beyond the male-female binary and seek to represent speakers of all gender identities, including agender speakers.

On the other hand, the arbitrary view maintains that there is no association between grammatical gender and biological gender.[9] Therefore, "grammatical gender is regarded as an exclusively formal feature; gender assignment of nouns is believed to be arbitrary."[10] In other words, the labels masculine, feminine, and neuter, are categorical terms which would be perhaps more

---

[5] James Stratton, "The Use of the Generic Masculine, the Derivational Morpheme -in and Gender-Fair Innovations in Unrehearsed Spoken Dialogue in Modern Standard German," *Interdisciplinary Journal for Germanic Linguistics and Semiotic Analysis* 23, no. 1 (2018): 5.
[6] See Friederike Braun, Sabine Sczesny and Dagmar Stahlberg, "Cognitive effects of masculine generics in German: An overview of empirical findings," *Communications*, 30, (2005): 1–21; Sabine Sczesny, Magdalena Formanowicz and Franziska Moser, "Can Gender-Fair Language Reduce Gender Stereotyping and Discrimination?" *Frontiers in Psychology*, 7 (2016): 1-11.
[7] See Lisa Horvath and Sabine Sczesny, "Reducing the lack of fit for women with leadership positions? Effects of the wording in job advertisements," *European Journal of Work and Organizational Psychology* 25, no. 2 (2015): 316-328.
[8] Friedrich Marcus and Elke Heise, "Does the use of gender-fair language influence the comprehensibility of texts? An experiment using an authentic contract manipulating single role nouns and pronouns," *Swiss Journal of Psychology*, 78, no. 1-2 (2019): 51–60.
[9] Hartwig Kalverkämper, "Die Frauen und die Sprache," *Linguistische Berichte* 62 (1979): 55-71.
[10] Friederike Braun, Sabine Sczesny and Dagmar Stahlberg, "Cognitive effects of masculine generics in German: An overview of empirical findings," 4.

adequately described as "Group I" "Group II" "Group III." In fact, many languages of the world use such labels. For instance, Swahili has eight noun classes and Zulu has 16 noun classes. In this view, grammatical categories do not necessarily reflect inherent biological or societal categories just like different noun classes have no bearing on or association with sex and gender in the real world. As mentioned in Stratton (2018), "one of the main reasons why many forms in Modern Standard German are "androcentric" is due to the morphological history of the language itself and not so much the intention of individual speakers."[11] Plurals that are so-called "androcentric" are often, from a historical perspective, an artifact of the grammatical and morphological structure.[12] Even if speakers conflate grammatical gender with biological gender, the large majority of speakers who use the generic masculine are not intentionally trying to be sexist.[13] Instead, speakers are using the linguistic resources at their disposal, which they have obtained through the natural process of language acquisition.

The arbitrariness of gender assignment is observable throughout the history of Germanic languages. For instance, in Modern Standard German, the derivational suffix -*heit* is grammatically feminine (e.g. *die Krankheit* 'illness'), but the cognate counterparts in respective Germanic languages are not (e.g. Norwegian *en skjønnhet* 'beauty.masc' versus German *die Schönheit* 'beauty.fem'). Even though German -*heit* and Scandinavian -*het/hed* are reflexes of Proto Germanic *haidus, their grammatical gender has changed throughout history (e.g. masculine in Norwegian, feminine in German, and non-gender-specific in English). Variation in grammatical gender can even be found in early Germanic languages (e.g. Old Saxon *magaðhed* 'virginity.fem', Old English *mægðhad* 'virginity.masc', see also Old English *se cildhad* 'childhood.masc' and German *die Kindheit* 'childhood.fem', Old Saxon *lefhed* 'illness/sickness.fem' and German *Krankheit* 'illness/sickness.fem') and the same level of variability can be found with other derivational suffixes (e.g. German -*tion*: *die Information, die Conversation*, Norwegian -*sjon*: *en informasjon, en konversasjon*). Gender assignment with clothing in Modern Standard German also illustrates this arbitrariness (e.g. *der Rock* 'skirt.masc,' *der Bikini* 'bikini.masc').

Regardless of whether one adopts the semantic view or the arbitrary view, several innovations have entered the German language over the last five

---

[11] Stratton, "The Use of the Generic Masculine, the Derivational Morpheme -in. and Gender-Fair Innovations in Unrehearsed Spoken Dialogue in Modern Standard German," 6.
[12] Ibid., 6.
[13] Dagmar Stahlberg, Friederike Braun, Lisa Irmen and Sabine Sczesny, "Representation of the sexes in language" in *Social Communication*, ed. Klaus Fiedler (New York: Psychology Press, 2007), 17.

decades due to feminist and LGBTQIA+ advocacy work. Typographically, efforts toward achieving more overt linguistic gender equality have resulted in the development of several linguistic conventions, such as the *Paarform* 'pair form' (e.g. *Lehrerinnen und Lehrer* 'female teachers and male teachers'), the *Binnen-I* 'the capital I' (e.g. *LehrerInnen*), the *Schrägstrich* 'forward slash' (*Lehrer/innen*), the *Bindestrich* 'hyphen' (e.g. *Lehrer-innen*), *Klammern* 'parentheses' (e.g. *Lehrer(innen)*), the *Gendergap* 'the gender gap' (e.g. *Lehrer_innen*), the *Doppelpunkt* 'hyphen' (e.g., *Lehrer:innen*), the *Gendersternchen* 'genderstar' (e.g. *Lehrer*innen*), and more recently, the *X-Form* 'x-form' (e.g. *Lehrx*).[14] Of these innovations, only the latter two are thought to include non-binary, trans, intersex, and agender speakers. Although the majority of the typographic conventions have become frequent in formal written registers, i.e. bureaucratic and educational settings, because most of them are not easily pronounceable (e.g. *Lehrer/innen*), it is reasonable to hypothesize that they have had little effect on everyday spoken German.[15] However, it should be noted that some attempts have been made to oralize the written conventions, such as the insertion of a glottal stop between the gendered morpheme boundary.[16] While the original goal in the 1970s into the late 20th century was to increase the visibility of women, in recent years the discourse has moved beyond the male-female binary to include speakers of all sexes and gender identities, with innovations such as non-binary pronouns (e.g. *xier* 'they') and the adoption of English singular *they*.[17] *Hen* is another example of a gender-neutral pronoun in German, which can be inflected for case (*hen* 'accusative, *hem* 'dative,' and *hens*

---

[14] The use of the genderstar (e.g., *Politiker*innen*) includes non-binary speakers (e.g., transgender or intersex), but Pusch (2019) criticizes its use because they are not morphologically visible whereas men (e.g., -*er*) and women (e.g., -*innen*) are.

[15] For information on the use of these innovations in formal settings, see: Estrella Castillo Días, "Der Genus/Sexus-Konflikt und das generische Maskulinum in der deutschen Gegenwartssprache," PhD diss., University of Passau, 2003; Hanna Acke, "Sprachwandel durch feministische Sprachkritik." *Zeitschrift für Literaturwissenschaft und Linguistik*, 49, no. 2 (2019): 303-320.

[16] For information on pronunciability, please see: Hadumod Bußmann and Marlis Hellinger, "Engendering Female Visibility in German" in *Gender across Languages*, ed. Marlis Hellinger and Hadumod Bußmann. (Amsterdam and Philadelphia, PA: John Benjamins, 2003), 155. Stratton, "The Use of the Generic Masculine, the Derivational Morpheme -in. and Gender-Fair Innovations in Unrehearsed Spoken Dialogue in Modern Standard German," 11; see also Anatol Stefanowitsch's *Sprachlog*, "Gendergap und Gendersternchen in der gesprochenen Sprache," 2018, http://www.sprachlog.de/2018/06/09/gendergap-und-gendersternchen-in-der-gesprochenen-sprache/.

[17] For more information, see https://geschlechtsneutralesdeutsch.com/das-nona-system/

'genitive').[18] Nevertheless, despite increasing efforts to create more gender-inclusive language, proposals have been and still are met with some resistance.[19]

Because most of the earlier proposals created a problematic binary distinction (e.g. *Lehrerinnen und Lehrer* 'female teachers and male teachers'), additional strategies have been employed, such as the substantivization of verbs, as in *die Studierenden* 'the ones who study' (derived from *studieren* 'to study'), the substantivization of participles, as in *die Angestellten* 'the employees' (derived from *anstellen* 'to employ'), and the substantivization of adjectives, as in *die Jugendlichen* 'the adolescents' (from *Jugend* 'youth' + derivational suffix *-lich* + plural morpheme *-en*). Other strategies include the use of relative clauses in lieu of noun phrases (e.g. *die Personen, die studieren* 'the people who study') and the use of gender-neutral lexemes, such as *Person* 'person,' *Fachkraft* 'specialist,' *Arbeitskraft* 'workforce,' *Feuerwehrleute* 'fire brigade people,' and *die Redaktion* 'editorial staff' as opposed to generic masculine counterparts.[20] In recent years, some gender-neutral nouns have been neologized through linguistic resources such as clipping (e.g. see *Studis* as an alternative to *Studenten* 'students').

Despite the ubiquity of gender-inclusive language constructions in formal spoken and written discourse, little is known about their frequency in informal spoken German.[21] To date, to the best of my knowledge, only one study has attempted to tap into this empirical question, albeit with a number of shortcomings.[22] Since these prescriptive forms were imposed on the German language, it is reasonable to hypothesize that in unrehearsed speech, namely vernacular speech, they are used less frequently.[23] In a previous study, 30 native

---

[18] An example of its use is: *Hans is eine nicht-binäre Person – hen ist* [...] 'Hans identifies as non-binary – they are [...]'.
[19] See, for instance, signatures collected from over 90,000 people against the *Gender Unfug*, https://vds-ev.de/aktionen/aufrufe/schluss-mit-gender-unfug/
[20] Guentherodt et al., "Richtlinien zur Vermeidung sexistischen Sprachgebrauchs," 15–21; Gabriele Diewald and Anja Steinhauer, *Gendern – Ganz einfach!* (Berlin: Duden, 2019).
[21] For information on their use in formal written registers, see Bußmann and Hellinger, "Engendering Female Visibility in German;" Victoria Lamb and Filippo Nereo, "Equality amongst citizens? A study of how the German basic law and the German version of the Swiss constitution exhibit and avoid sexist language," 109–126; Franziska Moser and Bettina Hannover, "How gender fair are German schoolbooks in the twenty-first century? An analysis of language and illustrations in schoolbooks for mathematics and German," *European Journal of Psychology of Education* 29, no. 3 (2014): 387-407.
[22] Stratton, "The Use of the Generic Masculine, the Derivational Morpheme -in. and Gender-Fair Innovations in Unrehearsed Spoken Dialogue in Modern Standard German," 1-52.
[23] Vernacular speech is defined as "the style in which the minimum attention is given to the monitoring of speech." (William Labov, *Sociolinguistic patterns* [Philadelphia: University of Pennsylvania Press, 1972], 208).

speakers of Modern Standard German were asked to describe eight referents in both singular and plural conditions. When describing a mixed-sex group (specifically, a stereotypical group of cisgender male and female referents), responses fell into three categories: the generic masculine (e.g. *die Lehrer* 'the teachers'), a gender-neutral variant (e.g. *die Lehrkraft* 'teaching force'), and a gender-fair variant (e.g. *Lehrerinnen und Lehrer* 'female teachers and male teachers').[24] Except for the female singular condition, the generic masculine was the preferred variant, suggesting that the use of more gender-inclusive language is register-specific and is, therefore, rarely used in unrehearsed informal spoken German. The present study builds on this previous study by adding new data and taking a different methodological approach, namely variationist sociolinguistic methods.

Methodology

Participant profiles

The corpus for the present study consists of 48 speakers of Federal and Swiss Standard German (23 from Germany, 25 from Switzerland). Speakers from Germany came from an East Frisian speech community (Westoverledingen, Lower Saxony) and speakers from Switzerland lived in the Basel speech community. Stratified sampling was carried out where possible to keep the age and sex of the speakers proportionate. The distribution by sex and age is reported in Tables 6.1 and 6.2. For recruiting speakers younger than 18 years of age, a school from both speech communities with a comparable academic standing was selected, and stratified random sampling was carried out within the two schools. To recruit participants over the age of 18, flyers and word of mouth were used.[25]

---

[24] Gender-neutral and gender-fair language are both types of gender-inclusive language. The difference is that gender-neutral language circumvents mentioning the gender (e.g. *Lehrpersonen* 'teaching people') whereas gender-fair language includes both male and female referents in the noun phrase (e.g. *Lehrer und Lehrerinnen* 'male and female teachers'). However, gender-fair constructions are not always "gender-fair" in the sense that they do not necessarily include non-binary, intersex, or agender speakers.

[25] This study was first carried out in Germany in 2016 and was then extended to include a Swiss sample in 2017. Speakers ages 11-12 took part in the initial study in Westoverledingen (Germany), but due to recruitment problems and the structure of Swiss schools, speakers 11-12 were not included in the Swiss sample. Following the suggestion of a reviewer, to ensure comparability of age groups, data from 11–12-year-old speakers from Germany are not included in the present analysis. However, for information on 11–12-year-old speakers, please see: Stratton, "The Use of the Generic Masculine, the Derivational Morpheme -in. and Gender-Fair Innovations in Unrehearsed Spoken Dialogue in Modern Standard German," 1-52. The study was approved by the

Table 6.1: German Participant Profiles

($n = 23$)

Age	Male	Female	Total
13-15	3	3	6
16-18	3	3	6
19-39	3	3	6
40+	3	2	5
TOTAL	15	14	23

Table 6.2: Swiss Participant Profiles

($n = 25$)

Age	Male	Female	Total
13-15	3	3	6
16-18	3	3	6
19-39	3	3	6
40+	3	4	7
TOTAL	12	13	25

Design and procedure

The approximate duration of the study was 10-15 minutes. Participants were asked to describe images containing referents in four conditions: the male-only condition (e.g. *Lehrer*), the female-only condition (e.g. *Lehrerin*), the mixed-sex group condition (e.g. *Lehrerinnen und Lehrer*), and the female-only group condition (e.g. *Lehrerinnen*). However, in line with variationist sociolinguistics practices, the variable context was circumscribed to a comparable uniform context, namely the description of mixed-sex plural referents.[26] For the speakers from Germany, images were deliberately chosen to elicit a response using six target (real) lexemes (*Schüler* 'pupil,' *Lehrer* 'teacher,' *Tourist* 'tourist,'

Institutional Review Board (IRB). Participants who were minors had to receive written permission from their parents or legal guardian to participate in the study.

[26] For information on the other three conditions, see Stratton, "The Use of the Generic Masculine, the Derivational Morpheme -in. and Gender-Fair Innovations in Unrehearsed Spoken Dialogue in Modern Standard German," 1-52.

Spion 'spy,' *Bundeskanzler* 'chancellor,' *Präsident* 'president') as well as two pseudowords (*Selfiemacher* 'a selfie-taker' and *Iphoner* 'an iPhone user'). Pseudowords were included in the design to examine potential differences between established and less established words with respect to their use as gender-inclusive or gender-exclusive realizations. The pseudowords were introduced using the following verbal prompt in (2).

(2) *Viele Wörter kommen jeden Tag in die deutsche Sprache hinein. Jetzt erfinden wir zwei neue Wörter in diesem Zimmer: ein Selfiemacher und ein Iphoner (also Iphone, mit 'r' am Ende). Ein Selfiemacher ist jemand, der ein Selfie macht und ein Iphoner ist jemand, der ein Iphone benutzt. Kannst du bitte das Wort Selfiemacher/Iphoner benutzen, um die folgenden Bilder zu beschreiben.*

['Lots of words enter the German language every day. Now we're going to coin two new words right here in this room: a selfie-taker and an *iPhoner* (that's Iphone, with an 'r' on the end). A selfie-taker is someone who takes a selfie and an *iPhoner* is someone who uses an iPhone. Can you please use the words *Selfiemacher* or *Iphoner* to describe the following images.']

Because of elicitation challenges which became apparent after the initial part of the study in Germany, the target words were modified by the time this study was carried out in Switzerland (replacement words: *Schüler* 'pupil,' *Lehrer* 'teacher,' *Politiker* 'politician,' *Polizist* 'police officer,' *Soldat* 'soldier').[27] *Tourist* was removed because the images of tourists in the German sample rarely elicited a response using this target word.[28] Therefore, for the Swiss population, *Tourist* was replaced with *Polizist* 'police officer' because it is easier to elicit, but this word still ends in the morphological ending *–ist*. *Präsident* was replaced with *Soldat* because it was challenging to elicit *Präsident* in plural conditions.[29] Images of German *Bundeskanzler* were also replaced with images that were culturally relevant to the Swiss sample (thus, *Politiker* 'politician' as opposed to *Bundeskanzler* 'German federal chancellor'). The images, which were used to elicit the two original pseudowords, were used in the Swiss sample, but two additional words were also included, namely *Dabtänzer* 'someone who is

---

[27] Ibid., 20.
[28] Ibid., 20.
[29] Ibid., 18-19.

dabbing/the dab dance move' and *Schubbrettfahrer* 'someone who rides a hoverboard'; prompts for the latter two appear in (3) and (4). Additional pseudowords were included for the Swiss study because a speaker in the German sample claimed to have already heard *Selfiemacher* previously. The differences in prompts must therefore be taken into account when making comparisons between the two speech communities.

(3) *Jetzt erfinden wir (noch) ein Wort und zwar Dabtänzer. Ein Dabtänzer ist jemand, der so* (they were shown the hand movement which is used in the dance move) *tanzt.*

['Now we're going to coin a new word: *Dabtänzer*. A *Dabtänzer* is someone who does this with their hands when they dance.']

(4) *Jetzt erfinden wir (noch) ein Wort und zwar Schubbrettfahrer. Ein Schubbrettfahrer beschreibt jemanden, der mit einem Schubbrett fährt. Vielleicht haben Sie schon mal einen gesehen* (they were shown a picture). *Im Englischen heißt es ein Hoverboard.*

['Now we are going to coin yet another word, namely *Schubbrettfahrer*. A *Schubbrettfahrer* describes someone who travels by *Schubbrett*. Maybe you've seen one of these (shown an image). In English, it's called a 'hoverboard']

The image of two women taking a selfie in Figure 6.1 was used to elicit *Selfiemacherinnen* (female-only referents). Figure 6.2 shows the image of a *Dabtänzer*, that was used to elicit *Dabtänzer* (male-only referent). Participants were presented with visual stimuli (i.e. the appropriate images) one at a time, as in Figures 6.1 and 6.2, and were asked to describe what they saw. Efforts were taken to hinder speakers from discerning the study's purpose, although it was anticipated that speakers would discover its goal toward the end of the tasks. For example, the order of the images was counterbalanced for each speaker in order to minimize the chances of this occurring. After describing all images, the speakers were asked whether they had some inkling of the goal of the study. However, none of the 59 participants were able to identify its purpose.

Figure 6.1: Image R – *Zwei Selfiemacherinnen*[30]

Figure 6.2: Image T – *Ein Dabtänzer*

---

[30]As in the previous study from 2018, the images could not be included in the present publication due to copyright regulations. However, two of the images (Image R and Image T) do belong to the author and thus are reported in Figure 7.1 and 7.2. For more information on the images used, see: Stratton, "The Use of the Generic Masculine, the Derivational Morpheme -in. and Gender-Fair Innovations in Unrehearsed Spoken Dialogue in Modern Standard German," 36-38.

The linguistic variable is defined as two or more ways of saying the same thing.[31] These different ways are referred to as variants. To describe a group of mixed-sex referents, speakers of German have at least three variants at their disposal: a generic masculine variant (e.g. *die Schüler* 'the pupils'), a gender-neutral variant (e.g. *die Kinder* 'children'), and a gender-fair variant (e.g. *Schülerinnen und Schüler* 'female teachers and male teachers'). For the data analysis, each variant was coded with a number (generic = 1, gender-neutral = 2, gender-fair = 3). Coding the data in this way prepared the dataset for the distributional analysis. However, for the multivariate analysis, gender-fair and gender-neutral responses were concatenated into one level so that comparisons could be made between gender-inclusive language variants (i.e. the use of gender-neutral & gender-fair forms) and gender-exclusive language variants (i.e. the use of generic masculine forms).

In order to examine the factors conditioning the choice to use gender-inclusive versus gender-exclusive language when describing mixed-sex referents, a binary mixed effects logistic regression analysis was run in *Rbrul*.[32] The response, that is, the dependent variable, had two levels: [gender-inclusive language, gender-exclusive language]. One internal factor (morphological composition) and four external factors were run as independent variables (sex, age, education, geography). Morphological composition had three levels [*-er*, *-ist*, other], sex had two [male, female], age had four [13-15, 16-18, 19-39, 40+], geography had two [Germany, Switzerland], and education had two [higher education, no higher education].[33] Each participant was also run as a random intercept in the model to account for idiosyncratic intra-speaker variability.

Results

Distributional analysis

Table 6.3 reports the distribution of variants used to describe mixed-sex referents in the East Frisian and Basel speech communities, excluding pseudowords. The generic masculine was used over 70% of the time, followed by use of gender-neutral variants (used over 20% of the time), with gender-fair forms (e.g., *Lehrerinnen und Lehrer* 'female and male teachers') ranking the least frequent. Overall, the generic masculine was used more frequently by

---

[31] William Labov. *Sociolinguistic patterns*, 188.
[32] Daniel Johnson, "Getting off the GoldVarb standard: Introducing Rbrul for mixed-effects variable rule analysis," *Language and linguistics compass* 3, no. 1 (2009): 359-383.
[33] For MORPHOLOGICAL COMPOSITION, the endings *-at*, *-ent* and *-ion* were included in the OTHER category given that *-at* only appeared in the Swiss sample and *-ion* and *-ent* only appeared in the German sample.

speakers from East Frisia than speakers from Basel, and speakers from Basel used gender-neutral and gender-fair forms more frequently than those from East Frisia. Table 6.4 relays the distribution of the three variants used to describe mixed-sex referents using the four pseudowords. The distribution indicates that the generic masculine was almost always used when referring to or describing a mixed-sex group of *Selfiemacher, iPhoner, Dabtänzer,* and *Schubbrettfahrer.*

Table 6.3: Distribution of Variants for Describing Mixed-Sex Referents (real words)

	Generic Masc		Gender-Fair		Gender-Neutral	
	N	%	*N*	%	*N*	%
East Frisia	125/160	78	1/160	.6	34/160	21.4
Basel	84/125	71	5/125	4	31/125	25

Table 6.4: Distribution of Variants for Describing Mixed-Sex Referents (pseudowords)

	Generic Masc		Gender-Fair		Gender-Neutral	
	N	%	*N*	%	*N*	%
East Frisia	60/60	100	0/60	0	0/60	0
Basel	94/96	98	0/96	0	2/96	2

Only one instance of the *Paarform* was found in the German sample, see (5). When the speaker was informed after the study that they were the only person to use the *Paarform*, the speaker suggested that their occupation may have played a role in its use, as their occupation may have made them more sensitive to the importance of linguistic, social equality, see (6). In contrast, there were five instances of the *Paarform* used by the Swiss sample, see (7). However, in both speech communities, whenever the *Paarform* was used, it was produced by participants whose occupation may have required them to use legalese and gender-inclusive language, i.e., professions such as government and postal clerks, teachers, and lawyers. As for the use of gender-neutral forms (excluding pseudowords), these were used approximately 20% of the time when describing a mixed-sex group. For instance, to describe a group of both male and female teachers, some speakers used the gender-neutral forms *Lehrkräfte, Kollegium,* and *Lehrpersonen* 'teaching force/faculty.' In the Swiss sample, mixed-sex groups of police officers and soldiers were frequently described using gender-neutral constructions (e.g. *Polizeibeamten* 'police officials,' *Polizei* 'police,' *Polizeistreife* 'police patrol'). For the soldiers, speakers often used the gender-neutral word *Militär* 'military' as opposed to the lexical item *Soldaten* (e.g. *sie sind im Militär*). On the one hand, using *Militär* over *Soldaten* may point to some attempt to acknowledge that soldiers do not have to be cisgender men. However, on the other hand, *Soldatinnen* 'female soldiers' was never used to describe a group of female-only soldiers. Participants circumvented this word form by using the word *Militär* 'military' (e.g. *die Frauen sind im Militär* 'the women are in the military'). Since *Soldatinnen* would have been a grammatical and felicitous response, avoidance of this term may be indicative of the social expectations with respect to the roles women are stereotypically thought to perform. On the other hand, avoiding a gendered term may also suggest that speakers are acknowledging the diverse gender identities that soldiers can have.

(5) *Ich sehe Schülerinnen und Schüler*

'I see female pupils and male pupils'

(6) *Die Tatsache, dass ich Sozialarbeiter bin, spielt vielleicht eine Rolle, weil ich der Wörter bewusst bin, die ich benutze – vielleicht bewusster als andere Leute*

'The fact that I'm a social worker perhaps plays some role because I'm more aware of the words that I use – perhaps more aware than others'

(7) (a) *Ich sehe ein Klassenzimmer mit jungen Schülern und Schülerinnen*

'I see a classroom with young male pupils and female pupils'
[Basel, male, 52, insurance adjuster]

(b) *Das ist eine Versammlung von Lehrerinnen und Lehrern*

'That is a gathering of female and male teachers'
[Bern, male, 83, retired, former postal worker]

(c) *Das sind Lehrer und Lehrerinnen*

'Those are male teachers and female teachers'
[Basel, female, 53, secretary]

(d) *Das sind Lehrerinnen und Lehrer*

'Those are female teachers and male teachers'
[Basel, 52, male, teacher]

(e) Ich sehe Lehrer und Lehrerinnen. Also die Lehrkräfte

'I see male teachers and female teachers. So the faculty'
[Basel, 52, male, insurance adjuster]

The frequency of the generic masculine is plotted in apparent time in Figure 6.3. The apparent time distribution shows that younger speakers relied more frequently on the generic masculine than older speakers. In contrast, older speakers used more gender-inclusive language than younger speakers. As for gender differences, five of the six speakers who used gender-fair forms were male, but there were few differences in the use of gender-neutral language.

Figure 6.3: The Use of the Generic Masculine in Apparent Time

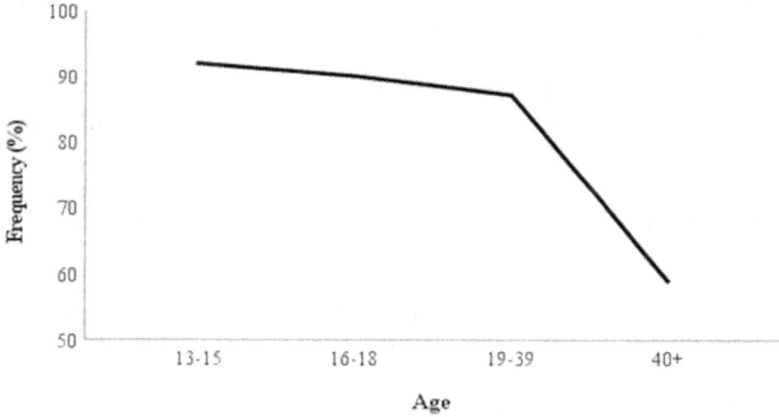

Multivariate Analysis

A logistic regression analysis was run in *Rbrul* to examine the factors influencing the use of gender-inclusive and gender-exclusive language when describing a mixed-sex group. The generic masculine (or gender-exclusive language) was run as the application value and five factors (independent variables) were included in the model: internal (morphological composition) and external (age, sex, education, geography), with speaker run as a random intercept. The output of the model, reported in Table 6.5, contains factor weights for each factor group, which range from 0-1; a numeric value closer to 1 indicates the favoring of the application value (in this case, the use of the generic masculine).

Table 6.5: Logistic Regression of Factors Conditioning Use of Generic Masculine to Describe Mixed-Sex Referents

| Input | .71 | | |
| Total N | 455 | | |
	N	%	FW
MORPHOLOGY (5.77e-06)			
-er	317	89.9	.71
-ist	54	68.5	.37
OTHER	84	72.6	.42
Range			*34*
SEX (0.211)			
Male	229	80.8	.43
Female	226	87.6	.56
Range			*13*
AGE (8.13e-11)			
13-15	158	92.4	.67
16-18	102	90.2	.60
19-39	101	89.1	.57
40+	94	58.5	.19
Range			*48*
EDUCATION (7.4e-07)			
Higher education	92	58.7	.26
No higher education	363	90.6	.73
Range			*47*
GEOGRAPHY (0.66)			
Germany	232	84.9	.51
Switzerland	223	83.4	.48
Range			*3*

Random Effect (Speakers *n* = 54)

The model found three of the five factors to be statistically significant. First, morphological composition was significant, indicating that lexical items ending in *-er* were more likely to appear in the generic masculine than lexical items containing other morphological suffixes. Second, age was significant, confirming that younger speakers used the generic masculine more frequently than older speakers, as the distributional evidence suggested. Third, education was significant, indicating that speakers with a higher level of education were less likely to use the generic masculine than speakers with jobs without higher education. In contrast, speakers with higher education used more gender-inclusive language than speakers without higher education. The range for the factor groups indicates that age (48) and education (47) had the strongest effect on the use of gender-inclusive and gender-exclusive language.

Discussion

Although the use of gender-inclusive language has become common practice in formal written and formal spoken German, little was known about its frequency in unrehearsed spoken German. To address this gap in research, the present study used variationist methods to examine its frequency relative to gender-exclusive language and to examine the factors that may influence its use or absence of use in unmonitored language. Through an elicited production task, the present study found that, despite its increase in frequency in formal registers, the generic masculine was still by far the number one variant in informal spoken German. In both the East Frisian and Basel speech communities, the generic masculine was used over 70% of the time to describe a group of mixed-sex referents. Moreover, younger speakers used the generic masculine more frequently than older speakers, potentially suggesting that the generic masculine is becoming more dominant in vernacular spoken German.[34] However, that said, gender-neutral constructions were used over 20% of the time, suggesting some linguistic awareness of the need to overtly include speakers of diverse gender identities. In contrast, gender-fair constructions, such as the so-called *Paarform*, were used rarely. On the one

---

[34] Higher frequency among younger generations can indicate language change in progress, whereas higher frequency in older cohorts typically indicates receding use. For more information, please see: William Labov, "The social motivation of a sound change," Word, 19, no. 3, (1963): 273-309; William Labov *The social stratification of English in New York City*, (Washington. D.C.: Center for Applied Linguistics, 1966); Guy Bailey, Tom Wikle, Jan Tillery, and Lori Sand, "The apparent time construct," *Language Variation and Change*, 3, no. 3, (1991): 241-264; Guy Bailey, "Real and apparent time," in *The handbook of language variation and change*, eds. Jack K. Chambers, Peter Trudgill, and Natalie Schilling-Estes. (Oxford: Blackwell, 2003), 312–332.

hand, the low frequency of binary gendered constructions could suggest that this type of language has not become a common part of the vernacular. However, on the other hand, avoiding binary gendered constructions in favor of gender-neutral constructions may suggest that speakers are aware of the issues concerning the use of binary forms in the context of non-binary, agender, or intersex speakers. Therefore, when speakers do choose to use gender-inclusive language, they opt for forms that are more gender-inclusive (i.e., gender-neutral language), and when they do not choose to use gender-inclusive language, they use the generic masculine; with binary gendered forms rarely being utilized.

In terms of absolute frequency, the generic masculine was used less frequently in Basel than in East Frisia, and gender-inclusive language occurred more frequently in Basel than East Frisia. By itself, this finding could suggest that urbanity is having some effect on the use of gendered language. As one might expect, speakers in urban environments may have a higher level of awareness of the issues concerning the use of the generic masculine than speakers in (semi-)rural environments; urban planes have larger populations, which could mean more diversity and thus the need for linguistic representation of a broader range of groups. Moreover, urban environments house more formal professions, which, in turn, means speakers may be more accustomed to formal language. However, contrary to these hypotheses, geography was not identified as a statistically significant factor. Instead, linguistic (morphological composition) and social factors (age and education) were identified as significantly influencing gendered language.

In terms of age, older speakers used gender-inclusive language at a significantly higher frequency than younger speakers. One possible explanation may be that the movement toward using prescriptive gender-inclusive linguistic forms has been ongoing for quite some time, meaning that older speakers are likely to have had longer exposure to this type of language than younger speakers, specifically insofar as the inclusion of cisgender women is concerned.[35] Only

---

[35] It should be noted, however, that attempts have been made to employ gender-neutral strategies throughout the history of Germanic and despite recent innovations, such attempts are not a recent phenomenon. For instance, Gothic had *frauja* 'lord' which surfaces as *frō* 'lord' and *frouwa* 'woman' in Old High German, where only the latter lives on today in Modern Standard German (other than in retentions such as *Fronleichnam* 'lord's body'). The fact *Frau* 'woman' has become more common than the masculine counterpart points toward the change in social roles over time. Similarly, Old English had *man* which had both a generic masculine and non-generic masculine interpretation, but *wer* 'man' and *wif* 'woman' were available for disambiguating the two (note that *wer* only remains in retentions such as *werewolf* but *wif* remains as *wife* having undergone semantic narrowing). However, due to the Anglo-Saxon patriarchal society, *wer* 'man' was

six of the 48 speakers used the *Paarform* to describe a group of seemingly male and female referents. The fact that all six speakers were over the age of 50 suggests that age plays an important role in its use. However, it is likely that age is interfering with education, as speakers with higher education (i.e., those in the 19-39 age category or above) were found to use more gender-inclusive language than speakers without higher education (i.e., below the age of 19). Since speakers in the 13-15 and 16-18 age groups were still in secondary education, age is flagged as a factor even though it is likely education that is conditioning the use of gender-inclusive language.

With respect to education, and in part, occupation, all speakers who used gender-fair language had higher education and worked in some official formal capacity, which arguably required them to use or be exposed to gender-inclusive language regularly, as evidenced in the example in (6). Although speakers who had less formal and arguably blue-collar professions (e.g., baker, construction worker) were found using some gender-neutral forms (e.g., *Leute* 'people'), more specialized choices (such as *Lehrkräfte* 'teaching force,' *Polizeibeamte* 'police official') were reserved to the speech of speakers who were highly educated and held white-collar jobs. This finding is in line with Sczesny, Moser & Wood, who found that the use of gender-inclusive language is "a product of both deliberate and habitual factors."[36] In other words, speakers who are regularly exposed to gender-fair and gender-neutral language are more likely to internalize these forms and use them in vernacular speech. That is not to say that speakers without higher education and formal professions never use gender-inclusive language but there is a correlation between the use of gender-inclusive language and a speaker's education level, and thus, in turn, often occupation. Because of the relationship between education and prescriptivism, it seems only natural that a speaker's education would play a role in the use of prescriptively imposed gender-inclusive language. Moreover, given that administrative and higher educational settings are loci in which gender-inclusive guidelines have been promoted, it is also not

---

still used in arguably sexist ways in Old English (e.g., *werleas* 'unmarried' - literally 'man-less'). For more information on the history of *man* and *wer* in English, see Stratton (2023). The derivational suffix –*in* was also used in Old High German for overtly marking female referents (e.g., *friuntin* 'female friend'). To provide one more example, unlike Old English, Old Norse plural articles were declined for gender (*þeir* 'masculine plural', *þær* 'feminine plural', *þau* 'neuter plural'), and the neuter plural was often used when referring to a group of both male and female referents.
[36] Ibid.

surprising that speakers being educated or working in these settings use this type of language most frequently.

Although register was not included as a factor in the quantitative analysis, a comparison of the present results with the reported frequency of gender-inclusive language in formal registers suggests that register is a factor conditioning the use of gendered language in Federal and Swiss Standard German. After all, when writing, speakers have the time to monitor or edit their speech consciously so that it conforms with gender-inclusive guidelines, a statement which is also true for rehearsed spoken language. In contrast, in unrehearsed speech, speakers do not have this luxury. Despite the significant progress toward using gender-inclusive language in written registers, the present study indicates that gender-inclusive language is rarely used when little to no monitoring occurs. Studies on gender-inclusive forms in formal written language have found that the generic masculine is still used more frequently than gender-fair and gender-neutral forms.[37]

Despite the evidence of the use of some gender-neutral language, the overall low frequency of gender-inclusive language may be indicative of the limited effects of prescriptivism on naturally occurring speech, as prescriptivism is known to have a larger effect on written language than vernacular language.[38] Many examples of the failings of prescriptivism on naturally occurring speech are observable, such as the prescribed attempt to remove double negation in English, which still nevertheless appears in the vernacular.[39] The prescribed pronunciation of the <ch> digraph in Federal Standard German is another example, which has many regional realizations which do not conform to the

---

[37] See for instance, Sabine Sczesny, Franzisker Moser and Wendy Wood, "Beyond sexist beliefs: How do people decide to use gender-inclusiv language?" *Personality and Social Psychology Bulletin*, 41, no. 7, (2015), 952.

[38] For work on the effects of prescriptivism in English, please see: Anita Auer, "University of Leiden Precept and Practice: The Influence of Prescriptivism on the English Subjunctive," in *Syntax, style and grammatical norms: English from 1500-2000*, ed. by D. Kastovsky (Berne: Peter Lang, 2006), 33-54; David Crystal, *The Fight for English: How language pundits are, shot, and left*, (Oxford University Press, 2006). For French, please see: Shana Poplack and Nathalie Dion, "Prescription vs. praxis. The evolution of future temporal reference in French," *Language* 58, no. 3 (2009): 557-587; Lieselotte Anderwald, *Language Between Description and Prescription. Verbs and Verb Categories in Nineteenth-Century Grammars of English*, (Oxford, Oxford University Press, 2016).

[39] Walt Wolfram and Natalie Schilling Estes, *American English: Dialects and Variation*, 3rd ed. (Oxford: Blackwell, 2015), 47-48.

standard.[40] Even if prescriptive rules are monitored in written language, in unmonitored speech, the true vernacular surfaces, and efforts to suppress such language can often result in hypercorrection. For instance, speakers of German who pronounce <ch> as a postalveolar fricative following front vowels as opposed to the palatal fricative make a conscious effort to replace their vernacular pronunciation with the prescribed (palatal) pronunciation. However, this prescribed self-monitoring often results in hypercorrection (e.g. *komisch* 'strange' [komɪʃ] becomes [komɪç]).

Finally, to examine whether novel words are more propitious to the process of *gendern* 'gendering,' four pseudowords were included in the study. The study found that speakers were less likely to realize the pseudowords in a gender-inclusive format than real words. No speakers attempted to use the pseudowords in a gender-fair format (e.g. *sie sind Selfiemacher und Selfiemacherinnen* 'they are male and female selfie-takers'), which provides additional support for the fact that gender-inclusive language has made little imprint on unmonitored speech production. While speakers have the linguistic capacity and resources to use novel words in a gender-inclusive way, speakers almost always realized them using the generic masculine. Given that older speakers used more gender-inclusive language than younger speakers, the results from the pseudowords words bring into question whether duration of exposure to the stimuli (i.e., the words) is a contributing factor. Since speakers had just encountered the words, despite having the linguistic resources to use them in gender-inclusive ways, such a process likely takes monitoring and therefore necessitates time.

Conclusion

Over the last five decades, several innovations have entered the German language as a result of feminist and LGBTQIA+ advocacy work. However, despite frequently occurring in formal discourse, little was known about the extent to which gender-inclusive language has been adopted in German vernacular speech. The present study tapped into this question using variationist sociolinguistic methods. Results indicated that with the exception of some gender-neutral constructions, overall, gender-inclusive language was rarely used in unrehearsed spoken German. Instead, the generic masculine was the norm. Although speculative, I see three possible explanations for the limited integration of gender-inclusive language in unmonitored speech.

---

[40] Please see: Joachim Herrgen, *Koronalisierung und Hyperkorrektion. Das palatale Allophon des /CH/-Phonems und seine Variation im Westmitteldeutschen.* (Stuttgart: Franz Steiner, 1986).

First, the absence of gender-inclusive constructions may not reflect disinterest toward gender equality social movements but rather a general product of ideologically-driven prescriptive attempts to change a language that speakers have already naturally acquired. Although prescriptivism can have an impact on written and prepared speech due to the time available for monitoring, when speakers have little to no time to monitor their speech, the vernacular is uttered, which, in the case of the present study, results in the output of the generic masculine.

However, on the other hand, there are two more optimistic explanations for the absence or low frequency of gender-inclusive language in vernacular speech. On the one hand, it is possible that progress toward gender equality has been so dramatic in different domains of society that the need for gender-inclusive language outside of legal and formal settings has been unnecessary. On the other hand, forms such as the *Paarform* (e.g. *Lehrerinnen und Lehrer* 'female and male teachers') may occur at a low frequency in everyday vernacular spoken German because speakers feel it is inadequate. Instead of using binary gendered forms, they turn to gender-neutral constructions to cater to a larger diverse group of identities. Nevertheless, even though gender-neutral language can be found in everyday spoken German, the generic masculine still prevails, suggesting that prescriptivism has had less effort on the vernacular than on writing.

Even though gender-inclusive language was rarely found in German vernacular speech, on the few occasions it was used its use was influenced by linguistic and social factors. First, words with particular morphological endings were found to be more amenable to being realized as a gender-inclusive form than others. Second, older speakers were found to be more likely to use gender-inclusive language than younger speakers, and finally, speakers with higher education were found to be more likely to use gender-inclusive language than speakers without higher education. Although, in terms of absolute frequency, the speakers from Switzerland used gender-inclusive language more frequently than the speakers from Germany, this difference was not statistically significant.

This latter finding is important in the larger context of German sociolinguistics since traditionally, geography has been referenced as one of the most central explanatory factors influencing German variation and change.[41] However, at least in terms of the two speech communities sampled in the present study, geography played less of a role, whereas social factors such as education had a larger effect. Therefore, a broader contribution of the present study is the finding that factors other than geography condition and constrain German

---

[41] For a list of studies on geography, see Stratton, "Tapping into German Adjective Variability: A Variationist Sociolinguistic Approach," *Journal of Germanic Linguistics*, 63-101.

variation and change, a finding which is in line with recent variationist work on German.[42] The higher weighting of the effects of social factors over geography on the use of the generic masculine is not entirely surprising given the social nature tied to the importance of linguistic gender equality movements.

The goal of these studies is not to downplay or de-emphasize the role of geography as a conditioning factor since geography has inevitably played a crucial role in German dialectology.[43] However, instead, the point is that a common finding which emerges from these studies is that other factors, both linguistic and social, also operate on various aspects of German variation and change. Awareness of this finding could pave the way for future research on the social correlates of German variation and change.

Bibliography

Acke, Hanna. "Sprachwandel durch feministische Sprachkritik." *Zeitschrift für Literaturwissenschaft und Linguistik*, 49, no. 2, (2019): 303-320.

Anderwald, Lieselotte. *Language Between Description and Prescription. Verbs and Verb Categories in Nineteenth-Century Grammars of English*. Oxford, Oxford University Press, 2016.

Auer, Anita. "University of Leiden Precept and Practice: The Influence of Prescriptivism on the English Subjunctive." In *Syntax, style and grammatical norms: English from 1500-2000*, edited by D. Kastovsky, 33-54. Berne: Peter Lang, 2006.

Bailey, Guy, Tom Wikle, Jan Tillery, and Lori Sand. "The apparent time construct." *Language Variation and Change*, 3, no. 3, (1991): 241-264.

———. "Real and apparent time." In *The Handbook of Language Variation and Change*, edited by Jack K. Chambers, Peter Trudgill and Natalie Schilling-Estes, 312-332. Oxford: Blackwell, 2003.

Beaman, Karen. "Swabian relatives: Variation in the use of the wo-relativiser." In *Advancing Socio-grammatical Variation and Change*, edited by Karen V. Beaman, Isabelle Buchstaller, Sue Fox, James A. Walker, 134-164. New York: Routledge, 2021.

Braun Friederike, Anja Gottburgsen, Sabine Sczesny, and Dagmar Stahlberg. "Können Geophysiker Frauen sein? Generische Personenbezeichnungen im Deutschen." *Zeitschrift für germanistische Linguistik*, 26, no. 3, (1998): 265-283.

Braun Friederike, Sabine Sczesny, and Dagmar Stahlberg. "Cognitive effects of masculine generics in German: An overview of empirical findings." *Communications*, 30, (2005): 1–21.

Busse, Ulrich, and Anne Schroeder. "Problem areas of English grammar between usage, norm, and variation." In *Grammar between Norm and*

---

[42] Ibid.; James Stratton, "Adjective Intensifiers in German," 183-215; Karen Beaman, "Swabian Relatives: Variation in the Use of the wo-relativiser," 134-164.

[43] Stratton, "Tapping into German Adjective Variability: A Variationist Sociolinguistic Approach," 63-101.

Variation, edited Alexandra Lenz and Albrecht Plewnia, 87-102. Frankfurt: Peter Lang, 2010.

Bußmann, Hadumod, and Marlis Hellinger. "Engendering Female Visibility in German." In *Gender across Languages*, edited by Marlis Hellinger and Hadumod Bußmann, 141-174. Amsterdam and Philadelphia, PA: John Benjamins, 2003.

Bülow, Lars, Andrin Büchler, Nicolai Timon Rawyler, Christa Schneider, and David Britain. "Linguistic, social, and individual factors constraining variation in spoken Swiss Standard German." In *Intra-individual Variation in Language*, edited by Alexander Werth, Lars Bülow, Simon E. Pfenninger and Markus Schiegg, 127–173. Berlin: De Gruyter Mouton, 2021.

Crystal, David. *The Fight for English: How language pundits ate, shot, and left.* Oxford University Press, 2006.

Días Castillo, Estrella. "Der Genus/Sexus-Konflikt und das generische Maskulinum in der deutschen Gegenwartssprache." PhD diss., University of Passau, 2003). Accessed May 1, 2017. https://opus4.kobv.de/opus4-uni-passau/files/33/ECastillo.pdf

Diewald, Gabriele, and Anja Steinhauer. *Gendern – Ganz einfach!* Berlin: Duden, 2019.

Friedrich, Marcus, and Elke Heise. "Does the use of gender-fair language influence the comprehensibility of texts? An experiment using an authentic contract manipulating single role nouns and pronouns." *Swiss Journal of Psychology*, 78, no. 1-2, (2019): 51–60.

Grabrucker, Marianne. *Vater Staat hat keine Muttersprache*. Frankfurt: Fischer, 1993.

Guentherodt, Ingrid, Marlis Hellinger, Luise Pusch F., and Senta Trömel-Plötz. "Richtlinien zur Vermeidung sexistischen Sprachgebrauchs." *Linguistische Berichte*, 69, (1980): 15–21.

Herrgen, Joachim. *Koronalisierung und Hyperkorrektion. Das palatale Allophon des /CH/-Phonems und seine Variation im Westmitteldeutschen.* Stuttgart: Franz Steiner, 1986.

Horvath, Lisa, and Sabine Sczesny. "Reducing the lack of fit for women with leadership positions? Effects of the wording in job advertisements." *European Journal of Work and Organizational Psychology* 25, no. 2, (2015): 316-328.

Johnson, Daniel, E. "Getting off the GoldVarb standard: Introducing Rbrul for mixed-effects variable rule analysis." *Language and linguistics compass* 3, no. 1 (2009): 359-383.

Kalverkämper, Hartwig. (1979). "Die Frauen und die Sprache." *Linguistische Berichte* 62, (1979): 55-71.

Labov, William. "The social motivation of a sound change." *Word*, 19, no. 3, (1963): 273-309.

———. *Sociolinguistic patterns*. Philadelphia: University of Pennsylvania Press, 1972.

———. *The social stratification of English in New York City*. Washington. D.C.: Center for Applied Linguistics, 1966.

Lamb, Victoria, and Filippo Nereo. "Equality amongst citizens? A study of how the German basic law and the German version of the Swiss constitution exhibit and avoid sexist language." *German Life and Letters* 65, no. 1, (2012): 109–126.

Moser, Franziska, and Bettina Hannover. (2014). "How gender fair are German schoolbooks in the twenty-first century? An analysis of language and illustrations in schoolbooks for mathematics and German." *European Journal of Psychology of Education* 29, no. 3 (2014): 387–407.

Poplack, Shana, and Nathalie Dion. "Prescription vs. praxis. The evolution of future temporal reference in French." *Language*, 58, no. 3, (2009): 557-587.

Pusch, Luise F. "Der Mensch ist ein Gewohnheitstier, doch weiter kommt man ohne ihr." *Linguistische Berichte* 63, (1979): 84–101.

———. *Die Frau ist nicht der Rede wert*. Frankfurt am Main: Suhrkamp, 1999.

———. "Das Gender-Sternchen ist nicht die Lösung." https://www.jetzt.de/hauptsache-gendern/gendern-linguistin-luise-f-pusch-ueber-das-gendersternchen-und-geschlechtergerechte-sprache

Sczesny, Sabine, Magdalena Formanowicz, and Franziska Moser. "Can Gender-Fair Language Reduce Gender Stereotyping and Discrimination?" *Frontiers in Psychology*, 7, (2016): 1-11.

———, Franziska Moser, and Wendy Wood. "Beyond sexist beliefs: How do people decide to use gender-inclusive language?" *Personality and Social Psychology Bulletin*, 41, no. 7, (2015): 943-954.

Stahlberg, Dagmar, Friederike Braun, Lisa Irmen, and Sabine Sczesny. "Representation of the sexes in language." In *Social Communication*, edited by Klaus Fiedler, 163-187 (New York: Psychology Press, 2007).

Stefanowitsch, Anatol. "Gendergap und Gendersternchen in der gesprochenen Sprache." Written in 2018.http://www.sprachlog.de/2018/06/09/gendergap-und-gendersternchen-in-der-gesprochenen-sprache/

Stratton, James. "The Use of the Generic Masculine, the Derivational Morpheme -in. and Gender-Fair Innovations in Unrehearsed Spoken Dialogue in Modern Standard German." *Interdisciplinary Journal for Germanic Linguistics and Semiotic Analysis* 23, no. 1, (2018): 1-52.

———. Adjective Intensifiers in German. *Journal of Germanic Linguistics*, 32, no. 2, (2020): 183-215.

———. Tapping into German Adjective Variability: A Variationist Sociolinguistic Approach. *Journal of Germanic Linguistics*, 34, no. 1 (2022): 63-101.

———. Where did wer go? Lexical variation and change in third-person male adult noun referents in Old and Middle English. *Language Variation and Change*, no. 35 (2023): 199-221.

Stratton, James, and Karen Beaman. *Expanding Variationist Sociolinguistic Research in Varieties of German*. London: Routledge, 2024.

Trömel-Plötz, Senta. *Linguistik und Frauensprache*. Frankfurt am Main: Fischer Taschenbuch Verlag, 1978.

Whorf, Benjamin. *Language, thought, and reality: Selected writings*. J. B. Carroll (Ed.), Cambridge, Mass: Technology Press of Massachusetts Institute of Technology, 1956.

Wolfram, Walt, and Natalie Schilling Estes. *American English: Dialects and Variation*. (3rd ed.). Oxford: Blackwell, 2015.

Chapter 7

Dialect contact and language death: Morphological leveling in an Indiana German heritage variety

Karen Rösch
Indiana University - Purdue University in Indianapolis

Abstract: Case syncretism in German-American heritage varieties and its contributing factors have been the subject of much research in past decades, e.g., Gilbert (1972) on Texas German, Huffines (1989) on Pennsylvania German, Keel (1994) on Kansas Volga German. However, Indiana German has received little scholarly attention over the past thirty years. Salmons' incisive 1986 article, *Hoosiers* Do *Speak German,* issues a call for much-needed research in this state which results in two detailed studies documenting linguistic features in Indiana German. This study is the first to revisit the Jasper-Ferdinand (JF) variety in almost three decades based on new data collected by this author between 2015 and 2017.

Freeouf's (1990) Jasper-Ferdinand data collected in Dubois County, Indiana, provides a rich source of antecedent data in order to establish further reduction of case marking in the noun phrase (NP) for this last generation of JF speakers. In his 1990 study, he notes "an apparent tendency toward a one-case system in the NP in J-F (1990: 181)," i.e., a system marked by nominative forms, as indicated in Examples (1) and (2). Representative 2017 samples are shown below Freeouf's 1990 data.

2017 datasets are from fifteen (15) fluent and semi-fluent speakers in order to provide the most accurate account of these varieties as they are currently spoken. The focus in this analysis is on determiner markings in the NP, i.e., definite and indefinite articles and possessive determiners. A shared methodology in data collection strengthens the analysis of this comparative study: both Freeouf's and this study utilize Gilbert's (1963) translation tasks and open-ended interview techniques.

This article first provides an overview of past research on case marking in three U.S. German varieties and in Indiana German, followed by a brief description of the Indiana German Dialect Project and its methods. Following Freeouf's methodology, I subsequently present and analyze fifteen (15) 2017 JF re-samplings of Gilbert's (1963) translation tasks and/or narrative samples in four syntactic environments. I conclude with a discussion of possible internal and external factors influencing leveling of the JF case system.

Keywords: Heritage German; Case Syncretism; Indiana German dialect project; sociolinguistics

***

1. Introduction

Case syncretism, or the merging or leveling of multiple cases into a single form, in German-American heritage varieties and contributing factors have been the subject of much research in previous decades on Texas German, Pennsylvania German, and Kansas Volga German.[1] German-American heritage varieties refer

---

[1] Unless otherwise noted with page numbers, all citations in this chapter refer to complete studies and their content. For Texas German, see Glenn Gilbert, *Linguistic Atlas of Texas German* (Austin: University of Texas Press, 1972) and Hans Boas, "Case Loss in Texas German: The Influence of Semantic and Pragmatic Factors," ed. Johanna Barðdal and Shobhana L. Chelliah (Amsterdam; Philadelphia: John Benjamins, 2009). For Pennsylvania German, see Marion Lois Huffines, "The Dative Case of Pennsylvania German: Diverging Norms in Maintenance and Loss," in *Yearbook of German-American Studies*, ed. William Keel, 22 (Kansas: Lawrence State UP, 1987), 173–81; as well as her book chapter "Case Usage among the Pennsylvania German Sectarians and Nonsectarians," in *Investigating Obsolescence: Studies in Language Contraction and Death*, ed. Nancy Dorian (Cambridge: Cambridge University Press, 1989), 211–26. Seiler has also conducted a study on Swiss German varieties in Adams County in Indiana, see Guido Seiler, "If Dialects Are Languages, Then Dialect Contact Is Language Contact: To the Amish 'Schwitzer' in Adams County (Indiana, USA)," *Zeitschrift Für Dialektologie Und Linguistik* 84 (2017): 202–31. For Kansas Volga German, see William Keel, "Reduction and Loss of Case Marking in the Noun Phrase in German-American Speech Islands: Internal Development or External Interference?," in *Sprachinselforschung: Eine Gedenkschrift Für Hugo Jedig*, ed. Nina Berend and Klaus Mattheier (Frankfurt: Peter Lang, 1994), 93–104; also note his book chapter "German Settlement Varieties in Kansas: Some Unusual Phonological and Morphological Developments with the Approach of Language Death,"

to the German varieties (i.e. local and regional dialects) spoken in early German settlements established in the U.S. in the nineteenth century. Most of these German heritage varieties are now endangered, with the exception of Pennsylvania German, but there are still small pockets throughout the U.S. where "the old German" is spoken by aging speakers.

This chapter presents a synchronic look (i.e. in today's time and space) at an endangered German heritage language spoken in southwestern Indiana and situates this variety and its aging speakers within the cultural, social, and historical framework of their childhood and adulthood through their tales of yesteryear—times when their language and community were vibrant and uniquely German. This study offers a unique perspective within the field of philology that presents new possibilities for research and study of moribund and endangered languages (cf. also 5.0 for a description of data collection methods).

German heritage varieties in Indiana have received little scholarly attention in the past thirty years. Salmons' incisive article, *Hoosiers* Do *Speak German*,[2] issued a call for much-needed research in Indiana that resulted in two studies documenting sociolinguistic and linguistic features of two Indiana German heritage varieties: 1) a study conducted by Freeouf documenting a possible "Franconian-type koiné"[3] of western middle and upper German varieties which he terms Jasper-Ferdinand *Daitsch* (hereafter J-F),[4] so named after the

---

in *Perspectives on Phonological Theory and Development*, ed. Ashley Farris-Trimble and Jessica Barlow (Amsterdam: John Benjamins, 2014), 155–72.

[2] Joseph Salmons, "But Hoosiers Do Speak German: An Overview of German in Indiana," ed. William Keel (Lawrence: Kansas State UP, 1986), 155–66. Salmons' own work on Indiana German concentrated mainly on register, lexicon, and descriptions of the sociohistorical and sociolinguistic contexts in the two Indiana communities of Jasper and Ferdinand. See also Joseph Salmons, "Issues in Texas German Language Maintenance and Shift," *Monatshefte* 75 (1983): 187–96; Joseph Salmons, "Register in the Formation and Evolution of an Immigrant Language: Evidence from Some Indiana German Dialects," *WORD* 42 (1991): 31–56.

[3] Peter Frank Freeouf, "Religion and Dialect: Catholic and Lutheran Dialects in the German of Dubois County" (Ph.D., Indiana, 1990), 7. Siegel defines a koiné as "a stabilized result of mixing of linguistic subsystems such as regional or literary dialects...and is characterized by a mixture of features of these varieties, most often by reduction or simplification," ("Koines and Koineization," *Language in Society* 14, no. 3 (1985): 363.

[4] Altenhofen also uses the same term for a Brazilian koiné of Middle German Franconian that its speakers term *Hunsrückisch*, see Cléo Altenhofen, "Standard Und Substandard Bei Den Hunrückern in Brasilien: Variation Und Dachsprachenwechsel Des Deutschen Im Kontakt Mit Dem Portugiesischen," in *German Abroad: Perspektiven Der*

communities in southern Indiana in which it is spoken, and 2) Nutzel's study in 2009 that documents an East Franconian variety in northern Dubois County.[5]

Using data I recorded between 2015 and 2017, my study revisits the J-F variety some 20 years later to investigate case syncretism in the J-F nominal system. My analysis here focuses on morphological leveling, i.e., the reduction or simplification of case markings in the noun phrase. This study informs research on several levels. It not only contributes to a large corpus of linguistic studies on the leveling of structural features, e.g. case marking in language contact situations associated with language shift and death in U.S. German heritage varieties, but it is also relevant to U.S. migrant languages.[6] It also contributes to a broader corpus of international research on case maintenance and loss in moribund German varieties worldwide, such as those in Russia and Brazil.[7]

I rely on Freeouf's study from 1990 as a rich source of antecedent data to ascertain the current status of case marking in the noun phrase (hereafter NP) in this last generation of speakers. I first describe the sociohistorical and sociolinguistic contexts of German heritage languages in Sections 2 and 3. An overview of past research on case marking and syncretism in the now endangered U.S. German heritage varieties follows in Section 4. Section 5 presents the methodology I used to collect samples from J-F speakers from 2015 to 2017 and Section 6 describes language use of the J-F variety today and various difficulties J-F speakers encountered during the interview process that affected data collection. Section 7 defines the scope of my study and presents

---

Variationslinguistik, Sprachkontakt- Und Mehrsprachigkeitsforschung, ed. A. Lenz (Göttingen: Vienna University Press, 2016), 103–30.

[5] Daniel Nutzel, *The East Franconian Dialect of Haysville, Indiana* (Regensburg: Edition Vulpes, 2009).

[6] See Paul Kerswill, "Dialect Levelling, Koinéisation and the Speech of the Adult Migrant," *University of Pennsylvania Working Papers in Linguistics* 3, no. 1 (1996): 1–12.

[7] See Nina Berend, "Zur Vergleichbarkeit von Sprachkontakten: Erfahrungen Aus Wolgadeutschen Sprachinseln in Den USA Und Russland," in *German Language Varieties Worldwide: Internal and External Perspectives*, ed. William Keel and Klaus Mattheier (Frankfurt: Peter Lang, 2003), 239–68; Peter Rosenberg, "Comparative Speech Island Research: Some Results from Studies in Russia and Brazil," in *German Language Varieties Worldwide: Internal and External Perspectives*, ed. William Keel and Klaus Mattheier (Frankfurst: Peter Lang, 2003), 199–238; Altenhofen, "Standard Und Substandard Bei Den Hunrückern in Brasilien: Variation Und Dachsprachenwechsel Des Deutschen Im Kontakt Mit Dem Portugiesischen"; Anne Pauwels, "Diglossia, Immigrant Dialects and Language Maintenance in Australia: The Case of Limburgs and Swabian," *Journal of Multilingual and Multi-Cultural Development*, no. 71 (1986): 13–30; Michael Clyne, *Deutsch Als Muttersprache in Australien* (Wiesbaden: Franz Steiner Verlag, 1981).

biographical information on the informant pool (e.g., fluency, year of birth, gender, etc.).

Section 8 is divided into two sub-sections that focus on my comparative analysis with Freeouf's 1990 findings on determiner markings in the NP:

8. provides samples from two Rösch 2017 fluent speakers.

8.1 is dedicated to a quantitative comparison with Freeouf's 1990 findings to Rösch's 2017 J-F re-samplings of Gilbert's translation tasks.[8]

I conclude with a discussion of potential internal and external factors influencing case leveling in the J-F varieties in Section 9 and a summary of my 2017 findings in Section 10.

2. Nineteenth Century German Immigration to the U.S.

German immigration to the U.S. in the nineteenth century (~1820 – 1890) was mainly the result of economic and political push-and-pull factors in both Central Europe and the U.S. Push factors in Germany, as in most of Central Europe, included poor harvests, famines, overpopulation, and the effects of industrialization had created untenable conditions of widespread hunger, unemployment and poverty. In addition, inheritance laws, strict economic policies of authoritarian monarchies and the failure of the 1848 Rebellion left no choice for many but to emigrate in the face of imprisonment, conscription, and death. The lure of the U.S. with its freedoms, availability of land, employment opportunities—but most importantly, the impact of letters from immigrants such as Friedrich Ernst describing America's opportunities—ignited an immigration movement to the U.S. over the span of several decades.[9] Comprised mainly of farmers, craftsmen and merchants, these immigrants brought their traditions, cultural practices and German language varieties to their new home.[10] These language varieties spanned a wide geographic area and regional varieties at a point in time when there was still no widespread use of a standardized German and included varieties that were not always mutually intelligible.[11]

---

[8] Glenn Gilbert, "The German Dialect Spoken in Kendall and Gillespie Counties, Texas" (Ph.D., Harvard, 1963).
[9] Karen Rösch, *Language Maintenance and Language Death: The Decline of Texas Alsatian* (Amsterdam: John Benjamins, 2012), 40. See also, Hans Boas, *The Life and Death of Texas German* (Durham: Duke University Press, 2009).
[10] Rösch, *Language Maintenance and Language Death: The Decline of Texas Alsatian*, 40.
[11] See Stefan Elspass, "Standard German in the 19th Century? (Counter-) Evidence from the Private Correspondence of 'Ordinary People,'" in *Standardization: Studies from the*

Apart from several Pennsylvania German varieties, most German heritage varieties in the U.S. are now experiencing the last stages of language death, as these varieties are only spoken by a small number of speakers with limited fluency over the age of 80 and were not transmitted to the younger generations.[12] Such is also the case for the J-F variety in Indiana.

3. The J-F Variety and its Linguistic Roots

The Jasper-Ferdinand area was predominantly settled by Catholic Germans from five different areas in pre-unification Germany between 1836 and 1860: the Grand Duchy of Baden, the Principality of Hesse, the Kingdoms of Bavaria, Prussia, and Hanover.[13] Jasper was established in 1818 and predominantly settled by immigrants from Pfaffenweiler in the state of Baden, Germany.[14]

Jasper is located in central Dubois County and serves as its county seat. The town of Ferdinand to its south and founded in 1840 was mainly settled by immigrants from central and north-central German areas. Both areas span a large geographic area and encompass many local and regional dialects from Upper, Middle, and Low German varieties. Examples of regional varieties range from Low Alemannic[15] (Alsatian, *Badisch,* and Bavarian) in the southwestern German territories, Rhine Franconian (Palatinate and Hessian)[16] in west-central German-speaking areas, and Low German such as Westphalian[17] in northwestern areas as illustrated in Figure 7.1.

Germanic Languages, ed. Andrew Linn and Nicola McLelland (Amsterdam: John Benjamins, 2002), 43–65.

[12] See Mark Louden, *Pennsylvania Dutch: The Story of an American Language* (Baltimore: John Hopkins UP, 2016).

[13] For reference also see Freeouf, "Religion and Dialect: Catholic and Lutheran Dialects in the German of Dubois County"; Ruth Doane, *The History of St. Ferdinand Parish, 1940-1998* (Ferdinand: Herald Print, 1998).

[14] See also Doane, *The History of St. Ferdinand Parish, 1940-1998*; George Wilson, *Wilson's History of Dubois County, Indiana: From Its Primitive Days to 1910,* 2nd ed. (Jasper: Evansville Bindery, Inc., 2000); Elfrieda Lang, "German Immigration to Dubois County, Indiana during the Nineteenth Century," *Indiana Magazine of History,* no. June (1945): 131–51.

[15] See Marthe Phillip and Arlette Bothorel-Witz, "Low Alemannic," in *The Dialects of Modern German,* ed. Charles Russ (Stanford: Stanford University Press, 1989).

[16] See W.A.I. Green, "The Dialects of the Palatinate," in *The Dialects of Modern German,* ed. Charles Russ (Stanford: Stanford University Press, 1989).

[17] See Martin Durrell, "Westphalian and Eastphalian," in *The Dialects of Modern German,* ed. Charles Russ (London: Routledge, 1989).

Figure 7.1: Dubois County Townships: Location of Jasper and Ferdinand, IN

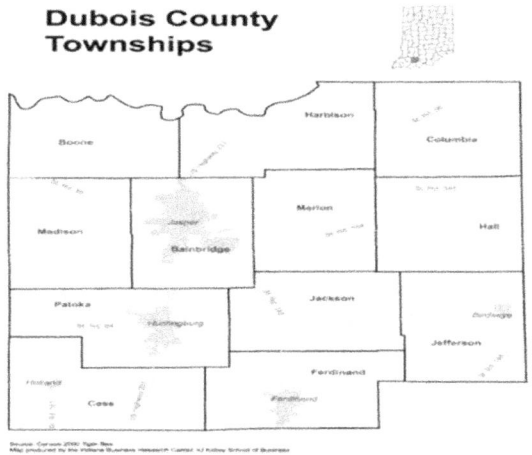

Source: Census 2000. Map produced by the IBRC atc Indiana University's Kelley School of Business; https://www.stats.indiana.edu/maptools/maps/boundary/townships_2000/dubois_township.gif

The regional language varieties brought to southern Indiana represent several types of case paradigms with different patterns of case mergers in nominal and pronominal systems[18] that make the task of identifying source dialects difficult. If one looks at the predominant case paradigm for territories clustered around the central Rhine in this area today, one finds two-case systems, i.e. a merger of the nominative and accusative (NA/D) versus an oblique form. However, this area also lies adjacent to Upper (High) German areas slightly to the east where all three cases occur.[19]

Both Freeouf and Salmons suggest that for the J-F variety, marked base dialectal features were leveled and a koiné developed that favored the prestigious Upper German varieties spoken in Jasper (first settled by families from Baden).[20] A closer examination of base dialectal features contributing to a J-F koiné would be helpful in the discussion on leveling, but due to its scope cannot be satisfactorily addressed here.

---

[18] Nominal mergers usually exhibit more reduction than the pronominal system.
[19] See Werner König, *Dtv-Atlas Zur Deutschen Sprache*, 16th ed. (Munich: Deutscher Taschenbuch Verlag, 2007).
[20] Freeouf, "Religion and Dialect: Catholic and Lutheran Dialects in the German of Dubois County"; Salmons, "Register in the Formation and Evolution of an Immigrant Language: Evidence from Some Indiana German Dialects."

4. Previous Research on Case Marking and Syncretism

Morphological leveling[21] of the case system in situations of language shift has been a topic of intense study in U.S. German heritage varieties. The focus has been on the "loss" of dative case markings and often attributed to contact-driven change (in this case, English, as well as with other German varieties). As Keel astutely points out, this rests on the assumption that these varieties possessed a more complex system before their arrival in the U.S.[22] In fact, several of the same regional varieties documented in the late 1800s and mid-1900s in Germany did exhibit a two-case system that Freeouf describes.[23]

As the scope of research on case syncretism in the nominal systems is too extensive to condense into a form that sufficiently acknowledges all past research on morphological reduction in U.S. heritage varieties, the following synopsis focuses on three varieties in addition to Indiana German: Texas German, Pennsylvania German, and Kansas Volga German. Texas and Pennsylvania German have received most of the scholarly attention in past decades, followed by German varieties in Kansas, Michigan, Wisconsin, and Iowa. Generally speaking, scholars have found the predominance of a two-case system mostly exemplified by a nominative and non-nominative distinction.

For Texas German, Eikel notes a two-case system consisting of a nominative and non-nominative in New Braunfels and determines that "the dative, it may be said, has been lost and replaced by the accusative"[24] In the 1960s, Gilbert conducts an extensive 31-county survey sampling lexical, phonological, and morphosyntactic features in Texas German varieties, the results of which he publishes in the 1972 *Linguistic Atlas of Texas German*.[25] He reports that the dative and accusative are merging into a "new" common object case generally characterized by accusative morphological markings."[26] Smaller-scale studies

---

[21] Other equivalent terms used by past scholars to describe case syncretism include morphological *reduction, simplification* and *loss* of case.
[22] Keel, "Reduction and Loss of Case Marking in the Noun Phrase in German-American Speech Islands: Internal Development or External Interference?," 96.
[23] Freeouf, "Religion and Dialect: Catholic and Lutheran Dialects in the German of Dubois County"; also see Martha Schrier, "Case Systems in German Dialects," *Language and Linguistics Compass* 41 (1965): 420–38.
[24] Fred Eikel, "The Use of Cases in New Braunfels German," *American Speech*, no. 24 (1949): 279.
[25] Glenn Gilbert, "English Loanwords in the German of Fredericksburg, Texas," *American Speech* 40 (1965): 102–12; Gilbert's *Linguistic Atlas of Texas German* made little distinction between German varieties in his analysis but did reference regional varieties such as Alsatian and Low German in his field notes on informants.
[26] Gilbert, "English Loanwords in the German of Fredericksburg, Texas," 109.

on case marking in Texas German varieties include Salmons, Guion, and Boas, who report similar tendencies toward a common oblique case.[27] Sixty years after Eikel's study, Boas conducts two studies--one large-scale, area-specific study of New Braunfels Texas German and another smaller study using data from the Texas German Dialect Archive (TGDA).[28] He notes a significant decline in dative case markings and attributes this mainly to internal processes of leveling and external factors of dialect contact and language shift.

For Pennsylvania German (PG), Louden and Huffines find reduction in both the nominal and pronominal systems in the speech of PG speakers.[29] Specifically, Huffines finds that, contrary to expectations, conservative sectarians who spoke little English produced far fewer dative-case markings than non-sectarians.[30] She therefore concludes that the external influence of English does not play an important role in the reduction of dative case markings. This is in accord with Rosenberg's findings on German speech islands in Russia, who found pronounced evidence of case reduction in these varieties despite intense contact with the Russian six-case system.[31]

For Kansas German, Keel defines a two-case system for the definite article in the nominal system of the Volga German variety in Ellis County.[32] Berend finds

---

[27] Salmons, "Issues in Texas German Language Maintenance and Shift"; Susan Guion, "The Death of Texas German in Gillespie County," in *Language Contact across the North Atlantic*, ed. P.S. Ureland and Clarkson (Tübingen: Niemeyer, 1996), 443–63; Hans Boas, "Tracing Dialect Death. The Texas German Dialect Project," in *Proceedings of the Twenty-Eighth Annual Meeting of the Berkeley Linguistics Society, February 15-18, 2002*, ed. Julie Larson and Mary Paster (Berkeley: Berkeley Linguistics Society, 2003), 387–98.
[28] Eikel, "The Use of Cases in New Braunfels German"; Boas, *The Life and Death of Texas German*; Boas, "Case Loss in Texas German: The Influence of Semantic and Pragmatic Factors."
[29] See Louden, *Pennsylvania Dutch: The Story of an American Language*; Huffines, "Case Usage among the Pennsylvania German Sectarians and Nonsectarians." Reed, however, finds a two-case distinction between a common and dative case in Lehigh and Berks County (Carroll E. Reed, *The Pennsylvania German Dialect Spoken in the Counties of Lehigh and Berks* [Seattle: University of Washington Press, 1949], 46).
[30] Huffines, "Case Usage among the Pennsylvania German Sectarians and Nonsectarians." Sectarian members live in a tight, closed (usually rural) community, whereas non-sectarians live in integrated open communities (usually urban) where English is the dominant language.
[31] Peter Rosenberg, "Vergleichende Sprachinselforschung: Sprachwandel in Deutschen Sprachinseln in Russland Und Brasilien," *Linguistik Online* 13, no. 1 (April 14, 2013): 288, http://dx.doi.org/10.13092/lo.13.881. See also Putnam (2003) for a discussion on a common oblique case in German-American dialects.
[32] William Keel, "On the Heimatbestimmung of the Ellis County (Kansas) Volga German Dialects," *Yearbook of German-American Studies* 17 (1982): 99–109.

a *Kasusmischung* in Volga German, e.g., a nominative versus oblique marking in the masculine, but a feminine demonstrative pronoun that retains its dative marking.[33] Khramova also finds a two-case system in the Volga German of Russell County, but one consisting of a merger of the nominative and accusative (i.e. a common oblique case).[34]

For Indiana German, initial research and analysis of German heritage varieties concentrates on register, lexicon, and descriptions of sociohistorical and sociolinguistic contexts in Dubois County.[35] Salmons later notes a "third significant variety, Westphalian Low German, spoken by far fewer, mostly older people scattered across the southwestern part of the county, including some in Ferdinand."[36] Nutzel's study centers on the moribund East Franconian variety spoken in Haysville in northern Dubois County, where he finds preservation of a two-case system with a nominative versus oblique distinction in the NP.[37]

Freeouf's dissertation study "Religion and Dialect" centers on religious social networks in Dubois County and their role in preserving the Franconian J-F variety of Indiana German. He describes a three-case pronominal system and a two-case nominal system with sporadic occurrences of dative case marking. Furthermore, he notes significant reduction in masculine accusative markings in the NP (shown after each example, i.e. (nom), which leads him to posit a possible collapse of the nominative and accusative into a common case marked by nominative forms. Freeouf notes that the J-F variety is closer to written Standard German (hereafter, SG) than the Haysville variety to the north.[38]

I replicate his four samples of substantiating data for nominative marking in Freeouf's four SG accusative and dative case environments in Examples (1) – (4) as shown in Figure 7.2 to set the stage for my analysis in Section 8. I do not compare my results with the SG form as Freeouf does, but instead utilize

---

[33] Berend, "Zur Vergleichbarkeit von Sprachkontakten: Erfahrungen Aus Wolgadeutschen Sprachinseln in Den USA Und Russland."

[34] Maria Khramova, "The Volga German Dialect of Millberger" (Ph.D., Kansas, 2011). For Texas Alsatian, Rösch traces this NA/D paradigm back to the base dialects of the speakers and establishes maintenance of the original pattern in current-day speakers in *Language Maintenance and Language Death: The Decline of Texas Alsatian* (2012).

[35] See Salmons, "But Hoosiers Do Speak German: An Overview of German in Indiana"; Salmons, "Register in the Formation and Evolution of an Immigrant Language: Evidence from Some Indiana German Dialects."

[36] Salmons, "Register in the Formation and Evolution of an Immigrant Language: Evidence from Some Indiana German Dialects," 35.

[37] Nutzel, *The East Franconian Dialect of Haysville, Indiana*, 124.

[38] Freeouf, "Religion and Dialect: Catholic and Lutheran Dialects in the German of Dubois County," 43–44.

Dialect contact and language death 147

Freeouf's 1990 descriptions of the J-F determiner system as the basis for the analysis of my 2017 J-F data as shown in Figure 7.2.

Figure 7.2: Occurrence of Nominative Forms in SG Accusative and Dative Contexts

Example (1): Direct objects (SG accusative)[39]
    a.   [dɛr hunt hat <u>dɛr be:sə man</u> gəbɪsə] (nom)
          'the dog bit that bad man'
    b.   [had <u>ə juŋər man</u> khat] (nom) @
          'he had a young man'

Example (2): Indirect or intransitive objects (SG dative)
    a.   [gɛp <u>di ku:</u> əmɔl ə bɪ̈səl hai] (nom)
          'give the cow a little hay'
    b.   [gɛp əmɔl <u>di andərə bu:bə ən me:dlə</u> ə bɪ̈səl gɛlt] (nom)
          'give the other boys and girls some money'

Example (3): Prepositional objects (SG accusative or dative)
    a.   [iç hap ɛtwas <u>ın mai lingəs aux</u>] (nom)
          'I have something in my left eye'
    b.   [ɛr fɔ:rt je:dər dɔ:x <u>tsu di štat</u>] (nom)
          'he drives to the city every day'

Example (4): possessive determiners (SG dative)[40]
    a.   [<u>mai</u> fadər sai ʃpro:x] @ (nom)
          'my father's language'
    b.   [<u>dem</u> ɛdgər sainə frau] (dat precedes nom)
          'Edgar's wife'

Freeouf's also provides additional sets of NP examples showing occurrences of accusative and dative case marking, as in [dɛn.MASC.ACC naiə fadər] 'the new priest (father),' [ım.NEUT.DAT haus] 'in the house,' and [dɛm.MASC.DAT sai eŋlıʃ] 'his English.'

---

[39] Translation, underlining and case notations in parentheses in these examples are Freeouf's (1990) notations; he used @ to denote a narrative example versus a Gilbert (1963) translation task. Source for Figure 7.2. is Freeouf, "Religion and Dialect: Catholic and Lutheran Dialects in the German of Dubois County," 77-79.

[40] Example (4) shows a possessive periphrastic construction usually expressed with DAT.DET + Possessor + Possessed occurs in many dialects, but which is unacceptable in SG. SG prescribes genitive case marking with articles *des/eines* and *der/einer* in a reversed positioning of Possessed + GEN.DET + Possessor.

5. Rösch 2015 - 2017 Data Collection Methods

I established the IUPUI[41] Indiana German Dialect Project (IGDP)[42] as Principal Investigator in January 2015 for the purpose of

1) documenting and preserving endangered Indiana German heritage varieties,

2) collecting phonological, morphological, and lexical data necessary to the analysis of various linguistic features for researchers, and

3) collecting important sociolinguistic and historical data (e.g. oral histories) for purposes of teaching and research. I recorded speaker data from 2015 – 2017 which spanned three geographical areas in Indiana: southwestern Indiana (e.g. Jasper and Ferdinand), central Indiana (e.g. Indianapolis metropolitan area), and northeastern Indiana (e.g. Fort Wayne).

Instruments for data collection were patterned after the Texas German Dialect Project, except for small changes that tailored questions to the sociolinguistic and sociohistorical contexts of Indiana.[43] Three methods provided sociolinguistic, phonological, morphological, and lexical data: 1) open-ended interviews, 2) Gilbert (1963) translation tasks, and 3) a biographical questionnaire.[44]

The open-ended interviews consist mainly of questions relating to informants' experiences of growing up in a German community as a child and young adult. A second part of the interview is a set of translation tasks from English to German, first used by Gilbert (1963) to collect phonological, morphological, and lexical data for Texas German (Gilbert 1972). In addition, a biographical questionnaire addresses language use, language attitudes, and biographical data such as birthplace, ancestry, and religious affiliation. This questionnaire is conducted together with the informant during the interview or, due to time constraints, given to the informant to complete and mail.

Freeouf utilized the same methods of data collection for the J-F variety as I employed, i.e., Gilbert's translations tasks and open-ended interview techniques.

---

[41] Indiana University-Purdue University Indianapolis.
[42] Generously funded by the Liberal Arts New Frontiers Experimentation Fellowship.
[43] Refer to Hans C. Boas et al., "The Texas German Dialect Archive: A Multimedia Resource for Research, Teaching, and Outreach," *Journal of Germanic Linguistics* 22, no. 3 (September 2010): 277–96, https://doi.org/10.1017/S1470542710000036.
[44] See also, Barbara Johnstone, *Qualitative Methods in Sociolinguistics* (Oxford: Oxford University Press, 2000); Lesley Milroy and Matthew Gordon, *Sociolinguistics: Method and Interpretation* (Malden, Oxford, and Carlton: Blackwell, 2003); Sali Tagliamonte, *Analysing Sociolinguistic Variation* (Cambridge: Cambridge University Press, 2006).

Dialect contact and language death 149

This strengthens the analysis of my comparative study. I use the identical translation tasks and the four NP environments Freeouf employed to conduct his investigation of possible case syncretism in the J-F variety. I also interviewed speakers from the same areas in Dubois and Spencer counties as described by Freeouf.[45]

One major difference in data display distinguishes my study from that of Freeouf. Although he organizes his large corpus of phonological data under helpful headings, e.g. *Consonants, Phonemes, Pronominal Morphology*, Freeouf does not always identify the speaker source (e.g. F1, J1) after speaker samples. It is therefore not possible to determine which variant was produced by whom or how many of the informants consistently used a certain variant.[46]

6. J-F Language Use in the Twentyfirst Century

Most heritage varieties today are endangered due to an aging speaker population with little or no opportunity to speak it. Age-related conditions such as hearing impairment, physical endurance and memory often inhibited the completion of the interview tasks. Today in the 21st century, the typical J-F speaker is over 80 years of age and dominant in English. Most interviewees learned both English and German as a child but many now experience difficulty in conversing in their heritage language. Several participants note that they have not spoken their heritage language for several decades. This infrequent use of German often made it difficult to continue the data collection process and required longer response times, particularly during Gilbert's translation tasks.[47]

There are, however, still rare opportunities to speak the "old German:" Sister City partnerships with Pfaffenweiler (Jasper) and Dudenhofen (Ferdinand)

---

[45] Freeouf, "Religion and Dialect: Catholic and Lutheran Dialects in the German of Dubois County," 1. No recent German-born immigrants were included in this study, as this study focuses only on heritage speakers. Recent German-born immigrants acquire their respective German varieties in a different environment, where German is dominant and English is learned as a foreign language, usually beginning in the fifth grade.

[46] However, Freeouf does provide a detailed list of 'Selected Sentences from a Jasper Informant' identified as J3, which includes many of the Gilbert sentences and several narrative examples. In addition, Freeouf provides two lengthy phonetically transcribed texts for participants J1 and F4 in his Appendices.

[47] It was also necessary to schedule some interviews with 2 – 4 family members (one situation was a group of four Ferdinand speakers, where one speaker so dominated in answering that the other three had no opportunity to interject!).

bring visitors to their community that are housed with an Indiana German host. For some hosts, this offers them an opportunity to use their German. Informant F2 (90 years old) also speaks of a men's card group in Ferdinand where they all speak German. Information from the Indiana German questionnaire given to each participant supplies information on place and year of birth, religious affiliation, age the J-F heritage language was acquired, and fluency (cf. Section 5). Informant profiles for Jasper and Ferdinand are displayed in Figures 7.3 and 7.4:

Figure 7.3: Jasper Area Participants

IGDP#	Birth Year	Birthplace	Residence	Fluency	Age J-F Learned	Religious
JASPER AREA						
J1 (M) †	1925	Jasper	Jasper	FLUENT	0-5	Catholic
J2 (M) †	1927	Jasper	Jasper	Rememberer	N/A	Catholic
J3 (M) †	1927	Jasper	Jasper	FLUENT (no Gilbert tasks)	0-5	Catholic
J4 (F)	1933	Jasper	Jasper	Semi (no Gilbert tasks)	0-5	Catholic
J5 (F)	1933	Celestine	Ferdinand	Semi /partial Gilbert tasks	0-5	Catholic
J6 (M)	1943	Huntingburg	Jasper	Semi / no Gilbert tasks	0-5	Catholic
J7 (F)	1944	Celestine	Jasper	Semi	0-5	Catholic
J8 (M)	1948	St. Anthony	St. Marks	FLUENT	0-5	Catholic
J9 (M)	1959	Jasper	Indianapolis	Rememberer	N/A	Catholic
J10 (M)	1959	Jasper	Indianapolis	Rememberer	N/A	Catholic

Dialect contact and language death 151

Figure 7.4: Ferdinand Area Participants

FERDINAND AREA						
IGDP#	Birth Year	Birthplace	Residence	Fluency	Age J-F Learned	Religious
F1 (F)	1925	Ferdinand	Ferdinand	Rememberer	N/A (Eng only)	Catholic
F2 (M)	1927	Ferdinand	Ferdinand	FLUENT	0-5	Catholic
F3 (M)	1928	Spencer County	Ferdinand	FLUENT (partial Gilbert tasks)	0-5	Catholic
F4 (F)	1932	Spencer County	Ferdinand	Semi	0-5	Catholic
F5 (M)	1936	Fulda	Ferdinand	Semi (no Gilbert tasks)	0-5	Catholic
F6 (M)†	1940	Fulda	Ferdinand	Semi (Group Interview)	0-5	Catholic
F7 (M)	1940	Ferdinand	Jasper	Semi	0-5	Catholic
F8 (M)	1942	Ferdinand	Ferdinand	FLUENT	0-5	Catholic
F9 (F)	1942	Ferdinand	Ferdinand	Semi	0-5	Catholic
F10 (M)	1947	Mariah Hill	Mariah Hill	FLUENT	0-5	Catholic
F11 (M)	1948	Mariah Hill	Ferdinand	Semi	0-5	Catholic
F12 (M)	1950	Huntingburg	Ferdinand	FLUENT	0-5	Catholic

Between July 2015 and July 2017, I interviewed 21 informants[48] born between 1925 and 1959 in Dubois and Spencer counties for the purpose of collecting linguistic and sociolinguistic data on the J-F heritage variety. Four speakers (F1, J2, J9, J10) were only able to conduct the sociolinguistic interview in English. These I designate as "rememberers" and are shown in gray.[49] They are not included in this linguistic analysis for obvious reasons, but still provide

---

[48] Spouse and siblings often asked to be able to sit in on the interviewed. I scheduled them for an individual interview at a later date and time.
[49] See also Colette Grinevald, "Linguistics of Classifiers," in *International Encyclopedia of the Social and Behavioral Sciences*, ed. N.J. Smelser and P.B. Baltes (Elsevier Sciences Ltd, 2001).

important sociohistorical and biographical data. Four additional informants (**J3, J4, F3, F5**) completed the open-ended interview in the heritage language but were unable to complete the lengthy Gilbert translation tasks comprised of 80+ items[50] due to advanced age, health issues, fatigue, or time constraints.[51] I provide narrative samples from the open-ended interviews for these four speakers in the Appendix. Unfortunately, one interview session with speaker J6 was not recorded due to an unnoticed glitch with my recorder. The final informant (F6) participated in a family group interview where his brother so dominated the conversation with the effect that he rarely interjected comments. Because of this, I scheduled a separate interview with him, but unfortunately, F6 passed away a week later before I could conduct the interview.

This accounts for all informants interviewed.

7. Rösch 2017 J-F Data and Analysis

My study relies on 18 data sets based on the open-ended interview and Gilbert's translation tasks after omitting the "rememberers" who completed the interview in English. These 18 fluent and semi-fluent informants are comprised of seven Jasper (three female and four male) and 11 Ferdinand (two female and nine male) speakers. To provide a general distinction between speaker fluency, I make two here: *fluent*, i.e. where the informant can converse easily in the heritage language on common topics without hesitation, and *semi-fluent*, where the informant has some difficulty in speaking continuously and sometimes switches to English due to lexical gaps.

Most linguistic studies on German-American heritage varieties include data on determiners that provide additional data for comparison. Determiner marking is also obvious—it is one of the first grammatical features with which learners of German have difficulty, as nouns in SG exhibit three genders and function in four cases. One only has to glance at the prescribed SG masculine definite article forms in Figure 7.5 to understand why.

---

[50] Gilbert's translation tasks were often repeated in the list and spaced at intervals to allow for confirmation of the item. It was often necessary to skip over some of these repetitions to accommodate aging participants.

[51] The open-ended interviews often lasted 1 ½ - 3 hours depending on the number of participants. Ferdinand and Jasper also lie 2 ½ - 3 hours by car away from IUPUI. As sole investigator, this necessitated a 6-hour return trip. I was not always able to return to re-interview informants due to the excessive travel time required as well as time restrictions of my position and duties at the university.

Dialect contact and language death

Figure 7.5: SG Masculine Definite Article Declinations for 'The Man'

der Mann 'the man'	definite article	indefinite article	Plural
NOM	der Mann	ein Mann	die Männer
ACC	den Mann	einen Mann	die Männer
DAT	dem Mann	einem Mann	den Männer<u>n</u>
GEN	des Mannes	eines Mannes	der Männer

The focus in my comparative analysis with Freeouf's findings is also on determiner markings in the NP, i.e. definite articles, indefinite articles, and possessive determiners. Demonstratives and pronouns are also included for the additional information they contribute.[52]

The following quantitative and qualitative data analysis is structured as follows:

(1) Quantitative data from eleven (11) informants who completed the Gilbert translation tasks is presented in Tables (7.1) – (7.8) in Section 8.2.

(2) Qualitative data in the form of narrative examples from the sociolinguistic interview from four of the five informants (the fifth informant deceased before the scheduled interview) who could not complete the translation tasks is provided in Examples (5) – (8) in the Appendix.

(3) Qualitative analysis of internal and external factors that account for variation, leveling, and decline of the J-F variety are discussed in Section 9.

8. J-F Narrative Samples of Two (2) Fluent Speakers

Two narrative excerpts taken from my 2015 - 2017 data in Example (5) provide an introductory look at the J-F variety as still spoken by two fluent speakers in 2015 - 2017:

Example (5): Rösch 2017 J-F narrative excerpts

   a.   F1: "*Wurscht moche*"

[vo mir gəbutʃtə hɛn, də hɛn mə moɑgɛns uːf, UH, ausəm bɛt gɔŋgə un UH, un ə haufə peːls un faier gəmɔxt, un ə keːsl fiːəs wɔsr hais mɔxə. wo sie kəm hɛn,

---

[52] Demonstratives are the antecedents of the definite article and are generally more resistant to leveling, as is also the case with pronouns. See for reference, Salmons, *A History of German*.

dɛn hɛn di: dəs ʃwain (pause) ɪn də woɑdə fɛr di ho:ɑ opne:mə un dɛn hɛn si o:fgəmɔxt un di dɛ:rmə rausgəno:mə un di le:və un di hɛ:ɑts un dɛs hɛn zi UH kɔ:lt fi:ɑ UH vuɑʃt mɔ:xən, un ʃwɔɑdəmɔ:xn. un dan hen si dɛɑ, vo si ɔvə di gɔ:ntsə ausgəno:mə hɛn, dɛn hɛn si si: fɛrʃnɪtə, di ɪnɑʃtə ɛ:ɑst un dɛn fon u:nɑ WELL, dɛn hɛn si di foɑdə LEG, bain rapgənomə un dɛn hɛn si di mɪdəl . . .]

'When we butchered, we (got) up out of bed in the morning and so, and (got) a lot of pails and made a fire and a kettle for heating water. When they came, then they (put) the pig in the water to take off the hair…and then they opened it up and took out the intestines and the liver and the heart and they picked it up for making sausage and Schwartemagen.[53] *And then they (took) the (pause) after they had taken out everything, then they cut it (pig) all up—first the insides and then from beneath. Then they took off the front leg and then they (cut) the mid-section…'*

b. J3:[54] *"Balle spiele"*

[mir hɛn ɪmə kʃpi:lt als ʃu:l aus vɔr un di me:dl fu nubədran… da sɪn mir drүbə zu dɛs ʃu:lhaus kʃpruŋə. mir hɛn ə bɔlə khɔt un mɪt də bɔl kʃmɪsə un wu ɪmə mir gətrɔfə hon, da hɔt dɛr mүsə dɛs bɔlə nɛmə un ʃmai:sə. (fɛrʃte:ən zi dɛs?) un dan hɛnɑmə ɑ plɔts khɔt, vo məs ko:l hɪnai gədu: hɛn ɪn vɪndə vɛns…un mir hɛns də bɔlə i:bə də, i:bə də gəval kʃmɪsə un WHATEVER'N KIDS (ɪn) kʃɔŋən hɔt…na dɛr tɛts nɛmə un danubə ʃmaisə, vɛr dɛr ɛs trɛfə hɔt kɛnə (pause) mir hɛns (pause) vi: hɛn si ɛs khaisə? ANDY OVER]

'We always played when school was over and the girls from next door, we ran over to the schoolhouse. We had a ball and threw the ball and whoever we hit, then he had to take the ball and throw it. (Do you understand that?) An' then we had a place where we put coal in the winter when it (pause) and we threw the ball over the, over the wall and whatever'n kids caught (it) (pause) well, he would take it an,' an' throw it over…whoever he was able to hit (pause) we called (pause), what did they call it? Andy Over!'

---

[53] A type of sausage made from innards, stuffed in pig's stomach, and smoked

[54] J3 completed the sociolinguistic interview, but due to illness and a hearing impairment was unable to complete Gilbert's translation tasks.

8.1. Quantitative Data Analysis: Gilbert Translation Tasks

Freeouf describes the following commonly occurring forms for J-F definite articles in the NP:[55]

        1. [dɛr]   (masc.nom);

        2. [də]   (masc.acc);

        3. [dɛs]   (neut.nom/acc) and

        4. [di]   (fem.nom/acc and plural).[56]

I base the comparative analysis of my 2015-2017 data using Freeouf's description above. Tables (7.1) - (7.8) display case-marking data from six fluent (J1, J8, F2, F8, F10, F12) and five semi-fluent informants (J5, J7, F4, F9, F11) for Gilbert's translation tasks that Freeouf also employed for his 1990 study. These tables also correspond to Freeouf's four nominal environments of the definite article identified in Examples (1) - (4) in Section 4.

I display the J-F article variations using an IPA notation and note the speaker's assignment of gender (masculine, feminine, neuter), case (nominative, accusative, dative) and determiner constituents, i.e. definite article (*def.*); demonstrative (*dem.*); possessive determiner (*poss.*), and pronoun case (*pro.*). Each table displays the English translation task followed by either a Freeouf (1990) sample when available or a sample from my 2017 J-F data. I designate Rösch 2017 occurring forms that match Freeouf's description above with the symbol ʲᶠ.

Tables (7.1) - (7.8) exhibit definite article and demonstrative markings in the NP that function in nominative (subject), accusative (direct object), or dative contexts (e.g. indirect objects or two-way prepositions) for the Gilbert translation tasks. I provide a short analysis after each Table showing participant responses to Gilbert's translation tasks in their heritage varieties.

---

[55] Freeouf, "Religion and Dialect: Catholic and Lutheran Dialects in the German of Dubois County," 147.

[56] Freeouf notes other infrequent case forms, such as masc.ACC [dɛn], masc. and neut.DAT [dɛm, ɛm, m], and fem.ACC [də].

Table 7.1: Gilbert Translation Task: 'he's putting the chair under the tree'

F10 (2017): [ɛr du:t də ʃtu:l une də baum]	
Target: J-F masculine definite article [də] (direct object environment/accusative)	
[dɛr] (def.masc.nom.)	J1, F2, F8
ʲᶠ [də] (def.masc.acc)	J5, J8, F4, F10, F12
[di] (def.fem.nom/acc/dat.)	F11
[dɛt] (dem.masc.acc)	J7
did not complete task	F9

Five Jasper/Ferdinand speakers produce the accusative [də] definite article described by Freeouf for the direct object, while the remaining five who completed the task produce variants.

The following Tables (7.2) and (7.3) target demonstrative forms ('this/that; these/those') that Freeouf (1990, 170-3) describes as either identical to the definite articles or as separate J-F demonstratives. He also notes Low Alemannic forms (hereafter LAlem), masculine and neuter forms of [sɛlə(r)] (masc.nom/acc) and [sɛl] neut.nom/acc.

Table 7.2: Gilbert Translation Task: 'the dog bit that bad man'

F9:	[dɛr hunt hɔt dɛt, dɛs mɔn gəbɪsə]
Target: J-F demonstrative masculine [dɛt] (direct object)	
[dɛr, de:r] (def.masc.nom)	F2, F10
[dɛs] (def.neut.nom/acc)	J8
[də] (def.masc.acc)	J7
ʲᶠ [dɛt] (J-F dem.masc.acc.)	J5, F4, (F8),[57] F9
[dat] (no mention by Freeouf)	F11
[sɛlə(r)] LAlem (dem.masc.nom)	F8, F12
[sɛlən] LAlem (dem.masc.acc)	J1

---

[57] Informant J8 produced both ʲᶠ [dɛt] and [dɛs]

Dialect contact and language death 157

Table (7.2) samplings depict a wide range of individual variants. Four J-F speakers produce the demonstrative variant described by Freeouf for this direct object context. Table (7.3) shows responses for the neuter noun [ai] Eng 'egg' for the J-F demonstrative article [dɛs] and LAlem [sɛl] for this accusative environment. The neuter demonstrative differs from its masculine counterpart but shares a common form for both nominative and accusative contexts.

Table 7.3: Gilbert Translation Task: 'boil that egg in hot water'

F4:	[kox dɛs ai ɪn haisə vɔ:sər]
Target: J-F neuter demonstrative article [dɛs] (direct object)	
ʲᶠ [dɛs] (dem.neut.nom/acc)	J8, F2, F3, F4, F9, F11
[də] (def.masc.acc)	J7
[dɛt] (masc.dem.acc/dat)	F4, F9
ʲᶠ [sɛl] (dem.neut) (LAlem)	J1, J5
[sɛlə] (dem.fem.) (LAlem)	F12
[s] (con.neut.acc)	F10

Unfortunately, no Gilbert items polled the definite article in an indirect object context, but Gilbert's translation tasks did target pronoun forms as in 'he's helping me' and 'give her two pieces.'

Pronominal systems are historically robust and usually the most resistant to reduction.[58] Thus, one might expect several dative pronoun forms to appear if still extant. Therefore, Tables (7.4) and (7.5) look to the realization of the pronoun in these two contexts that sample production of either the accusative or dative pronoun *mir* or accusative pronoun *mich*, Eng 'me.' Freeouf notes both accusative and dative forms for all personal pronouns, i.e. [hɛlft miç, hɛlft mir] 'he's helping me now.'[59]

---

[58] For reference, Salmons, *A History of German*.
[59] Freeouf, "Religion and Dialect: Catholic and Lutheran Dialects in the German of Dubois County," 165–66.

Table 7.4: Gilbert Translation Task: 'he's helping me now'

J3: (Freeouf 1990)	[ɛr duːt mir hɛlfə jɛts]
F10: (Roesch 2017)	[dɛr hiːlft mɪç jɛts]

Target: J-F accusative *mich* or dative pronoun *mir* (Freeouf 1990) (indirect or intransitive objects)

ʲᶠ [miç] (pro.me.acc)	J8, F2, F4, F5, F8, F9, F10, F12
[mɪʃ] pro.me acc)	J7
[miː] (pro.me.reduced)	F11
[diç] (you,acc)	J1

None of the eleven J-F speakers (seven of these who reside in Ferdinand) produce a dative form for Eng 'me.' All but one speaker produces an accusative variant (including J7 who produces [mɪʃ] 'misch' typical of Palatinate varieties up through the Rhineland brought by the immigrants who settled Ferdinand.[60] Table (7.5) exhibits the responses for the expected accusative or dative form of 'me' described by Freeouf:

Table 7.5: Gilbert Translation Task: 'he came with me'

F2 [ɛr ɪs mɪt mɪç kɔmə]	
Target: personal pronoun [mɪç] as accusative or dative object	
ʲᶠ [miç]	J1, F2, F4, F8, F9, F10, F11, F12
[mir]	J8
[mɪʃ]	J7
[miː]	J5

Only one J-F speaker in Table (7.5) produces a dative form for the pronoun *mir* 'me.'

The results of these two tables indicate a probable leveling and merging of the dative and accusative forms in the J-F variety that support the koinéization posited by Freeouf and Salmons, but do not currently favor the early prestigious

---

[60] J1 produces the pronoun for 'you' [diç] in accusative form and F11 produces a reduced form, a possible misspeak due to similarity to Eng 'me.'

Dialect contact and language death 159

Upper German Jasper variety's three-case system three decades later.[61] It is not possible to posit any far-reaching conclusions considering the small sampling size of this last generation of J-F speakers.

I next examine a Gilbert translation task that elicits a dative form for the pronoun *ihr* (Eng 'her') in an indirect object environment. Table (7.6) exhibits the speaker results for a second Gilbert translation task that targeted this SG feminine dative form.

Table 7.6: Gilbert Translation Task: 'give her two pieces'

J7: (Roesch 2017):	[gɪp i:rə tsuai ʃtɪ:kə] (dat)
F8: (Roesch 2017):	[gɛp zi: tsuai ʃtʏkɛ] (acc)
Target: J-F accusative or dative pronoun (Freeouf 1990) (indirect object, personal pronouns)	
ʲᶠ [zi:] (pro.acc)	J1, F8, F9
ʲᶠ [si:] (pro.acc)	J8, F12
[zə] (pro.acc)	F2
ʲᶠ [i:rə] (pro.dat)	J7
ʲᶠ [gɛb]'ər (pro.dat)	F10
[miç] (acc) ('me.'pro.add)	F4
'she' (Eng.nom.)	J5
'her' (Eng.acc/dat.)	F11 [gɪp hɚ tsuai ʃtʏkə]-- I don't know what 'her' is

Table (7.6) exhibits multiple variants for the SG dative feminine pronoun [i:r] 'her.' Only one Jasper and one Ferdinand informant produce a dative form for the above task. In addition to the above results, F11's honest statement, "I don't know what 'her' is" indicates a loss of this dative pronoun in progress for this speaker. Rösch's Texas Alsatian samplings for 'her' showed similar results.[62] Reviewing the responses above, several informants produce the accusative form *sie* equivalent to the English pronouns 'she' and 'her.' Freeouf, too,

---

[61] Freeouf, "Religion and Dialect: Catholic and Lutheran Dialects in the German of Dubois County"; Joseph Salmons and Daniel Nutzel, "Language Contact and New Dialect Formation: Evidence from German in North America," *Language and Linguistics Compass* 5, no. 10 (2011): 705–17.
[62] Rösch, *Language Maintenance and Language Death: The Decline of Texas Alsatian*, 146-49.

provides examples where speakers rephrased this item, e.g. [si hɛns iːrə gɛbə, si gɛps miç, dan hat si mir dɛs gɛwə].⁶³

Tables (7.7) and (7.8) exhibit speaker productions of the definite article as the object in a prepositional phrase. Here it is important to note that this context contains a two-way preposition, i.e., a preposition that dictates both dative and accusative forms depending on stating location (where?) requiring a dative form or a 'change of location' (where to?) that requires an accusative form. Again, many regional dialects often favor one or the other: *mich* or *mir*, Eng *me* despite the prescriptive insistence of SG.

Table 7.7: Gilbert Translation Task: 'he is already in the room'

J3 (Freeouf 1990):	[ɛr is jɛts in <u>di</u> ʃtuːp]
J1 (Roesch 2017):	[ɛr ɪs jɛts ʃoː <u>ɪm</u> tsɪːmə] (dat); [ɪn <u>di</u> ʃtup] (acc)

Target: J-F accusative *die (Stube)* or dative definite article *dem (Zimmer)* also contraction *im*, Eng 'in the'(definite article, prepositional object)

ʲᶠ [ɪ<u>m</u> tsɪːmə] (con.neut.dat)	J1
[ɪn də tsɪmə] (def.masc)	F9
ʲᶠ [ɪn <u>di</u> ʃtuːp] (def.fem.acc)	J1, J5, J8, F4, F10,
[ɪn də ʃtuːp] (def.masc.acc.)	F8, F12
ʲᶠ [ɔ<u>m</u> ʃtuːp] (con.masc/neut.dat)	F2
[ɪn <u>di</u> room] (def.fem.acc)	F11

Freeouf observes that dative-marked contractions only occur sporadically and notes that the majority of his informants produce the feminine article [di] for the lexical item *die Stube* 'room.'⁶⁴ Not surprisingly, responses show several definite article variants given by J-F speakers. J1 produces both dative and accusative forms. F2 produces a dative contraction similar to J1. Table (7.8) elicits data for the possessive determiner [dai].

---

⁶³ Freeouf, "Religion and Dialect: Catholic and Lutheran Dialects in the German of Dubois County," 166–67.
⁶⁴ Ibid., 147–48.

Dialect contact and language death 161

Table 7.8: Gilbert Translation Task: 'there is something in your left eye'

	Freeouf (1990):	[iç hap ɛtwas ın mai lingəs aux]
	J8 Roesch (2017):	[ɛs ıs ɛːbıs ın dai lıŋstɛs augə]
	Target: (Possessive determiner JF 'dai' object)	
ʲᶠ [dai] 'your'		J1, J8, F2, F8, F12
[mai] 'my'		J7, F4, F9
[sai] 'his'		F11
[də]		J5
omitted determiner:		F10 [i hɔp ɛtvɑz ıns liːŋə aux]

Trudgill's model of stages in New Dialect Formation describes the second stage of koinéization as characterized by extreme variability, which is evidenced here in (7.8).[65] Five speakers produce the expected possessive determiner [dai], four speakers produce other possessive determiner variants. J5 produces a definite article, and F10 omits it altogether. Previous data in Tables (7.1) – (7.8) show that these J-F informants produce a range of determiner variants with only occasional dative forms.

9. Internal and Externals Factors Contributing to Morphological Leveling in Case Marking

This section posits plausible internal and external processes that account for the morphological leveling in the case marking of the J-F variety. I begin with interrelated internal and external processes that apply to the J-F context: base dialect paradigms, dialect contact and language death—the boundaries of which are often indistinguishable from each other.

Intermarriage between a non-speaker and a speaker can result in the German heritage variety not being acquired or only partially acquired. However, intermarriage between speakers who spoke different German varieties presents an interesting example of close and intense dialect contact.

Several speakers (e.g. J8, F3, F5) mention that father and mother spoke different types of German. J8 (b.1948), notes that his mother from the Alsace (i.e. a LAlem variety), spoke differently from his father. This was the case for J8, who remembered and produced both demonstrative variants of the mother *sel-* and father *des, det* in the translation tasks.

---

[65] Peter Trudgill, *New-Dialect Formation: The Inevitability of Colonial Englishes* (New York: New York UP, 2004), 110–12.

A third factor contributing to morphological "leveling" or reduction is the external factor of changing social and linguistic contexts associated with language shift. The shift from German to English in formerly monolingual German communities has been well documented in U.S. German speech islands and associated with political ideologies around the beginning of the twentieth century.[66] Together with the increasing stigmatization of German varieties during the course of two World Wars with Germany, this resulted in English-only laws for education and news media (e.g., newspapers). As a result, German was rarely spoken in public domains and retreated into private domains of family and friends. Here, it survived in isolated, rural communities with tight social networks among German-speaking neighbors. The incomplete acquisition of this last generation during this shift is evident in several semi-speaker responses shown above.

Current J-F speakers (J3, F3, F4, F5) born in the 1920s and 1930s mention the difficulty they experienced in first grade where English was legally mandated and attest that parents often spoke German when they did not want to be understood. Some recount experiences where older siblings made fun of their "strange" German (F4).

The last generation of fluent speakers in the J-F communities was born in the late 1940s (J8, J10, F10, F12). The language is still extant due only to the longevity of its speakers and individual familial circumstances. For example, fluent speaker F10 (b.1947) never married, but conversed in German with his father while working the farm together. Fluent speaker F12 (b.1950) and figurehead for the German-speaking Ferdinand community also spoke only German with his father while farming and working in the dairy. F12 regularly communicates in German with close friend and fluent speaker F8 (b.1942). F2 (b.1927) is one of nine children, who still speaks German with his one surviving sister.

In essence, the predominance of English in most domains created a context where the once-fluent speaker rarely had the opportunity to "really speak" German aside from brief pleasantries, e.g., greetings, weather, health (J3). Several speakers commented that they had not spoken it "in decades" and though first slow in responding, were able to recall more as the interview progressed. This disuse and infrequent opportunity to use the language has now progressed to a critically endangered stage where only a limited number of fluent speakers remain but who have not transmitted it to the next generation.

---

[66] For reference, see Klaus Mattheier, "Sprachinseltod: Überlegungen Zum Entwicklungsdynamik von Sprachinseln," in *In German Language Varieties Worldwide: Internal and External Perspectives*, ed. William Keel and Klaus Mattheier (Frankfurt: Peter Lang, 2003), 13–51.

Next, I look to the external factor of English. All J-F speakers today are unequal bilinguals, i.e. English is their dominant language. Determiners in the English nominal phrase exhibit a one case system: the definite article *the*, and indefinite article *a*. English demonstratives (*this/these, that/those*) and possessive determiners (*my/our; his/their*) show only number. It is possible that English reduced forms account for a reduction in certain forms, such as the reduced form *de* in J-F definite article forms. It is more likely that either reduced base dialect features are being preserved or that internal processes of leveling are at work. I refer here again to Rosenberg's findings on German speech islands in Russia, who presented evidence of pronounced case syncretism in these varieties despite intense contact with the Russian six-case system.[67]

I also briefly address the external factor of Standard German here. Schools, churches, and newspapers are the most important institutions that support language maintenance. Salmons reports that German newspapers and German in Indiana schools disappeared completely from public and most private schools during WWI and did not reappear until decades later.[68] Dubois County did not reinstate German in the schools until the 1970s. Freeouf reports that the last German newspaper disappeared in 1914, but usage of German in church services continued a bit longer.[69] I was able to locate one German clergy in Jasper who still speaks German. For current J-F speakers (born 1925 - 1950), it is highly unlikely that Standard German played any significant role in their language development.

The four speaker narratives in Examples (5) - (8) (see Appendix) demonstrate that these are fluent speakers who produce complex constructions and have little difficulty with extended conversations. These speakers, who represent some of the eldest in my 2017 J-F dataset still produce occasional dative forms, usually as contractions, as in *mei Mom wɔr gut im Koche*, literally 'my mother was good in cooking.' I conclude that these dative contractions produced by speakers have become lexicalized, as also shown in previous examples of <u>am</u> *helfe*, <u>am/im</u> *Zimmer*, <u>am</u> *Bode*. Although not frequently, these determiner contractions are produced by fluent speakers in the translation tasks.

Determiner forms of J-F speakers can be summarized as follows:

- The J-F reduced article [də] in unstressed positions is frequently produced in lieu of nominative, accusative and dative determiner forms.

---

[67] "Comparative Speech Island Research: Some Results from Studies in Russia and Brazil."
[68] "But Hoosiers Do Speak German: An Overview of German in Indiana," 159–60.
[69] "Dialect Leveling and Preservation in the German of Dubois County, Indiana," in *Studies in Indiana German-Americana*, vol. 1 (Madison: Max Kade Institute, 1988), 14.

- J-F demonstrative forms of both [dɛr, dɛs, di], Eng 'the' and LAlem [sɛl-], Eng '*this/that; these/ those,*' in the noun phrase have been preserved, but rarely occur.

- Demonstrative pronouns [dɛr, dɛs, diː] are also frequently produced by fluent speakers, with occasional occurrences of LAlem [sɛl] and the masculine accusative [deːn]. In general, internal leveling of marked dialectal features in J-F has been at work here.

- The J-F reduced form for the indefinite article [ə], Eng '*a*' as well as reduced possessive determiners that exhibit final -*n* apocope, e.g. [*mai, dai, sai*] Eng 'my, your, his'—not an uncommon occurrence in several German regional dialects—are as Freeouf described three decades ago and are the preferred form for most speakers.⁷⁰

- Within the possessive determiner set, however, the 'polite' plural forms [*unsə, airə, irə*] (Eng 'our, your, their') were only produced by two fluent speakers during my interviews (see Example 15c).

- However, the neuter definite article [*dɛs*] and feminine and plural article [*diː*] occur frequently and alternate with reduced form [*də*] in all morphosyntactic positions. The masculine definite article [*dɛr*] and [*də*] in unstressed positions occurs in nominative, accusative and dative contexts.

- In addition, Freeouf mentions additional though infrequent use of accusative *den* and dative *dem* forms.

These two masculine accusative and dative forms, as well as formal forms, rarely occur in my 2017 data. It is evident that speakers today have "lost" certain accusative and dative forms in favor of a common case form [də] in the J-F nominal system.

10. Summary

To summarize, the wide variation of base dialects contributing to the J-F variety makes case assignment often difficult to determine. Specifically, reduced forms found in many of the base dialects argue for retention and not leveling of dialectal features:

1) the retention of LAlem *sel* demonstrates that several last-generation speakers have preserved some marked dialectal features;

---

⁷⁰ "Religion and Dialect: Catholic and Lutheran Dialects in the German of Dubois County," 148, 168.

2) the definite article *de* and demonstratives *det* and *dat* produced by some speakers are also characteristic of Low German and Franconian varieties;

3) the reduced possessive determiners [*mai, dai, sai*] and indefinite article *a* are characteristic of several regional dialects mentioned in §3; and

4) base dialect varieties identified in Section 3 exhibit a predominant paradigm of NA/D that several of the Rösch 2017 J-F narrative examples mirror. My 2017 data show only sporadic occurrences of dative case markings as also described by Freeouf.

The 2017 J-F variety is experiencing the beginning stages of koinéization as evidenced by my 2017 data in Tables (7.1) – (7.8), which exhibited a range of variants for determiners, but also frequent use of the reduced "default" form [də] in unstressed positions in the NP contexts as Freeouf designates in Examples (1) – (4) in Fig. 7.2.

I conclude that the leveling of case markings (reduction, simplification, coalescence) in the J-F variety described and presented here is now much removed from the influence of language / dialect contact. Instead, it is associated with the processes of a dying language in its final stages spoken by only a handful of fluent and semi-fluent speakers who did not transmit this variety to the next generation. The life of this variety now depends solely on the longevity of these last remaining speakers. The death of this J-F heritage variety is now imminent.

Appendix: Rösch 2017 Narrative Samples

Examples (5) - (8) provide samples from two semi-fluent (J4, F5) and two fluent speakers (J3, F3), who were not able or only partially able to complete the translations tasks due to health constraints. Three contexts (direct object, prepositional object, possessive determiner) are shown here, as the occurrence of definite articles in the indirect object position used by Freeouf are pragmatically rare. Designations identify the case form produced, not an expected SG form. I have bolded the determiners to facilitate identification and tagged reduced forms with (*red*).

Example (5): **J3 (b.1927),** Narrative examples for determiners

a. NP as direct object:

  i. [ɛs ɪs ɛtvɑs ɪn **mai**.POSS.DET lɪŋksɛ ɔːk] (*red*)

  'there is something in my left eye'

  ii. [mir hɛns **də balə**.DEF.MASC.iːbə də gval gəʃmɪːsə] (*red*)

  'we threw the ball over the wall'

      iii. [iç hab <u>den</u>.DEMONS.MASC.ACC nıt gəkant, der.DEMONS.MASC.NOM wa: ʃo: gəʃtoːɑvə]

          'I didn't know him, he had already died'

  b. NP as prepositional object:

      i. [vu iç zɛks ja: alt wa: hɛn iç mʏsə <u>ın di ʃuːl</u>.DEF.FEM.ACC geːn]

          'when I was six years old I had to go to school'

      ii. [da hat ziːs mıt <u>də eːdlə</u>[71] <u>ʃʊvɛtsə</u>.DEF.NEUT.] *(red)*

          'she liked to speak nobly'

      iii. [mir vaːn <u>ın di gɔtsaker</u>.DEF.FEM.ACC gɔŋə]

          'we had gone to the cemetery'

  c. NP with possessive determiner:

      i. [<u>mai faːdə</u>.1PERS.POS.DET.MASC.NOM un <u>mə muder</u>.1PERS.POS.DET hɛn ın daitʃ gəbɛt]

          'my father and my mother prayed in German'

      ii. [varɛn <u>airə faːdə un mudə</u> 2PERS.FORM.POS.DET.NOM daitʃ]

          'were your (formal) father and mother German'

      iii. [<u>mai groːsgroːsfadə</u>.1PERS.POS.DET.NOM ıs kʊme fu dadrʏbə]

          'my great-grandfather came from over there'

        Example (6): **J4 (b.1933)**, Narrative examples

  a. NP as direct object:

      i. [du haʃ auxə, du haʃ hɛnt un du haʃ <u>a mauəl</u>.INDEF] *(red)*

          'you have eyes, you have hands, and you have a mouth'

      ii. [<u>dɛs</u>.DEM.NEUT hap iç glɛrnt ın ɔːxt tɔk]

          'that I learned in eight days'

      iii. [iç glaub mai bruːdə.1PERS.POS.DET.NOM hat <u>iːnə</u>.3PERS.PL.PRON gəfuːnə]

          'I believe my brother found them'

  b. NP as prepositional object:

      i. [du kanʃ ʃprɛçə <u>mıt diː</u>.3PERS.DEM.PRON.PL.*red*]

---

[71] This seems to be how this speaker refers to a more "prestigious" form of German.

Dialect contact and language death 167

   'you can speak with them'
  ii. [mir varn gətaxt ɪn dɛs kiːrç.DEM.NEUT.]
   'we were baptized in that church'
  iii. [doː ɪn dɛr klai ʃulhaus.DEF.FEM.DAT mir hɛn ɔːxt klase khapt]
   'there in the little schoolhouse we had eight grades'
 c. NP with possessive determiners:
  i. [mai fatə 'n muder.1PERS.PL.POSDET.NOM hɛn daitʃ ʃprɔçə]
   'my father and mother spoke German'
  ii. [un i hab ksakt, vas ɪs dai nɔːmə.2PERS.POSDET.NOM]
   'and I said, what is your name'
  iii. [der.3PERS.DEM.PRON.MASC.hat sai fervanʃaf.3PERS.POSDET.gəfunə]
   'he found his relatives'

    Example (7): **F3 (b.1928)**, Narrative examples
 a. NP as direct object:
  i. [dan hən mə aux kholfə, FRY de flaiʃ.DEF.NEUT] (*red*)
   'then we also helped fry the meat'
  ii. [vəns gəreːgən hɔt, hɛn mə a ʃirm.INDEF.MASC.mɪtnemə] (*red*)
   'when it rained, we took an umbrella with us'
  iii. [mir hɛn kai TRACTOR.INDEF.khat] (*red*)
   'we didn't have a tractor'
 b. NP as prepositional object:
  i. [dan sin mir yːbə di PASTURE.DEF.FEM.ACC geːhn]
   'then we went over the pasture'
  ii. [mə.1PERS.DEF.NOM.RED hen just a hɔlf a mail kvoːnt fu də ʃuːl.DEF.FEM.] (*red*)
   'we lived just a half a mile from the school'
  iii. [vɛns tsait vɔr fɛr di klaidə.DEF.PL.ACC vɛʃə jedə moːntax]
   'when it was time for washing clothes every Monday'
 c. Possessive determiners in the NP:
  i. [zi un sai mɔn.3PERS.POSDET.NOM]
   'she and his husband' ("incorrect" determiner)

ii. [vɔs maːnə vɔr un <u>vɔs Papps sai vɔr</u>.3PERS.POSDET] *(red)*
'what was mine and what was Papps'

iii. [<u>mai tsvait ɛltʃtə ʃvɛster</u>.1PERS.POSDET.NOM. ɪs gəʃtorbə]
'my second-eldest sister died'

Example (8): **F5 (b.1936)**, Narrative examples[72]

a. NP as direct object:

   i. [iç hab <u>iːn</u>.PRON.MASC gəfraːkt, hɛt iːr.2PERS.PL.PRON.ʃtinkats ɪn daitʃlant]
'I asked him, do you have skunks in Germany'

   ii. [da haʃ du <u>di lait</u>.DEF.PL so fiːl bətsaːl mʏsə fɛr dɛs tuə]
'you had to pay the people so much for doing that'

   iii. [ai aiçhorn.INDEF.].ɑs;dɛr.3PERS.DEM.PRON frɛst aiçlə--<u>di nʏs</u>.DEF.PL]
'a squirrel; it eats acorns--the nuts'

b. NP as prepositional object:

   i. [vi iç <u>ɪn di</u>.DEF.FEM.ACC ʃuːl gɔŋə bɪn]
'when I went to school'

   ii. [iç vais vo iç mol haimkɔmə bɪn <u>fun di ʃuːl</u>.DEF.FEM.ACC]
'I remember once when I came home from school'

   iii. [un dɛs.DEM.NEUT hɛn mə gɛsə <u>mɪt də</u>.DEF.PL.rɛtɪçə] *(red)*
'and we ate that with the radishes'

c. Possessive determiners in the NP:

   i. [<u>mai</u> mutə.POSDET.FEM.NOM, di hɔt a bɪsəl ɔnrs daitʃ gəʃprɔːçə]
'my mother, she spoke German a little differently'

   ii. [<u>mai grosfadər</u>.1PERS.POSDET.MASC. hɔt a bɪsəl eːŋlɪʃ ʃprɛçə kɛnə]
'my grandfather could speak a little English'

   iii. [abə <u>sain fader</u> hɔt nɛt.3PERS.MASC.NOM]
'but his father couldn't'

---

[72] This speaker vacillates between producing the [n] after possessive determiners or dropping it. In double infinitives, this speaker consistently produces the [n] in the first infinitive of the "double infinitive, but not after the auxiliary, e.g. *schreiben muesse* 'had to write'

The narratives in Examples (6) - (8) demonstrate that these are fluent speakers who produce complex constructions and have little difficulty with extended conversations. These speakers, who represent some of the eldest in my 2017 J-F dataset, still produce occasional dative forms, usually as contractions, as in *mei Mom wɔr gut im Koche*, literally 'my mother was good in cooking.' I conclude that these dative contractions produced by speakers have become lexicalized, as also shown in previous examples of *am helfe, am/im Zimmer, am Bode*.

These determiner forms are consistently produced by fluent speakers in the translation tasks, so that determiner forms of J-F speakers can be summarized as follows:

The J-F default article [də] in unstressed positions is frequently produced indicative of internal leveling due to infrequent use coupled with the limited number of fluent speakers. J-F demonstrative forms of both [dɛr, dɛs, di], Eng '*the*' and LAlem [sɛl-], Eng '*this/that; these/ those,*' in the noun phrase have been preserved, but rarely occur. Demonstrative pronouns [dɛr, dɛs, di:] are also frequently produced by fluent speakers, with occasional occurrences of LAlem [sɛl] and the masculine accusative [de:n]. In general, internal leveling of marked dialectal features in J-F has been at work here.

The uni-form for the indefinite article [ə], Eng '*a*' and reduced possessive determiners that exhibit final *-n* apocope, e.g. [*mai, dai, sai*] Eng '*my, your, his*'—not an uncommon occurrence in several German regional dialects—are as Freeouf (1990, 148, 168) described three decades ago. Within the possessive determiner set, however, the 'polite' plural forms [*unsə, airə, irə*] (Eng '*our, your, their*') were only produced by two fluent speakers during my interviews (see Example 15c).

However, the neuter definite article [*dɛs*] and feminine and plural article [*di:*] occur frequently and alternate with reduced form [*də*] in all morphosyntactic positions. The masculine definite article [*dɛr*] and [*də*] in unstressed positions occurs in nominative, accusative and dative contexts (cf. Tables in §, which Freeouf also describes. In addition, he mentions additional though infrequent use of accusative *den* and dative *dem* forms. These two masculine accusative and dative forms as well as formal forms rarely occur in my 2017 data. It is evident that speakers today have "lost" certain accusative and dative forms in favor of a common case form [də] in the J-F nominal system.

Rösch 2017 Narrative Samples from J3, J4, F3, F5

Examples (6) - (9) provide samples from four fluent speakers (J3, J4, F3 and F5), who were not able or only able to partially complete the translations tasks due to time constraints. Three contexts (direct object, prepositional object, possessive determiner) are shown here, as the occurrence of definite articles in the indirect object position used by Freeouf is pragmatically rare. Designations identify the case form produced, not an expected SG form. I have bolded the determiners to facilitate identification and tagged reduced forms with (*red*).

Example (6): **J3** (b.1927), Narrative examples for determiners

i. [ɛs ɪs ɛtvɑs ɪn **mai**.POSS.DET lɪŋksɛ ɔːk] (*red*)

'there is something in my left eye'

ii. [mir hɛns **də balə**.DEF.MASC.iːbə də gval gəʃmɪːsə] (*red*)

'we threw the ball over the wall'

iii. [iç hab **den**.DEMONS.MASC.ACC nɪt gəkant, **der**.DEMONS.MASC.NOM waː ʃoː gəʃtoːɑvə]

'I didn't know him, he had already died'

i. [vu iç zɛks jaː alt waː hɛn iç mʏsə **ɪn di ʃuːl**.DEF.FEM.ACC geːn]

'when I was six years old I had to go to school'

ii. [da hat ziːs mɪt **də eːdlə**[73] **ʃʊvɛtsə**.DEF.NEUT.] (*red*)

'she liked to speak nobly'

iii. [mir vaːn **ɪn di gɔtsaker**.DEF.FEM.ACC gɔŋə]

'we had gone to the cemetery'

i. [**mai faːdə**.1PERS.POS.DET.MASC.NOM un **mə muder**.1PERS.POS.DET hɛn ɪn daitʃ gəbɛt]

'my father and my mother prayed in German'

ii. [varɛn **airə faːdə un mudə** 2PERS.FORM.POS.DET.NOM daitʃ]

'were your (formal) father and mother German'

iii. [**mai groːsgroːsfadə**.1PERS.POS.DET.NOM ɪs kʊme fu dadrʏbə]

'my great-grandfather came from over there'

Example (7): **J4** (b.1933), Narrative examples

i. [du haʃ auxə, du haʃ hɛnt un du haʃ **a mauəl**.INDEF] (*red*)

'you have eyes, you have hands, and you have a mouth'

ii. [**dɛs**.DEM.NEUT hap iç glɛrnt ɪn ɔːxt tɔk]

---

[73] This seems to be how this speaker refers to a more "prestigious" form of German.

'that I learned in eight days'

iii. [ɪç glaub mai bruːdə.1PERS.POS.DET.NOM hat iːnə.3PERS.PL.PRON gəfuːnə]

'I believe my brother found them'

i. [du kanʃ ʃprɛçə mɪt diː.3PERS.DEM.PRON.PL.*red*]

'you can speak with them'

ii. [mir varn gətaxt ɪn dɛs kiːrç.DEM.NEUT.]

'we were baptized in that church'

iii. [doː ɪn dɛr klai ʃulhaus.DEF.FEM.DAT mir hɛn ɔːxt klasə khapt]

'there in the little schoolhouse we had eight grades'

i. [mai fatə 'n muder.1PERS.PL.POSDET.NOM hɛn daitʃ ʃprɔçə]

'my father and mother spoke German'

ii. [un i hab ksakt, vas ɪs dai nɔːmə.2PERS.POSDET.NOM]

'and I said, what is your name'

iii. [der.3PERS.DEM.PRON.MASC.hat sai fervanʃaf.3PERS.POSDET.gəfunə]

'he found his relatives'

Example (8): **F3** (b.1928), Narrative examples

i. [dan hən mə aux kholfə, FRY de flaiʃ.DEF.NEUT] (*red*)

'then we also helped fry the meat'

ii. [vəns gəreːgən hɔt, hɛn mə a ʃirm.INDEF.MASC.mɪtnemə] (*red*)

'when it rained, we took an umbrella with us'

iii. [mir hɛn kai TRACTOR.INDEF.khat] (*red*)

'we didn't have a tractor'

i. [dan sin mir yːbə di PASTURE.DEF.FEM.ACC geːhn]

'then we went over the pasture'

ii. [mə.1PERS.DEF.NOM.RED hen just a hɔlf a mail kvoːnt fu də ʃuːl.DEF.FEM.] (*red*)

'we lived just a half a mile from the school'

iii. [vɛns tsait vɔr fɛr di klaidə.DEF.PL.ACC vɛʃə jedə moːntax]

'when it was time for washing clothes every Monday'

i. [zi un sai mɔn.3PERS.POSDET.NOM]
'she and <u>his</u> husband' ("incorrect" determiner)

ii. [vɔs ma:nə vɔr un <u>vɔs Papps sai vɔr</u>.3PERS.POSDET] *(red)*
'what was mine and what was Papps'

iii. [<u>mai tsvait ɛltʃtə ʃvɛster</u>.1PERS.POSDET.NOM. ɪs gəʃtorbə]
'my second-eldest sister died'

Example (9): **F5** (b.1936), Narrative examples[74]

i. [iç hab <u>i:n</u>.PRON.MASC gəfra:kt, hɛt i:r.2PERS.PL.PRON.ʃtinkats ɪn daitʃlant]
'I asked him, do you have skunks in Germany'

ii. [da haʃ du <u>di lait</u>.DEF.PL so fi:l bətsa:l mʏsə fɛr dɛs tuə]
'you had to pay the people so much for doing that'

iii. [ai aiçhorn.INDEF.].ɑs; dɛr.3PERS.DEM.PRON frɛst aiçlə--<u>di nʏs</u>.DEF.PL]
'a squirrel; it eats acorns--the nuts'

i. [vi iç <u>ɪn di</u>.DEF.FEM.ACC ʃu:l gɔŋə bɪn]
'when I went to school'

ii. [iç vais vo iç mol haimkɔmə bɪn <u>fun di ʃu:l</u>.DEF.FEM.ACC]
'I remember once when I came home from school'

iii. [un dɛs.DEM.NEUT hɛn mə gɛsə <u>mɪt də</u>.DEF.PL.rɛtɪçə] *(red)*
'and we ate that with the radishes'

i. [<u>mai</u> mutə.POSDET.FEM.NOM, di hɔt a bɪsəl ɔnrs daitʃ gəʃprɔ:çə]
'my mother, she spoke German a little differently'

ii. [<u>mai grosfadər</u>.1PERS.<u>POSDET.MASC.</u> hɔt a bɪsəl e:ŋlɪʃ ʃprɛçə kɛnə]
'my grandfather could speak a little English'

iii. [abə <u>sain fader</u> hɔt nɛt.3PERS.MASC.NOM]
'but his father couldn't'

---

[74] This speaker vacillates between producing the [n] after possessive determiners or dropping it. In double infinitives, this speaker consistently produces the [n] in the first infinitive of the "double infinitive, but not after the auxiliary, e.g. *schreiben muesse* 'had to write'

Bibliography

Altenhofen, Cléo. "Standard Und Substandard Bei Den Hunrückern in Brasilien: Variation Und Dachsprachenwechsel Des Deutschen Im Kontakt Mit Dem Portugiesischen." In *German Abroad: Perspektiven Der Variationslinguistik, Sprachkontakt- Und Mehrsprachigkeitsforschung*, edited by A. Lenz, 103–30. Göttingen: Vienna University Press, 2016.

Berend, Nina. "Zur Vergleichbarkeit von Sprachkontakten: Erfahrungen Aus Wolgadeutschen Sprachinseln in Den USA Und Russland." In *German Language Varieties Worldwide: Internal and External Perspectives*, edited by William Keel and Klaus Mattheier, 239–68. Frankfurt: Peter Lang, 2003.

Boas, Hans. "Case Loss in Texas German: The Influence of Semantic and Pragmatic Factors." edited by Johanna Barðdal and Shobhana L. Chelliah. Amsterdam; Philadelphia: John Benjamins, 2009.

———. *The Life and Death of Texas German*. Durham: Duke University Press, 2009.

———. "Tracing Dialect Death. The Texas German Dialect Project." In *Proceedings of the Twenty-Eighth Annual Meeting of the Berkeley Linguistics Society, February 15-18, 2002*, edited by Julie Larson and Mary Paster, 387–98. Berkeley: Berkeley Linguistics Society, 2003.

———, Marc Pierce, Hunter Weilbacher, Karen Roesch, and Guido Halder. "The Texas German Dialect Archive: A Multimedia Resource for Research, Teaching, and Outreach." *Journal of Germanic Linguistics* 22, no. 3 (September 2010): 277–96. https://doi.org/10.1017/S1470542710000036.

Eikel, Fred. "The Use of Cases in New Braunfels German." *American Speech*, no. 24 (1949): 278–81.

Freeouf, Peter Frank. "Dialect Leveling and Preservation in the German of Dubois County, Indiana." In *Studies in Indiana German-Americana*, 1:14–24. Madison: Max Kade Institute, 1988.

———. "Religion and Dialect: Catholic and Lutheran Dialects in the German of Dubois County." Ph.D., Indiana, 1990.

Gilbert, Glenn. "English Loanwords in the German of Fredericksburg, Texas." *American Speech* 40 (1965): 102–12.

———. *Linguistic Atlas of Texas German*. Austin: University of Texas Press, 1972.

———. "The German Dialect Spoken in Kendall and Gillespie Counties, Texas." Ph.D., Harvard, 1963.

Guion, Susan. "The Death of Texas German in Gillespie County." In *Language Contact across the North Atlantic*, edited by P.S. Ureland and Clarkson, 443–63. Tübingen: Niemeyer, 1996.

Huffines, Marion Lois. "Case Usage among the Pennsylvania German Sectarians and Nonsectarians." In *Investigating Obsolescence: Studies in Language Contraction and Death*, edited by Nancy Dorian, 211–26. Cambridge: Cambridge University Press, 1989.

Johnstone, Barbara. *Qualitative Methods in Sociolinguistics*. Oxford: Oxford University Press, 2000.

Keel, William. "German Settlement Varieties in Kansas: Some Unusual Phonological and Morphological Developments with the Approach of

Language Death." In *Perspectives on Phonological Theory and Development*, edited by Ashley Farris-Trimble and Jessica Barlow, 155–72. Amsterdam: John Benjamins, 2014.

———. "On the Heimatbestimmung of the Ellis County (Kansas) Volga German Dialects." *Yearbook of German-American Studies* 17 (1982): 99–109.

———. "Reduction and Loss of Case Marking in the Noun Phrase in German-American Speech Islands: Internal Development or External Interference?" In *Sprachinselforschung: Eine Gedenkschrift Für Hugo Jedig*, edited by Nina Berend and Klaus Mattheier, 93–104. Frankfurt: Peter Lang, 1994.

Kerswill, Paul. "Dialect Levelling, Koinéisation and the Speech of the Adult Migrant." *University of Pennsylvania Working Papers in Linguistics* 3, no. 1 (1996): 1–12.

Khramova, Maria. "The Volga German Dialect of Millberger." Ph.D., Kansas, 2011.

Louden, Mark. *Pennsylvania Dutch: The Story of an American Language*. Baltimore: John Hopkins UP, 2016.

Mattheier, Klaus. "German." In *Germanic Standardizations. Past to Present*, edited by Ana Deumert and Wim Vandenbussche, 211–44. Impact, Studies in Language and Society 18. Amsterdam ; Philadelphia: JBenjamins, 2003.

Nutzel, Daniel. *The East Franconian Dialect of Haysville, Indiana*. Regensburg: Edition Vulpes, 2009.

Reed, Carroll E. *The Pennsylvania German Dialect Spoken in the Counties of Lehigh and Berks*. Seattle: University of Washington Press, 1949.

Rösch, Karen. *Language Maintenance and Language Death: The Decline of Texas Alsatian*. Amsterdam: John Benjamins, 2012.

Rosenberg, Peter. "Comparative Speech Island Research: Some Results from Studies in Russia and Brazil." In *German Language Varieties Worldwide: Internal and External Perspectives*, edited by William Keel and Klaus Mattheier, 199–238. Frankfurt: Peter Lang, 2003.

———. "Vergleichende Sprachinselforschung: Sprachwandel in Deutschen Sprachinseln in Russland Und Brasilien." *Linguistik Online* 13, no. 1 (April 14, 2018). http://dx.doi.org/10.13092/lo.13.881.

Salmons, Joseph. *A History of German: What the Past Reveals about Today's Language*. Oxford: Oxford University Press, 2018.

———. "But Hoosiers Do Speak German: An Overview of German in Indiana." edited by William Keel, 155–66. Lawrence: Kansas State UP, 1986.

———. "Issues in Texas German Language Maintenance and Shift." *Monatshefte* 75 (1983): 187–96.

———. "Register in the Formation and Evolution of an Immigrant Language: Evidence from Some Indiana German Dialects." *WORD* 42 (1991): 31–56.

———, and Daniel Nutzel. "Language Contact and New Dialect Formation: Evidence from German in North America." *Language and Linguistics Compass* 5, no. 10 (2011): 705–17.

Siegel, Jeff. "Koines and Koineization." *Language in Society* 14, no. 3 (1985): 357–78.

Trudgill, Peter. *New-Dialect Formation: The Inevitability of Colonial Englishes*. New York: New York UP, 2004.

Wilson, George. *Wilson's History of Dubois County, Indiana: From Its Primitive Days to 1910*. 2nd ed. Jasper: Evansville Bindery, Inc., 2000.

Chapter 8

Nineteenth-Century American Translations of German Philology

Ulrike Wagner
Bard College Berlin

Abstract: It is no news that the philological techniques developed by late eighteenth- and nineteenth-century German scholars of religion and classical culture had enormous reach and reputation. Numerous sources such as those collected in the recently published *The Rise of the Research University* (Chicago UP, 2017) give evidence to how American higher education and its characteristic division into the undergraduate college and university grew out of a complex web of transatlantic dialogue and exchange. While abundant, however, these sources have sparked few deeper critical examinations going beyond general appraisals of the importance of German research, references to Humboldt or investigations of institutional changes. But as the editors of the sourcebook highlight, to truly understand what lies at the heart of this period of cross-cultural intellectual exchange, we ought to go further and delve "(…) into questions about the ends of scholarly inquiry and education" (5). I take this crucial remark on the far-reaching implications of nineteenth-century research practices in the humanities as a point of departure. Discussing textual materials from both sides of the Atlantic – some of which barely or not at all explored – this essay allows readers to track trajectories of influence, correspondence and dialogue that took place inside as well as outside of the halls and walls of colleges and universities. I suggest that philological practices made decisive contributions to forming conceptions of the self and to modes of cultural and religious renewal centered on the individual's ceaselessly active engagement.

Always with an eye toward recent critical literature on philology and its history, the essay's first part brings into focus the ongoing battles over the method and scope of philology as determined by figures such as Arnold Ludwig Heeren, Johann Gottfried Eichhorn, Christian Gottlob Heyne, F.A. Wolf, Johann Gottfried Herder and Johann Joachim Winckelmann. I bring them into dialogue with American intellectuals like George Bancroft, James Marsh, and George Ripley who studied in Germany and/or engaged with German philological research in essays, translations, and text collections. The second part centers on Herder's collection *Von deutscher Art und Kunst* (1773). The collection's contribution to aesthetic theory and programmatic role for the *Sturm und Drang* movement is well known and researched; the position of Goethe's and Herder's text in the context of debates over the practice and scope of philology, by contrast, has not been thematized. Drawing on current criticism (i.e. Gumbrecht: *The Power of Philology*, 2003; Turner: *Philology: The Forgotten Origins of the Modern Humanities*, 2014; Pollock: *Philology and Freedom*, 2016), I argue that their texts feature key aspects of what reading philologically meant at the time. I bring their approach into conversation with American texts crucial for the rise of the idea of liberal learning and for the religious and cultural reform projects, growing out of classical and theological research. Finally, I will turn to Emerson's aesthetics of the common, draw out its relation to the scholarly discourse of his time and ask in what ways Nietzsche's thoughts on philology and its pedagogic value echo Emerson.

Keywords: Historical overview; philological practices; 18th and 19th centuries; translation

***

Philological techniques developed by late eighteenth- and nineteenth-century German scholars of religion and *Altertumswissenschaften* (the science of antiquity) had enormous reach and reputation. Numerous sources, such as those collected in the recently published book on *The Rise of the Research University* provide evidence of how American higher education and its characteristic division into the undergraduate college and university grew out of a complex web of transatlantic dialogue and exchange.[1] While abundant, however, these sources have sparked few deeper critical examinations going beyond general appraisals of the importance of German research, references to Humboldt, or investigations of institutional changes. As the editors of the text collection emphasize, such broad assessments stop short of bringing to light the wide-ranging manifestations and spheres of impact sparked by activities at German research institutions and beyond; they suggest going further and delving "into questions about the ends of scholarly inquiry and education."[2] Similarly, Caroline Winterer argues that we will only begin to understand what humanist investigations meant for that generation of American scholars if we

---

[1] Louis Menand, Paul Reitter, and Chad Wellmon, eds., *The Rise of the Research University. A Sourcebook*, (Chicago: The University of Chicago Press, 2017).
[2] Menand, *The Rise of the Research University*, 5.

move beyond questions concerning the originality of their research and ask about the larger cultural and pedagogical bearings of their activities.[3]

I take these crucial remarks on the understudied cross-cultural implications of nineteenth-century research practices in Germany and America as a point of departure and examine questions concerning the nature and ends of research in the context of philological debates. The aim of *Germanic Philology: Perspectives in Linguistics and Literature* is not only to highlight the interdisciplinary manifestations of philology, but also, and more importantly, to illuminate the transnational dimension of the field and its broader cultural and social impact beyond institutional settings; in keeping with the editors' goal, this chapter discusses textual materials from both sides of the Atlantic— some of which have been entirely ignored or treated in a cursory manner—and allows readers to trace trajectories of influence and dialogue that have taken place both inside and outside the halls of colleges and universities. I suggest that philological practices developed by scholars with university appointments, as well as by those working and publishing outside of academic institutions, played an important role in the modern refashioning of conceptions of the self, notions of cultural value, and religious experience with wide reach. More specifically, I engage contemporary criticism on the history of philology and turn a philological lens on selected American translations and reviews concerned with the theological writings of Johann Gottfried Herder (1744- 1803). The translations and reviews by the Transcendentalists James Marsh (1794-1842) and George Ripley (1802-1880) are deeply concerned with the widely debated projects of American self-culture,[4] liberal learning, and

---

[3] Caroline Winterer, *The Culture of Classicism: Ancient Greece and Rome in American Intellectual Life, 1780 – 1910* (Baltimore: Johns Hopkins University Press, 2002), 3.

[4] The leading Unitarian preacher and Transcendentalist William Ellery Channing famously coined the term "Self-Culture" in his introductory address to the Franklin Lectures in Boston in 1838. In its most basic sense, Channing describes forms of cultivation directed at the self as "the care which every man owes to himself, to the unfolding and perfecting of his nature." According to his understanding, a subject who conceives of herself as a product of self-culture feels the duty to continuously "act upon [herself]," to "engage in the work of self-improvement," and to "strenuously…form and elevate [her] mind." William Ellery Channing, *Self-Culture. An Address Introductory to the Franklin Lectures. Delivered at Boston, September, 1838* (Boston: Dutton and Wentworth Printers, 1838), 11-12. To be sure, the details of Channing's understanding and treatment of self-culture in the antebellum contexts in which he found such efforts of cultivation flourishing are a complex and contested subject matter. It is therefore important to mention up front that I use the term in the most basic sense that Channing lays out—that is, as an umbrella term for strategies the self employs in order to work on itself. Self- culture, I suggest, sums up best the goal of the learning techniques a new generation of

religious and cultural renewal; I claim that their ways of treating these themes are underwritten by what Constanze Güthenke has shown to be a distinguishing quality of nineteenth-century German classical research: Scholars fashion the relationship with the past as a "quasi-personal" one, and this act of personification, of investing the past with attributes of a living being, has a feedback effect on the objects of inquiry as much as on the self-understanding of the modern practitioner and his field of research.[5] I demonstrate that this personal and personifying practice, imbued with a language of feeling and empathy, is crucial for understanding the nature and broader social significance of the translation of German philological research by nineteenth-century American scholars.

The end of the Napoleonic Wars and the publication of the first English translation of Germaine de Staël's *De l'Allemagne* in New York in 1814 marked the beginning of the travels and exchanges of German works and ideas across the Atlantic.[6] The first group of young American intellectuals came over to study in Germany, and between 1815 and 1850, around 225 American students attended German universities; 137 of them would later hold positions at American colleges and universities.[7] Among this group were figures like Edward Everett, George Ticknor, and George Bancroft who taught themselves German or took lessons with private tutors before and during their studies at the University of Göttingen, Germany's first proto-research university, where they joined seminars by scholars such as the classicist Arnold Ludwig Heeren and the Orientalist Johann Gottfried Eichhorn.[8] Heeren was a former student and son-in-law of the classicist Christian Gottlob Heyne, chair of Eloquence and Poetry at Göttingen and founder of the first university research seminar.[9]

---

scholars employs to highlight the benefits of studying past cultures and to consolidate their place at the heart of liberal education.

[5] Constanze Güthenke, *Feeling and Classical Philology: Knowing Antiquity in German Classical Scholarship, 1770 – 1920* (Cambridge: Cambridge University Press, 2020), 2.

[6] Anne Germaine de Staël, *Germany* (New York: Eastburn, Kirk and Co., 1814).

[7] Kurt Mueller-Vollmer, "'Every Ship Brings a Word': Cultural and Literary Transfer from Germany to the United States in the First Half of the Nineteenth Century," *KulturPoetik* 3, no. 2 (2003): 155-172.

[8] Armin Paul Frank and Kurt Mueller-Vollmer, *British America and the United States, 1770s-1850s*. Vol. 2 of *The Internationality of National Literatures in Either America: Transfer and Transformation* (Göttingen: Wallstein Verlag, 2000), 159-162.

[9] On Heyne's role for the discipline of *Altertumswissenschaften* and the rise of the research seminar, see Katherine Harloe, *Winckelmann and the Invention of Antiquity. History and Aesthetics in the Age of Altertumswissenschaften* (Oxford: Oxford University Press, 2013), 161-192; William Clark, *Academic Charisma and the Origins of the Research University* (Chicago: University of Chicago Press, 2006), 141-182.

During Heyne's tenure at Göttingen, the field of *Altphilologie* underwent a major paradigm shift, inspired by Johann Joachim Winckelmann's highly idealized and aestheticized view of ancient Greek culture. As Katherine Harloe details, Winckelmann has "the status of founding spirit of the university discipline of *Altertumswissenschaft*," despite never himself holding an official position at the university. His seminal role, however, is due not so much to "the enduring value of his scholarship," but rather to "the exemplarity of his life."[10] In other words, it is the close connection Winckelmann fashioned between his life, his character, and his scholarship that earned him his lasting reputation as a founding figure in the field of classical studies. Echoing Winckelmann in their research and pedagogy, Heyne and his former student Friedrich August Wolf studied the ancient past holistically: Rather than promoting a narrow, exclusively text-focused approach, they considered *Altertumswissenschaft* to be "the study of Graeco-Roman civilization 'in its essence and in every aspect of its existence.'"[11]

Such inclusive investigations of antiquity, employing different interpretive approaches and drawing on a wide range of ancient cultural productions were, however, also subject to vehement contestations reaching far beyond academic institutions. As Harloe's study demonstrates, Heyne was not only influenced by Winckelmann, he was also "one of [his] most skeptical eighteenth-century critics" and did not refrain from pointing out the methodological shortcomings and historical flaws of Winckelmann's reconstructions. Heyne found fault with Winckelmann's overactive imagination, making it obvious that the two "had very different ideas about the limits of permissible interpretation in the project of reconstructing antiquity as a whole." She highlights a similar tension between Wolf and Herder; the former felt deceived and professionally threatened by Herder's popular explications of the authorship of the Homeric poems in his essay "Homer und Ossian," published the same year as Wolf's *Prolegomena ad Homerum* (1795). In Wolf's eyes, Herder the amateur had not only plagiarized the findings outlined in the *Prolegomena* but had also misused and clumsily distorted the scientifically sound research methodology Wolf had developed to reveal the lack of a Homeric *Urtext*.[12] Like Heyne's critique of Winckelmann, Wolf's attack on Herder epitomizes the ongoing battle over the methods and scope of attempts to reconstruct the ancient past. Such disputes, which took place both within and outside the academy, were indicative of classical philology and the vicissitudes of its practice. Questions concerning the range of the objects

---

[10] Harloe, *Winckelmann and the Invention of Antiquity*, 5, 7.
[11] Ibid., 164.
[12] Ibid., 166, 188; 138-147.

of specialized research and the role that conjecture and intuition should play in recovering the ancient world were subject to constant negotiation.[13]

The nineteenth-century controversy echoes vibrantly in various shapes and forms throughout present-day criticisms of philology. Typically, we associate the philologist's tasks today in the first place with collecting, editing and commenting. In the eyes of many, professional philology is "the dutiful noting and cataloguing of alternative views, the compilation and responsible reporting of bibliographic references, and, in critical editions, the presentation of textual variants."[14] What unifies the diverse and growing body of leading critical approaches, however, is their critique of such narrow conceptions of philology.

The editors of the collected volume on *World Philology* belittle the field's current state: Today, "philology leads a pale, ghostly existence. All it has left are the fragments others have left behind: text criticism, bibliography, historical grammar, corpus linguistics."[15] This negligible status stands in stark contrast to a notable historical past when "philology was the queen of the sciences in the nineteenth-century university, bestriding that world like a colossus in its conceptual and institutional power. It set the standard of what scientific knowledge should be and influenced a range of other disciplines, from anthropology to zoology."[16] During these golden years, figureheads such as Friedrich August Wolf, Christian Gottlob Heyne, Friedrich Schlegel and August Boeckh formulated their grand, all-encompassing visions, which over the years would gradually give way to specialization and fragmentation. Against this backdrop, the contributors to the volume set out to reconstruct philology from different transcultural and transhistorical perspectives, to revive it as a comprehensive "discipline of making sense of texts" and to productively embrace its inherent tensions "between, for example, empirical depth and

---

[13] For a discussion of programmatic texts on the topic, see Constanze Güthenke, "'Enthusiasm Dwells Only in Specialization:' Classical Philology and Disciplinarity in Nineteenth-Century Germany" in *World Philology*, ed. Sheldon Pollock et al. (Cambridge: Harvard University Press, 2015), 265. On August Boeckh's impact on the discipline's historiography, see Güthenke, "Warum Boeckhs *Encyklopädie* lessen," *Geschichte der Germanistik* 51/52 (2017): 83-97 and Wilfried Nippel, "Philologenstreit und Schulpolitik: Zur Kontroverse zwischen Gottfried Hermann und August Böckh," in *Geschichtsdiskurs*, vol. 3 of *Die Epoche der Historisierung*, ed. Wolfgang Küttler et al. (Frankfurt am Main, 1997), 244-253.
[14] Sean Gurd, "Introduction," in *Philology and its Histories*, ed. Sean Gurd (Ohio: Ohio State University Press, 2010), 10.
[15] Pollock, *World Philology*, 9.
[16] Ibid., 2-3. On philology's transdisciplinary roles and functions present and past, see also Denis Thouard, ed., *Philologie als Wissensmodell / La philologie comme modèle de savoir* (Berlin/New York: De Gruyter, 2010).

conceptual breadth, the particular and the universal, and scientificity and creativity" with the aim of learning "how philology has made our world."[17]

To learn how philology has shaped the ways we view things is also a crucial incentive for James Turner's *Philology: The Forgotten Origins of the Modern Humanities*: "Because philology's legacy survives in ways we build knowledge today, the excavation of the philological past becomes an effort at once of historical reconstruction and present-day self-understanding."[18] According to Turner, distinct academic fields in the humanities, such as antiquarianism, classics, religious criticism, art history, and anthropology have a common root in philology, originally sharing as a result common methods and protocols of knowledge before fragmenting into separate disciplines over the course of the nineteenth-century. Swiftly moving from antiquity through the Middle Ages to the Renaissance and Reformation, the book focuses on the development and international expansion of new philological techniques after 1800. Turner acknowledges Germany's leading role in this period of philology's rapid growth and unprecedented intellectual dominance, yet his primary subject matter is the development of the modern humanities in England, Scotland, and America. He details how excavations from this shared history of humanist studies provide insights into the complex process of initiating and building modes of knowledge, and he suggests that engaging this past helps us see "strength and weaknesses" of today's disciplinary academic divisions and refine their quality.[19]

While different with regard to their specific objects of inquiry as well as the geographical and temporal scope of their research, Turner and Pollock both mobilize philology's extensive history as the intellectual historical foundation and inspiration for their respective projects of promoting new directions of philological inquiry in education, research, and society at large. *The Humanities and the Dream of America* by Geoffrey Galt Harpham concentrates in particular on the history of philological practices in America and zeroes in on the field's inherent methodological tensions. The duality between philology's "speculative boldness" and "a more subjective approach to questions of context, meaning, and value" on the one hand and its "commitment to an empirical attention to linguistic fact" on the other is rooted in the field's origins, and any

---

[17] Ibid., 21-24. On the topic of how philology might render us better agents and consumers of knowledge, see also Peter-André Alt, *Die Verheißungen der Philologie* (Göttingen: Wallsteinverlag, 2007).
[18] James Turner, *Philology: The Forgotten Origins of the Modern Humanities* (Princeton: Princeton University Press, 2014), xiii.
[19] Ibid., xiii.

investigation of the development of the humanities in higher education in America ought to take that into account.[20]

According to Harpham, America's humanist discourse, manifest in the country's unique liberal arts model of education, centers on the "activation of personal knowledge" sparked by a "sympathetic imaginative encounter with texts or artefacts."[21] More specifically, the text's property resides in its capacity to activate as well as enlarge and alter one's emotions, understanding, and experience. While we are "register[ing] our own half formulated thoughts and feelings," the encounter also "offer[s] us different ways of thinking or feeling that give us a perspective on our own lives and the lives of others, and thereby a sense of power over circumstances and freedom from mere contingency."[22]

Harpham's observations regarding the imperative of *Bildung* in nineteenth-century American discourses over the goals and directions of humanist *Wissenschaft* form a crucial backdrop for my own research.[23] His study covers a broad range of sources and stages in the career of philology and the humanities, leading up to the twenty-first century and referencing key actors of the German academic and public scene like F.A. Wolf, his student Philip August Boeckh, Wilhelm von Humboldt and Friedrich Nietzsche. Details and sources of the intellectual exchange with Germany in the early years, however, do not play a role in his account.

---

[20] Geoffrey Galt Harpham, *The Humanities and the Dream of America* (Chicago: The University of Chicago Press, 2011), 77.

[21] To corroborate his claim, Harpham considers seminal works from three centuries such as John Henry Newman's *The Idea of a University* (1852) which "set man of the terms of liberal education in the Anglophone world over a hundred years" (126), the *General Education in a Free Society*—the so called Harvard "Redbook"—published by a committee of Harvard professors in 1945, an essay by Richard J. Franke that exemplifies the discourse of private philanthropy concerned with supporting the humanities, and Andrew Delbanco's *The American Dream* (2000). For a detailed overview of sources and approaches to understanding the invention of the humanities in America, see chapter six in Harpham, *The Humanities and the Dream of America*, 145-190.

[22] Harpham, *The Humanities and the Dream of America*, 180.

[23] The terms *Wissenschaft* and *Bildung* are difficult to translate. Throughout this text, I will follow Menand, *The Rise of the Research University*, and stick either with the German term *Wissenschaft* or translate it as knowledge, scholarship, systematic knowledge, or science: "Broadly speaking, *Wissenschaft* refers in these late eighteenth-century and early nineteenth-century texts to any systematic way of knowing or the pursuit of such knowledge" (9). With *Bildung* (from *bilden*, to form) I will also either use the German term or translate it as self-culture, self-transformation or self-education. All these translational variants denote autonomy which is the key connotation of the term *Bildung* in German culture at the time.

American scholars came in contact with the controversy over the methods and reach of philology during their studies in Germany as well as through various other modes of intellectual transfer and organs of publication over the course of the nineteenth-century. The debate took on new forms and directions in New England, and it shaped the intellectual discourse as much as the development of institutions of learning. George Ticknor, a young graduate from Dartmouth College whose decision to study in Göttingen was motivated by Madame de Staël's account, remarks on the practice of humanistic scholarship at the university in a letter to Thomas Jefferson in 1816: "The men of letters here bring a philosophical spirit to the labor of exposition which is wanting in the same class in all other countries. The consequence is that the study of the classics has taken a new and more free turn within the last forty years (…)."[24] Upon his return, he was appointed the Smith Professor of French and Spanish Languages and head of the Department of Modern Languages at Harvard and attempted to model his teaching and research on what he had admired in Göttingen.[25]

George Bancroft, who had just graduated from Harvard and was well trained in classical languages like Ticknor, followed in his footsteps in 1818. Edward Everett, Harvard's first classics professor and recent returnee from Göttingen, had urged president Kirkland to send Bancroft abroad for a solid training in philological learning, and he received a fellowship "so that he could become [in Kirkland's words] 'an accomplished biblical critic,' able to expound and defend the Revelation of God."[26] After his studies in Göttingen, Bancroft left for the University of Berlin, which he found to be more intellectually stimulating and amenable to learning. Besides attending lectures by F.A. Wolf and Boeckh, Bancroft took courses with Friedrich Schleiermacher on the "science of education" which he praises highly: "I have taken a course of lectures with Schleiermacher on the science of education; it is the most interesting which I have as yet attended. (…) I honor Schleiermacher above all the German scholars, with whom it has been my lot to become acquainted."[27] After returning to America, Bancroft taught at Harvard for a few years but without becoming the theologian Kirkland had hoped for. He found the intellectual environment in Cambridge rather uninspiring and co-founded a private school near Boston modeled on the German gymnasium.[28]

---

[24] "Ticknor's Letter to Thomas Jefferson, Göttingen March 15, 1816," in Menand, *The Rise of the Research University*, 128.
[25] Menand, *The Rise of the Research University*, 124-125.
[26] Ibid., 125-126.
[27] "Letter from George Bancroft to President Kirkland, Berlin, November 5 (1820)," in Menand, *The Rise of the Research University*, 135.
[28] Menand, *The Rise of the Research University*, 127; see also Mueller-Vollmer, "'Every Ship Brings a Word': Cultural and Literary Transfer from Germany to the United States in the First Half of the Nineteenth Century," 155-172.

This cursory glance at the transatlantic sojourns of seminal figures active in the public sphere and New England's educational institutions suffices for gaining an impression of people's varied motivations for studying in Germany and of their later career paths. For the purpose of this study, I concentrate primarily on James Marsh, translator of Herder's major theological work *Vom Geist der Ebräischen Poesie* (1782-83), and on George Ripley, who published pioneering reviews of the translation. I selected these writings not because I regard them as generally representative of the incredibly diverse interests American intellectuals had in German scholarship. Rather, the texts under discussion are a good starting point for bringing into focus characteristics of what reading philologically implies for some of the period's leading scholars; and the writings disclose how critical techniques may generate new perspectives on matters of religion, culture, and individual *Bildung*.

Marsh was educated at Dartmouth College, and later he attended Harvard where he studied with Reverend Moses Stuart, head of Andover Theological Seminary, who introduced him to German literature and criticism. In 1812 Moses Stuart and Edward Everett became involved in a bidding war over the four volumes of Johann Gottfried Eichhorn's *Einleitung in das Alte Testament* (1780-83). Joseph Stevens Buckminster, one of New England's most influential and recently deceased ministers, had brought the Eichhorn volumes back from Europe. Stuart won the auction, but he gave Everett the permission to borrow his purchase.[29] Stuart had a further book that he wanted to make accessible to a larger circle of readers, and for which he was trying to find a translator: Herder's *Vom Geist der Ebräischen Poesie*. Everett turned the request down and focused on translating sections from Eichhorn instead. Stuart, however, did not give up and was able to win over his student James Marsh to take on the challenge. With few exceptions, critics rarely note his contributions to the spreading of Herderian thinking with his translation of Herder's fragment *The Spirit of Hebrew Poetry* (1833).[30] Rather, he is best known for his edition of Coleridge's *Aids to Reflection*, for which he wrote a "Preliminary Essay."[31]

---

[29] For further details of the bidding war, see Philip F. Gura, *American Transcendentalism: A History* (New York: Hill and Wang, 2007), 21-23.

[30] On the American reception of German historical scholarship in New England and at German universities, see Kurt Mueller-Vollmer, "American Students at the Center of Herderian Humanities in Germany," in *British America and the United States, 1770s-1850s*. Vol. 2 of *The Internationality of National Literatures in Either America: Transfer and Transformation* (Göttingen: Wallstein Verlag, 2000), 159-162; Barbara L. Packer's, *The Transcendentalists* (Athens, Georgia: University of Georgia Press, 2007), 14-19; Philip F. Gura, *American Transcendentalism: A History* (New York: Hill and Wang, 2007), 21-23, 25-31.

[31] There is no mention of Marsh's Herder translation in Louis Menand, *The Metaphysical Club* (New York: Farrar, Strauss and Giroux, 2001). Menand concentrates on Marsh's Coleridge edition, see 245-248.

Marsh was a Congregationalist minister and a key figure of the Vermont Transcendentalists. He served as president of the University of Vermont, took a chair in philosophy, and restructured the university's teaching curriculum during his tenure as president from 1826 – 1833. The new curriculum, as Harvey states in *Transatlantic Transcendentalism: Coleridge, Emerson, and Nature*, was premised on "Coleridgean principles" and revolutionized American higher education.[32] Inspired by Romantic idealism, Marsh introduced subject-centered practices of learning, leaving behind old rhetorical and grammar-oriented teaching models focused on memorization and recitation. Marsh, to be sure, was by no means alone in promoting curricular changes in higher education in the 1820s, yet according to Harvey's investigations, his curriculum turned out to be part of the most sustainable ones that would be adopted and modified by future generations of educators.[33] In reviewing Marsh's "An Exposition of the System of Instruction and Discipline Pursued at the University of Vermont," published in 1829 in defense of the new curriculum whose implementation had stirred much controversy, Harvey discusses its pedagogical focus on active learning and the processual, open-ended character of education promoted therein, echoing Romantic ideals of *Bildung* and continuous self-development.[34]

With this study's concentration on Marsh's translation of Herder and Ripley's discussion thereof, I now shift the focus from the conceptual realm of philosophy to concrete forms of critical labor. This turn to philological practices does not, however, introduce a revisionary view on the overall educational goals Marsh and his contemporaries formulated in response to their engagement with the philosophy of idealism. Rather, the shift to translations and textual criticism, I argue, contributes a detailed set of insights into *how* learning can be turned into an open-ended process, and *how* critical work can shape the individual as well as the social and cultural life they inhabit.

In the context of the American reception of German works and criticism, Ripley's reviews of Herder's works and of Marsh's translation of *The Spirit of Hebrew Poetry* stand out. Published in the May and November issue of the *Christian Examiner and General Review* in 1835, these texts provide the most

---

[32] Samantha C. Harvey, *Transatlantic Transcendentalism: Coleridge, Emerson, and Nature* (Edinburgh: Edinburgh University Press, 2013), 141.
[33] Ibid., 145.
[34] Ibid., 146-150.

nuanced and learned American investigation of Herder's thinking.[35] This journal was the most important mouthpiece of Unitarianism and the intellectual forum for the publication and broader circulation of key concerns of the Transcendentalist movement in the early years.[36] The Unitarian minister Ripley was a core figure of the Transcendentalist group. He had attended Harvard together with his cousin and friend Emerson, helped to found the Transcendental Club (a regular meeting point for anyone concerned with rethinking the premises of Unitarian theology in the movement's early years), and was a major force in translating and promoting German Biblical scholarship, literature, and philosophy among his contemporaries. He owned most of Herder's works in the original. Most famously, he edited a 14-volume series titled *Specimens of Foreign Standard Literature* between 1838 and 1842, which contains translations of what he considered canonical French and German writings.[37]

These reviews highlight the distinction Herder draws between religion and theology, and they make the claim that this difference is foundational to restoring faith in times of its crisis. According to Ripley, the research from the other side of the Atlantic provides new conceptual tools to reconstruct faith in times of its historico-critical deconstruction. Theology, Ripley writes referencing Herder, is not a field of inquiry "invested with any peculiar rights" but a science like any other with sets of "propositions for and against which we may dispute" and which need to be scrutinized and questioned like those of any other science. Religion, by contrast, "is a matter of inward nature."[38] Translating and paraphrasing Herder, Ripley locates God's "kingdom...among us" and emphasizes that it was Herder's central project "to bring the conviction of its truth to the individual consciousness of man."[39]

By introducing religion as a human disposition whose credibility is severed from specific historical incidents, Ripley opens up the Bible to rigorous and unrestricted critical examination, yet without weakening the subject's trust and

---

[35] George Ripley, "Review of *The Spirit of Hebrew Poetry*. By J. G. Herder. Translated from the German by James Marsh, 2 Vols., Burlington 1833," *Christian Examiner and General Review*, 18 (1835): 167-221; "Review of Johann Gottfried Herders Sämtliche Werke zur Religion und Theologie. Ed. By Johann Georg Müller. 18 Theile, Stuttgart-Tübingen 1827-1830," *Christian Examiner and General Review* 19 (1835): 172-204.
[36] On the journal's history, see Tiffany K. Wayne, *Encyclopedia of Transcendentalism* (New York: Facts On File, 2006), 47-48.
[37] Henry L. Golemba, *George Ripley* (Boston: Twayne Publishers, 1977).
[38] Ripley, "Review of Johann Gottfried Herders Sämtliche Werke" (Nov.1835), 180.
[39] Ibid., 196-197.

hope in the power of revelation in both past and present times: "Revelation pervades every age (…). Every age has had its mission in the unfolding of truth, and contributed its share towards the spiritual culture or man."[40] This distinction between the individual's spiritual disposition and historically specific manifestations of divine experiences allows for fundamentally new ways of thinking about relations between the spirit, matter and the letter.

Against this critical backdrop, Ripley introduces revelation as a lifelong educational process: "A ship on the ocean needs the wind; the human mind demands continued inquiry and discussion on both sides." This Herderian analogy illuminates cogently the demands placed on the individual with higher aspirations: For its divine potentials to unfold and to prevent falling into stagnation, the subject needs an environment acting on it like wind and water act on a ship; it has to expose itself and open up to the challenges posed by interrogations and debates. A powerful "aid" for the cultivation of such mental plasticity is "sound philological learning." One ought to bring an inquisitive and skeptical mindset to the writings of the Bible and all religious doctrines and "sacred records":[41]

> [Herder] desired to have all opinions confronted together, that their genuine character might be ascertained. The only security of the progress of science and the ultimate establishment of the truth was to be found, according to his view, in the calm comparison of different opinions, without excitement and without prejudice. He carried this principle so far, as to suppose that the best interests of religion were promoted by the free utterance of any doubts that were felt, either with regard to the received dogmas of the church, or the origin and character of Christianity itself.[42]

The individual gains freedom and integrity in matters of faith by comparing and critically scrutinizing different opinions about religious records and by questioning them. A person who calls into doubt his own propositions and the propositions of others acts in accordance with "the best interests of religion."

Through the lens of Herder's criticism, Ripley introduces a notion of religious integrity that places high demands on the individual. To be true to religion means to accept a life path centered on trial and error. Throughout his reviews, Ripley probes deeply into the details of *how* Herder seeks to accomplish the formation of a mind that integrates the unsettlement of propositions into his

---

[40] Ibid., 183.
[41] Ibid., 177.
[42] Ibid., 175.

modes of spiritual revival, into his return to "the consciousness of his own nature."[43] He identifies Herder's concept of empathy as a conduit for the formation of such a mind-set, and thereby picks up on what Marsh's "Translator's Preface" to *The Spirit of Hebrew Poetry* introduces as the lens for us to understand the characteristics of Herder's notion of religious recovery:

> The work, of which a translation is here offered to the public, has long been celebrated in Germany, as one of distinguished merit...It taught them [the Germans], too, in the study of Hebrew antiquity and Hebrew poetry, as the works of Lessing, Winkelmann, and others had done in regard to Grecian antiquity, to divest themselves of the conceptions, and modes of thought, which are peculiar to their own country and institutions, and of the peculiar spirit of their own age; by the force of imagination to place themselves in the condition of those ancient patriarchs and prophets...to see the world as they saw it, to feel as they felt, to imbibe and to express their spirit in its truth and simplicity.[44]

Marsh's preface to his translation of Herder's work is of great interest not only because of the methodological approach expressed therein, but also from a canonical point of view. By aligning Winckelmann's and Lessing's mode of reviving Greek antiquity with Herder's recovery of Hebrew poetry, he makes a case for the transferability of the exercises of empathy and self-abandonment to cultures other than Greek. Throughout the preface Marsh details what such acts of displacement mean for the modern reader and critic. He has to divest himself of everything he takes for granted and regards as normative in his own life world. He has to depart from habits and modes of thinking with which he is comfortable and try to abandon the range of emotions accompanying them.[45] By the same token, Ripley elaborates on Herder's modes of self-abandonment as the precondition for the modern mind's "pursuit of truth."[46]

According to Marsh and Ripley, it is by means of his practice of imaginary displacement that Herder sets himself apart from the text on which his reworkings of the Old Testament are modeled, Robert Lowth's *De Sacra Poesi Hebraeorum Praelectiones*. What diminishes the quality of Lowth's *De Sacra Poesi Hebraeorum* in Marsh's eyes is that he forms his opinions about Hebrew poetry too much against the backdrop of Greco-Roman standards of composition.

---

[43] Ibid., 201.
[44] James Marsh, "Translator's Preface" to Johann Gottfried Herder, in *The Spirit of Hebrew Poetry*, transl. James Marsh (Burlington: Edward Smith, 1833), 3.
[45] Ibid., 5.
[46] Riple, "Review of Johann Gottfried Herders Sämtliche Werke" (Nov.1835), 183.

The comparisons with Lowth's text help the American critics bring into focus the highly demanding nature of Herder's approach to the Hebrew Scriptures and demonstrate the method's advantages at the same time.[47] Ripley, above all, is concerned with exemplifying why Herder's "path of inquiry" is worth adopting and leads "students of the Bible" to "excellent success."[48] According to him, the exercise of divesting ourselves of what we take to be normative habits, emotions, and modes of thinking helps us to see the Hebrew verses as lively records, telling us of the ways in which ancient Hebrews experienced God's presence in their lives in numerous ways.

Against the backdrop of Ripley's and Marsh's explications of Herder's empathetic method, we gain a good sense of the critical labor needed to engage actively with a text, hone one's mental agility, and avoid the pitfalls of doctrinal imposition. This examination of the translator's preface and of Ripley's reviews sheds a fresh light on how the educational goal of engaging in an open-ended fashion with textual sources can be performed. Moreover, Ripley's text shows ways in which such intellectual labor can serve what takes center stage in the educational discourse at the time, that is the question of the self's formation. In the context of religious debates, this goal is associated with the restoration of man's faith in feeling and experiencing the divine and in acting as a "God-Man."[49] According to Ripley's reviews, Herder stands out because he does not just speak, but also *performs* his claim that the gift of revelation was no privilege of the past, but is potentially available to everyone at any time.

This topic leads to the heart of Ripley's review where he evaluates Marsh's translation. Ripley acknowledges "the literary enterprise and industry of an American scholar in undertaking and completing such a difficult task." At the same time, however, he is highly critical of the quality of Marsh's work as a translator:

> In justice to Herder it ought to be stated, that he suffers much under the hands of Professor Marsh. The vivacity and animation which breathe from every page of the original are evaporated in the translation. The spirited and graceful style of Herder, in the composition of this work, would hardly be recognized in the new costume which is given to his thoughts…[Marsh] often overlays the breathing life of the original with a thick shroud of words.[50]

---

[47] Marsh, "Translator's Preface," 6-7.
[48] Ripley, "Review of Johann Gottfried Herders Sämtliche Werke" (Nov.1835), 189-192.
[49] Ibid., 179.
[50] Ripley, "Review of *The Spirit of Hebrew Poetry*" (May 1835), 170.

According to Ripley, Marsh's English fails to bring out the vivacity of the original language. In large bodies of footnotes running over several pages, Ripley places his own translation side by side with Marsh's to exemplify his point. He shows how Marsh covers up Herder's "graceful" and "spirited" style that is "breathing with life" with a wordy translation, exhibiting grammatical flaws and a faulty diction. In short, Ripley resumes that "Herder's spirit is not in it."[51]

Ripley's critique draws attention to the complexity of Herder's philological practice. In Ripley's eyes Marsh's translation fails to convey that Herder combines the exercise of self-surrender with a strong formative impetus and a moment of self-discovery. Drawing on Madame de Staël's discussion of Herder's work in *Germany*, Ripley provides a detailed introduction to this creative dimension of Herder's approach to Hebrew poetry:

> It is seldom that we meet with a writer, whose soul is so penetrated with the true spirit of antiquity, and who is so capable of bringing up the faded past in vivid reality before the eye. "It seems, in reading him," says Madame de Staël, "as if we were walking in the midst of the old world with an historical poet, who touches the ruins with his wand and erects anew all the fallen edifices." He brings to his subject a freshness, a gushing enthusiasm, which spreads a charm over the driest details, and reminds us more of the eloquent conversation of a friend than of the learned discussion of a critic. Every thing is in motion, every thing has life, he is never languid himself, and he never permits languor in others; and we are led on from page to page of profound learning, of curious research, of wide and scholar-like investigation, with as little feeling and satiety or fatigue, as if we were reading a fascinating novel. He is unrivaled in the power of giving a picturesque beauty to the most barren subjects, so that the wilderness springs up into bloom and luxuriance under his magic touch. His own pure and noble spirit breathes through his productions. They seem to bring us into the presence of the author, where we hear his deep and thrilling voice, gaze upon his serene brow, and receive a revelation of his inmost heart. We cannot read them without knowing and loving the mind, from whose inspiration they proceeded. The great object of his life was the spiritual elevation of humanity; and, in his view, the means of his accomplishment was to infuse the spirit of Christ and his religion into the hearts of men. Such fervent love of man, such deep sympathy with Christ...these are so distinctly impressed on the whole face of his writings, that, in reading

---

[51] Ibid., 173.

them, we feel that we are enjoying the intimate communion of an exalted and holy mind.[52]

Ripley demonstrates through the lens of Herder's critical techniques how the modern reconstruction of a religious text can be turned into an instrument for man's "spiritual elevation." The passage details how Herder realizes his life's objective, the infusion of "the spirit of Christ into the hearts of men," by rendering the text a site for the critic to act as a "God-Man." Obviously convinced by the success of Herder's efforts, Ripley concludes that in reading *Vom Geist der Ebräischen Poesie* he feels as if he were witnessing an "intimate communion of an exalted and holy mind."

Ripley's enthusiastic championing of Herder's infusion of his spirit into his theological writings tallies with vital features of the concurrently emerging discipline of classical studies. In "The Potter's Daughter's Sons: German Classical Scholarship and the Language of Love Circa 1800," Güthenke details her claim that from the beginning "the life stories of individual scholars" are crucial for the consolidation of classical scholarship as a discipline, and she investigates the link between the personal and the emergence of classical studies in texts by Winckelmann, Herder, Schlegel, Humboldt, Wolf, Boeckh, and Schleiermacher.[53] While some of these figures determined the course and program of the field's professionalization directly by means of their institutional affiliations, others were not classical scholars in the professional sense. Both, however, had an equally significant impact on the consolidation and progress of the *Altertumswissenschaften* as a discipline whose historiography needs to be considered in terms of the individuals who shape it.

More specifically, what the works under scrutiny have in common is "the conception of the ancient past as a quasi-human figure vis-à-vis its observer."[54] In their accounts of antiquity, these scholars employ strategies of personification and express their reconstitutions in a contemporary language of interpersonal affection, attraction, and intimacy. Against the backdrop of her observation, Güthenke develops her central claim that this language of love and the imagery of affect has shaped individuals as much as the scholarly discourse that was establishing itself.

According to Güthenke, it was the rise of the idea of *Bildung* in Germany that informed classical scholarship's self-conception. The proliferation of the model of *Bildung* generated the turn toward individual experience and to questions of

---

[52] Ibid., 169.
[53] Constanze Güthenke, "The Potter's Daughter's Sons: German Classical Scholarship and the Language of Love Circa 1800," *Representations* 109 (2010): 122-147.
[54] Güthenke, "German Classical Scholarship," 122.

how engaging with classical antiquity facilitates self-formation and the formation of the discipline.[55] Ripley's discussion of Herder's theological writings addresses exactly the mutually transformative relationship Güthenke observes between self-formation and the emerging scholarly discourse in classical studies. In Ripley's eyes, Herder accomplishes the goal of making his readers feel that the divine resides in man himself by performing how to go beyond being a "learned critic" toward becoming a "historical poet," or what I would call a poet-philologist. In that function, Herder reveals powers that Ripley compares to those of a magician: like the magician with his "wand," the poet-philologist touches "the most barren subjects" and turns them into magnificent ones. He erects "ruins" and transforms the "wilderness" into a blossoming landscape. He endows the objects he singles out with a magical aura of exclusivity.

Through such acts of transformation, the past not only comes vibrantly alive, radically altering our perspective on it, but it also moves closer and becomes thereby more personal and accessible. Ripley writes that Herder's way of approaching his subjects reminds him of a conversation he would have with a friend. The author of the ancient writings himself seems to emerge as a friend, as a "mind" we cannot but love; through Herder's style of writing the author materializes as a person with physical characteristics, revealing his most intimate emotions to us. We can "hear his deep and thrilling voice," "gaze upon his serene brow" and gain insight into "his inmost heart."

What Ripley identifies here as features of Herder's method corroborates Güthenke's claim regarding the feedback effect that the discourse of interpersonal affection has on the scholar himself.[56] Ripley describes such a process of inventing the self when he observes that Herder impresses his "sympathy" and "intimate communion" with the divine "on the whole face of his writings" and thereby fashions himself as a "God-Man." Herder exhibits the scholar's ability to bring out his affinities with God vis-à-vis his activity as a poet-philologist. Through his intimate language and style, his strategy of zeroing in on individual objects he forges a personal perspective on the past which, in turn, enables him to fashion himself as a modern theologian able to turn religious records of the past into instruments for a timely and subject-centered mode of researching and of practicing religion.

Ripley's reviews and Marsh's translator preface give insight into how a mode of textual interaction structured around empathy and a language of intimacy and friendship may foster mental agility and an open-ended approach to

---

[55] Ibid., 122-123.
[56] Ibid., 126.

learning with bearings on the subject's self-understanding and the discipline of theology. In the final part of this chapter, I turn to Marsh's "Review of Stuart on the Epistle of the Hebrews," which offers a general account of philology's role in education and society. Stuart's *Commentary on the Epistle to the Hebrews* (1827-1828) is deeply informed by his detailed engagement with German philological methods; he had taught himself German just for that purpose and Marsh uses Stuart's hermeneutic approach in the *Commentary* as a forum to establish philology as *the* practice most suitable for the honing of one's emotional and cognitive faculties. The review also resonates with what Güthenke describes as a text's feedback effect on the self and the discipline. Marsh, however, limits his discussion of the impact of philological practices not to a specific field but broadens the perspective toward their role in a model of *Bildung* centered on liberal learning: "(...) every scholar, who is aiming at a liberal education, should be essentially a philologist," Marsh writes, looking to secure the field a place at the heart of liberal learning.[57]

In pursuit of this objective, Marsh elaborates on a key argumentative move familiar to readers of the translator's preface. Referring to Lessing and Winckelmann, he suggests that the critical techniques promoted by Herder are not tied to Hebrew culture but potentially applicable to other fields. In the review of Stuart he advises his readers to treat philology as an exercise whose usefulness is not contingent upon selected fields of application: "Let the question then be, whether philological pursuits and the critical study of language be *in themselves*, and without regard to the individual merits of the work or author read, a comparatively useful method of attaining knowledge and mental culture."[58] His primary interest lies in bringing into view and in promoting the value of the process of interpretation as such for the individual's development: "With this question [the question regarding the intrinsic use of philological pursuits] before us, we might...inquire whether the process, by which the meaning of the author's words is therein determined and knowledge acquired, be not as well suited as any other process, for developing and cultivating the best faculties of the mind."[59] What, then, are the characteristics of textual criticism that lead Marsh to hold it in such high esteem? Significantly, he proposes that the activities of "the philologist, the critical student of words" open up his mind to the relationship between how human modes of forming

---

[57] James Mars, "Review of Stuart on the Epistle to the Hebrews," *Quarterly Christian Spectator* (March 1829): 117.
[58] Ibid., 115. Marsh also suggests that there is no difference as to whether one employs philological methods in the realm of sacred or profane literature, compare 112-113.
[59] Ibid., 115.

language have altered frameworks of human life throughout history. He introduces the notion of words as archives, containing

> the notices of the senses generalized by the understanding, the collected results of the experience, not of one generation only, but of ages, the products of art, the acquisitions of science, the principles and ideas, which their philosophic minds may have unfolded, and which have a living and life-giving energy for the minds of every succeeding age.[60]

Languages are repositories of human experience and invention, telling those capable of unlocking their stories of the flourishing, decline, and transformation of human activity. The passage clearly indicates where the interests of a nineteenth-century American scholar engaging with languages and literatures lie. Marsh's primary question is not how such critical endeavors contribute to an existing body of philological scholarship but rather in what ways the works of others act upon the minds of those engaging them. He is interested in how a text's "living and life-giving energy" resonates with and forms the mind. So the objective of critical exercises such as immersing oneself in the past and of trying to "see with their [the ancients'] eyes and hear with their ears" is, first and foremost, a pedagogical one. Given that words record "the progress of the mind," Marsh declares, nobody can dispute that "these words and organized forms of language are necessary or useful to us in the cultivation of our minds."[61]

Besides its enriching functions, philological studies also confront students with the delimiting characteristics of language: "situated as we are in society, we unavoidably learn words before we can have much insight into the meaning of them and the consequence is, that we acquire a habit, of which the most critical and philosophical minds hardly divest themselves, of using them often without any definite and precise meaning." According to Marsh, drawing attention to such instances—and working toward the active dissociation of the semantic field a particular set of words has come to be associated with—forms an essential part of education.

Also, Marsh touches on the broader cultural implications of making philology the cornerstone of liberal learning. He proposes that American culture at large benefits from turning a vast variety of literatures and languages into objects of critical investigation: "Even the most uncultivated dialects of our western forests, or the islands of the Pacific, exhibit in their structures new and striking combinations of mental phenomena, which cannot but increase our admiration

---

[60] Ibid., 116.
[61] Ibid., 115-116.

of those principles of intellectual organization."[62] Utterances such as these implement philology as a practice that uncovers the value of languages, dialects and literary traditions of cultures that have so far been considered unworthy of becoming vital ingredients for the thriving of America's modern cultural life.

The essays, reviews, and translations I have discussed here provide first glimpses into the messy and extensive world of the transatlantic transmission of philological practices in the first half of the nineteenth-century. To date, however, most critical research on this vital period of intellectual history focuses on the links between the philosophical thinking and German Romanticism while the trafficking of philological practices and their translations have hardly received the same amount of attention. Winterer, who examines how a new generation of American classicists eroded old methods of classical learning by introducing German historical methods into the American college curriculum,[63] explains this neglect as a result of our own fixation on original scholarship rather than pedagogy and teaching: "Until the late nineteenth century, American professors would not have made such distinctions between scholarship and teaching. Their chief avenues for scholarly output were college textbooks, articles in literary and popular journals, and lectures directed at the learned public. In these venues they did not display the results of their own new research; rather, they distilled the fruits of German and English scholarship for a broadly educated American readership."[64] Hence, we can only begin to comprehend the roles and functions of publications by nineteenth-century American scholars if we refrain from evaluating them as scholarly contributions, aimed at sharing new findings. Rather, we ought to regard them as windows into the period's ideas of pedagogical reform and treat them as materials that provide insight into how teaching practices and goals in classical studies were transformed under the impact of German criticism.

What Winterer says about classical studies maps directly onto theological scholarship. Ripley and Marsh are not concerned with critically assessing and making an original contribution to Herder's research on the writings of the Old Testament; what they are interested in are the ends to which his critical techniques can be put. The current criticisms on the history of philology that I cite and think with here operate with capacious conceptions of the discipline and offer helpful frames for detailing the characteristics, objectives and modes of impact of the critical labor that figures like Marsh and Ripley bring into view. Notably, Güthenke's claim regarding the personal orientation of classical scholarship evident in an individualizing language of feeling and attachment

---

[62] Ibid., 116-117.
[63] Winterer, *The Culture of Classicism*, 3.
[64] Ibid., 3-6.

provides a useful frame of reference for analyzing and placing Marsh's and Ripley's engagement with Herder on the larger plane of academic trends at the time.

As I gestured at in the chapter's first section, Marsh and Ripley share their interest in German critical literature with a host of other scholars of their generation who used classical and theological research for the purpose of examining how philological labor may be utilized toward educational goals and larger reform projects in the fields of religion and culture. Hence, the feedback effects of philological work on the modern critic's self-understanding, the institutionalizing of liberal learning and its ties to broader socially relevant concerns warrant more extensive research.

As Harpham, Turner, Pollock, and Güthenke each highlight, the excavation of philological practices helps us gain a better understanding of philology's role in the production of knowledge. We see how that knowledge informs the subject, education, society, and disciplinary self-understanding at certain historical times and places; we witness the role of words in the de- and reconstruction of worlds.[65] While this chapter seeks to contribute to these existing excavation efforts and calls for more critical attention to the topic of nineteenth-century transatlantic philological transfer, it is crucial not to forget in this context that "there is no philology without the history of philology;"[66] philological practices change and so do the ways in which we construct their history. Employing philological methods therefore requires what Pollock terms "double historicization."[67] It requires a critical awareness that our own take on philology, on the "discipline of making sense of texts," is evidently shaped by where we are coming from, by our educational background, our experiences and by the historical time and place we inhabit.[68]

That said, most of the contributions to the growing body of research on philology's methodological pluralism and history is motivated by the current

---

[65] I adopt the phrase "from words to worlds" from Winterer: "Under the influence of German historical scholarship, they [classical scholars] encouraged students to reimagine their own relationship to antiquity, seeking not so much to imitate the ancients as to absorb their spirit through the critical, historical study of authentic ancient texts....[T]hey imagined the shift from words to worlds as a process of becoming Greek, literally of self-transformation through a historicized encounter with the classical past," Winterer, *The Culture of Classicism*, 77-78.

[66] Sean Gurd, "Introduction," in *Philology and Its Histories*, 6.

[67] Sheldon Pollock, "Future Philology? The Fate of a Soft Science in a Hard World," *Critical Inquiry* 35 (Summer 2009): 958.

[68] Ibid., 934.

crisis of the humanities.[69] To find a way out of this "crisis of rationale,"[70] scholars of the humanities must "reactivate the links between their practice and the larger interests of a society based on individual freedom and self-realization."[71] As I showed, the fashioning of such links are a central concern for leading nineteenth-century humanists, and I would suggest that further investigations of how their textual techniques informed other areas of life is a worthwhile undertaking, not just because we gain a better understanding of a vibrant period of intellectual transfer and transformation, but also because bringing the past in dialogue with today's debates may sharpen our views of philology's present role at educational institutions and beyond.

Bibliography

Alt, Peter-André. *Die Verheißungen der Philologie*. Göttingen: Wallsteinverlag, 2007.

Channing, William Ellery. *Self-Culture. An Address Introductory to the Franklin Lectures. Delivered at Boston, September 1838*. Boston: Dutton and Wentworth Printers, 1838.

Clark, William. *Academic Charisma and the Origins of the Research University*. Chicago: University of Chicago Press, 2006.

Frank, Armin Paul, and Kurt Mueller-Vollmer. *British America and the United States, 1770s-1850s*. Vol. 2 of *The Internationality of National Literatures in Either America: Transfer and Transformation*. Göttingen: Wallstein Verlag, 2000.

Golemba, Henry L. *George Ripley*. Boston: Twayne, 1977.

Gura, Philip F. *American Transcendentalism: A History*. New York: Hill and Wang, 2007.

Gurd, Sean, ed. *Philology and its Histories*. Ohio: Ohio State University Press, 2010.

Güthenke, Constanze. "The Potter's Daughter's Sons: German Classical Scholarship and the Language of Love Circa 1800." *Representations* 109 (2010): 122-147.

---

[69] In light of this crisis, a number of publications make a case for "returning" to philology. For references to and reviews of these recent publications, see Marcus Krause, "'The Return to Philology:' About the Eternal Recurrence of a Theoretical Figure," in *Philology in the Making. Analog/Digital Cultures of Scholarly Writing and Reading*, ed. Pál Kelemen (Bielefeld: Transcript-Verlag, 2019), 39-55. The volume *Philology Matters! Essays on the Art of Reading Slowly*, ed. Harry Lönnroth (Leiden/Boston: Brill, 2017) also provides comprehensive critical discussions of recent research on philology and contributes new perspectives to the growing field. See also Harpham, *The Humanities and the Dream of America*: Falling enrollments and humanist scholars who are "conflicted and confused about their mission," he suggests, "suffer from an inability to convey (...) the specific value they offer to public culture," 22.

[70] Louis Menand, cited in Harpham, *The Humanities and the Dream of America*, 22.

[71] Harpham, *The Humanities and the Dream of America*, 189.

---. "'Enthusiasm Dwells Only in Specialization.' Classical Philology and Disciplinarity in Nineteenth-Century Germany." In *World Philology*, edited by Sheldon Pollock, Benjamin A. Elman, and Ku-ming Kevin Chang, 264-284. Cambridge, MA: Harvard University Press, 2015.

---. Warum Boeckhs *Encyklopädie* lesen." *Geschichte der Germanistik* 51/52 (2017): 83-97.

---. *Feeling and Classical Philology: Knowing Antiquity in German Classical Scholarship, 1770 – 1920*. Cambridge: Cambridge University Press, 2020.

Harloe, Katherine. *Winckelmann and the Invention of Antiquity. History and Aesthetics in the Age of Altertumswissenschaften*. Oxford: Oxford University Press, 2013.

Harpham, Geoffrey Galt. *The Humanities and the Dream of America*. Chicago: The University of Chicago Press, 2011.

Harvey, Samantha C. *Transatlantic Transcendentalism: Coleridge, Emerson, and Nature*. Edinburgh: Edinburgh University Press, 2013.

Herder, Johann Gottfried. *The Spirit of Hebrew Poetry*. Translated by James Marsh. 2 vols. Burlington: E. Smith, 1833.

Krause, Marcus. "'The Return to Philology:' About the Eternal Recurrence of a Theoretical Figure." In *Philology in the Making. Analog/Digital Cultures of Scholarly Writing and Reading*, edited by Pál Kelemen and Nicolas Pethes, 39-55. Bielefeld: Transcript-Verlag, 2019.

Lönnroth, Harry, ed. *Philology Matters! Essays on the Art of Reading Slowly*. Leiden/Boston: Brill, 2017.

Marsh, James. "Stuart's *Commentary on the Epistle to the Hebrews*." *Quarterly Christian Spectator* 1 (1829): 112-149.

Menand, Louis, Paul Reitter, and Chad Wellmon, eds. *The Rise of the Research University. A Sourcebook*, Chicago: The University of Chicago Press, 2017.

---. *The Metaphysical Club*. New York: Farrar, Strauss and Giroux, 2001.

Mueller-Vollmer, Kurt. "'Every Ship Brings a Word': Cultural and Literary Transfer from Germany to the United States in the First Half of the Nineteenth Century." *KulturPoetik* 3, no. 2 (2003): 155-172.

Nippel, Wilfried. "Philologenstreit und Schulpolitik: Zur Kontroverse zwischen Gottfried Hermann und August Böckh." In *Geschichtsdiskurs*, vol. 3 of *Die Epoche der Historisierung*, edited by Wolfgang Küttler, Jörn Rüsen, and Ernst Schulin, 244-253. Frankfurt am Main, 1997.

Packer, Barbara L. *The Transcendentalists*. Athens: University of Georgia Press, 2007.

Pollock, Sheldon, Benjamin A. Elman, and Ku-ming K. Chang, eds. *World Philology*. Cambridge: Harvard University Press, 2015.

---. "Future Philology? The Fate of a Soft Science in a Hard World." *Critical Inquiry* 35 (2009): 931-961.

Ripley, George. "Review of *The Spirit of Hebrew Poetry*." *The Christian Examiner and General Review* 18 (May 1835): 167-221.

---. "Review of Johann Gottfried Herders *Sämtliche Werke zur Religion und Theologie*." *The Christian Examiner and General Review* 19 (November 1835): 172-204.

Staël, Anne Germaine de. *Germany*. New York: Eastburn, Kirk and Co., 1814.

Thouard, Denis, Friedrich Vollhardt, and Fosca Mariani Zini, eds. *Philologie als Wissensmodell / La philologie comme modèle de savoir*. Berlin/New York: De Gruyter, 2010.

Turner, James. *Philology: The Forgotten Origins of the Modern Humanities*. Princeton: Princeton University Press, 2014.

Wayne, Tiffany K. *Encyclopedia of Transcendentalism*. New York: Facts On File, 2006.

Winterer, Caroline. *The Culture of Classicism: Ancient Greece and Rome in American Intellectual Life, 1780-1910*. Baltimore: Johns Hopkins University Press, 2002.

Index

A

Abeles, Simon, 99, 100, 102
agender. *See* gender
alliteration, 8
Altertumswissenschaften, 178, 180, 181, 193, 200
Altphilologie, 181
Amish. *See* heritage varieties
analogy, xxix, 15, 17, 31, 36, 37, 39, 40, 81, 82, 189
androcentric, 113, 115
animate-to-animate transfer. *See* metaphor
anthropology, xxvii, xxxi, xxxv, 19, 182, 183
anti-Jewish. *See* anti-Semitism
antiphrasis, 51
antiquarianism, xxxii, 183
anti-Semitism, xxx, 92, 94, 98, 100, 105, 106, 107
antonomasia. *See* metonymy
Aristotle, 31, 36, 76, 101, 103, 104
art history, 183
Ashkenazi, 93, 96, 97
assimilation, 11, 105
authorial intent, 44, 52

B

Begriffsgeschichte, 18
Beowulf, xxviii, 12, 37, 40, 42, 49, 51, 52
Bildung, xxxii, 184, 186, 187, 193, 195
biological gender. *See* gender
blood libel, 106

Boeckh, August, 182, 184, 185, 193

C

calamo currente. *See* scribal error
Carolingian script, 66, 69, 71
case syncretism, xxxi, 138, 140, 144, 149, 163
Christian Yiddishist movement, 92, 96, 107
Christianization, 6, 98
cisgender. *See* gender
Codex Ambrosianus, 10
Codex Argenteus, 10
conversion, 6, 10, 104, 105, 107
  forced, 100, 102, 105
courtly love, 81, 86, 87, 88
courtly poetry, xxx, 88
Crimean Gothic, xxvi, 9, 10, 24
critical theory, xix, xxi, xxxii

D

dawnsong, 77, 78, 79
De l'Allemagne, 180
de Staël, Germaine, 180, 185, 192
digital philology, 56, 57, 61
digraphs. *See* scribal error
dittography, 69

E

emotive language, 103, 106
Encyclopaedia Brittanica, 14, 22
equity, xxx
etymology, xxi, xxxii, 49
eugenics, xx
euphemism, 44, 51

Exeter Book, xxviii, 60
extralinguistic criteria. *See* extralinguistic factors
extralinguistic factors, xxvii, xxxiii, xxxiv, 3, 5, 9, 13, 15

F

feminine. *See* gender
Fettmilch uprising, 94, 98
Fornaldarsögur, 12

G

gender, xxx, 141
   agender, 114, 116, 118, 129
   biological gender, 113, 114, 115
   cisgender, 114, 118, 125, 129
   feminine, xvii, 76, 81, 113, 114, 115, 130, 146, 155, 159, 160, 164, 169
   gender assignment, 114, 115
   gender bias, 113
   gender equality, 116, 133, 134
   gender gap, 116
   gender identity, 113, 114, 125, 128
   gendered language, xxvi, xxx, 112, 114, 129, 131
   gender-exclusive, 112, 114, 120, 123, 126, 128
   gender-fair, 112, 114, 118, 123, 126, 128, 130, 131, 132
   gender-inclusive, xxx, 112, 114, 117, 118, 120, 123, 124, 126, 128, 129, 130, 131, 132, 133
   gendering, 132
   gender-neutral, 112, 116, 117, 118, 123, 124, 126, 128, 129, 130, 131, 132, 133
   grammatical gender, 113, 114, 115, 152, 155
   intersex, 113, 114, 116, 118, 129
   linguistic gender equality, 116, 134
   male-female binary, xxx, 114, 116
   masculine, xxx, 112, 113, 114, 115, 117, 118, 123, 124, 126, 127, 128, 129, 131, 132, 133, 134
   neuter, xvii, 113, 114, 130, 155, 156, 157, 164, 169
   non-binary, xxx, 113, 114, 116, 117, 118, 129
   non-gender-specific, 115
   transgender, 113, 114, 116
Gendersternchen, 116, 136
German Romanticism, xv, 197

H

Hebraeisch-Teutsche, 95
Hêliand, xxviii, 6, 7, 8, 38, 39, 43, 44, 47, 48, 49, 52, 61
Herder, Johann Gottfried, xx, xxiii, xxiv, xxxii, 179, 181, 186, 187, 188, 189, 190, 191, 192, 193, 194, 195, 197, 198
heritage, 144
heritage varieties, xxx, xxxi, 138, 139, 140, 142, 144, 146, 148, 149, 152, 155
   Amish, xxx
   Kansas Volga German, 138, 145
   Pennsylvania German, 138, 142, 144, 145
   Texas German, xxx, 138, 144
Heyne, Christian Gottlob, xxxii, 180, 181, 182
Hildebrandslied, xxviii, xxix, 56, 57, 58, 59, 60, 61, 62, 64, 66, 71, 72
   transmission history, 72

Index 205

historical linguistics, xix, xxi, 2, 3, 14, 15, 18
history of philology, xxxiv, 179, 197, 198
Hugo von Montfort, xxix, 75, 76, 77, 88, 89
humanist studies, 183, 184
Humboldt, Wilhelm von, 178, 184, 193
hyperbaton, 34
hyperbole, 51
hypernymy, 48, 51
hyponymy, 48, 51

I

inanimate-to-inanimate transfer. *See* metaphor
Indiana German
  project, xxvi, 148
  variety, xxxi, 139, 144, 146, 148, 150
Indiana German Dialect Project. *See* Indiana German Project
insertions. *See* scribal error
Institutum Judaicum et Muhammedicum, 107
insular script, 56, 60, 68
intersex. *See* gender
intertextuality, xxvii
Íslendingasögur, 12

J

Jefferson, Thomas, 185
Jewish oath, 99
Juedisch-Teutsche, 95

K

Kabbalistic writings, 96

Kansas Volga German. *See* heritage varieties
kenning, xxvii, xxviii, 28, 29, 30, 32, 33, 34, 36, 37, 38, 39, 42, 43, 44, 48, 49, 50, 52
Koiné, 9
koinéization, 5, 158, 161, 165
Kurtzhandl, Löbl, 93, 99, 100, 101, 102, 103, 105, 106

L

Lakoff and Johnson, xxviii, 38, 48
language death, xxxi, 142, 161
language history, xxvi, 2, 3, 8, 11, 15, 19
liberal arts education, 184
liberal learning, xxxi, 179, 195, 196, 198
ligatures. *See* scribal error
linguistic relativism, 113
literary analysis, xxxii
literary history, 3, 11, 13, 14, 17, 20
litotes, 51

M

male-female binary. *See* gender
marginalia, 61
marginalized languages, xx
marginalized people, xxxiv
Marsh, James, xxxii, 179, 186, 187, 190, 191, 192, 194, 195, 196, 197, 198
masculine. *See* gender
Medienverschiebung, 82
metaphor, xxvii, xxviii, 28, 30, 31, 32, 33, 34, 35, 36, 38, 39, 40, 41, 43, 44, 45, 48, 50, 52
  analogical metaphor, 35, 36, 38, 39, 40, 41, 47, 48
  animate transfer, 35, 39, 41, 43

conceptual metaphor, 16
inanimate transfer, 35, 38, 44
objectification, 35, 36, 38, 39, 42
personification, 35, 36, 37, 38, 42, 43
qualitative metaphor, 35, 36, 39, 41, 43
spatial metaphor, 41
metonymy, xxvii, 28, 30, 31, 32, 33, 34, 35, 39, 44, 45, 48, 50, 51, 52
abstract-conceptual association, 45, 46
antonomasia, 45, 49, 50
metonymic association, 45
pars pro toto, 45, 48, 49
physical-spatial association, 45, 46
synecdoche, 31, 33, 38, 45, 48, 49
totum pro parte, 48, 49
minnesang, xxix, 77
minority groups, xxxiv, 93, 107, 108
minority status, of a language, xxix, 107
misogyny, xxxv
Montfort. *See* Hugo von Montfort

N

Napoleonic Wars, 180
neogrammarians, 5
neologisms, xxi, xxx, 117
neuter. *See* gender
Nietzsche, Friedrich, xix, xxi, 184
non-gender-specific. *See* gender
noun periphrasis, xxvii, 28, 29, 30, 31, 32, 34, 35, 37, 41, 42, 43, 45, 46, 48, 49, 50, 51, 52, 53

O

objectification. *See* metaphor

onomastics, 9

P

paleography, xxi, xxv, xxviii, 56, 57, 58, 60, 72
pars pro toto. *See* metonymy
Passover, 94, 106
patronym, 50, 51
penknife erasure. *See* scribal error
Pennsylvania German. *See* heritage varieties
periodization, xxvi, xxvii, xxxiii, 2, 3, 4, 5, 10, 11, 12, 13, 14, 15, 16, 17, 20, 21, 22
personification. *See* metaphor
philosophy, xxvi, 3, 21, 107
photography, 57, 61
prescriptivism, 130, 131, 133
Processus Inquisitorius, 100, 101, 102, 103, 104, 105, 106
Prolegomena ad Homerum, 181
psycholinguistics, 114

R

racism, xxi, xxiv, xxxv
religious criticism, 183
religious intolerance, xxix
rhetorical analysis, xxvii, xxviii
rhetorical modality, 34
rhetorical trope, 34, 50
Ripley, George, xxxii, 179, 186, 187, 188, 189, 190, 191, 192, 193, 194, 197, 198
Romantic idealism, 187

S

Schlegel, Friedrich, 182, 193
Schleiermacher, Friedrich, 185, 193

Index

scribal error, xxviii, 56, 60, 61
   calamo currente, 61, 62, 64, 67, 69, 70, 72
   digraphs, 61, 65, 66, 71
   insertions, 61, 62
   ligatures, 61, 65, 66
   penknife erasure, 61, 62, 64, 70
   stains, 61
scribal practices, 56, 70, 71, 72
Second Sound Shift, 59
semantic transfer, xxvii, 28, 32, 33, 34, 35, 36, 39, 40, 43, 44, 48, 53
skaldic writing, xxvii, 30, 44, 52
Social Darwinism, xx
social equality, 124
social history, xxvi, xxvii, 3, 8, 17, 18, 21
sociolinguistics, xxi, xxv, xxx, xxxi, 112, 119, 132, 133, 139, 140, 146, 148, 151, 153, 154
sociology, xxxv
Sonderegger, Stefan, 4
Stabreim. See alliteration
stains. *See* scribal error
substantivization of adjectives, 117
substantivization of participles, 117
substantivization of verbs, 117
Synecdoche. *See* metonymy

T

Talmud, 96, 102

Texas German, 144, 148, *See* heritage varieties
totem pro parte, 45, *See* metonymy
trans. *See* gender
transcendentalism, 179, 186, 187, 188, 197, 200
transculturalism, xxiv, xxv, 182
tropes, 28, 30, 31, 32, 34, 50
two-case system, 144, 145, 146

V

Vayber-taytsh, 95
Viduvilt, 94, 97
Vom Geist der Ebräischen Poesie, 186, 193
Vossian antonomasia. *See* metonomy

W

white supremacy, xxi
Wolf, Friedrich August, xxxii, 181, 182, 184, 185, 193
Wolkenstein, Oswald von, 88
Wulfila, 9, 10

Y

Yiddish, xxii, xxvi, xxix, xxx, 20, 91, 92, 93, 94, 95, 96, 97, 98, 99, 100, 101, 102, 103, 104, 105, 106, 107

www.ingramcontent.com/pod-product-compliance
Lightning Source LLC
Chambersburg PA
CBHW070602300426
44113CB00010B/1362